Come Along With Me

Madcap musings of gallivanting the globe

RUTH SIMKIN

BInk *Bink Books*

Bedazzled Ink Publishing Company • Fairfield, California

978-1-949290-54-7 paperback

Cover Design
by

Sappling
Studio

Bink Books
a division of
Bedazzled Ink Publishing Company
Fairfield, California
http://www.bedazzledink.com

Come Along With Me

To Judi Simkin,
My sister,
One of my favourite traveling companions,
Who can speak any language with her smile.

To Hu Ping Yu,
A cherished friend for over thirty years,
Who, together with her family,
Are some of the most generous people I know.

To Miwako Soejima,
A wonderful host,
A hospitable woman,
And a treasured friend.

To Natasha Sigaeva,
The most superlative guide I have ever encountered,
And a woman who has subsequently become
my friend and adopted sister.

To all four of you—
Thank you for the wonderful memories.

Acknowledgements

Books do not just suddenly appear on their own. A lot of people are involved in the process of a new book being published. It would be impossible to name every single person who contributed to the existence of Come Along With Me. It's not just the writing involved, but having the writer be in a position where writing becomes possible that is so important.

As I have done before in most books I've written, I would like to thank Dvora Levin for her encouragement and suggestions. She has been involved in all my writing and I can't imagine sending off work without her input.

My thanks and appreciation go to the people of my household: Estelle Kurier and my grandson Dante, for cheering up and helping me and my home; Ida Diaz and Felix Autenreith, particularly for their help with Kelly; Kathleen Lum for keeping my home functional; friends Jill Swartz and Mike Goldstein, for their support and their delicious food that finds its way into my kitchen and belly; the Hope Key gang, for always making sure I have food and lots of love; Marvin Kurier for everything he does and brings to me; and of course, my Golden Doodle Kelly, who makes me laugh daily and fills my heart, even though there are times when I wonder about her sanity and mine.

For those who do not live in Victoria, yet support me via email, Zoom, and other means of communication, I offer much gratitude and appreciation to my sister Judi Simkin, who is also a major part of this book. I receive encouragement and support from her on a daily basis. My cousin Em Cohen has been very supportive as well, and is another person who is very important to me. My entire family has always been very supportive of my writing and I will always be grateful for their presence and their love.

Lastly but by no means leastly, I express my thanks and gratitude to Bedazzled Ink Publishing—C.A. Casey, Claudia Wilde, and Liz Gibson. Now that we have published several books together, I have grown to trust them and appreciate their fine work as publishers. Once more, they have come up with a great cover, and all the editing, as usual, was perfect. They help bring my books to life and for that, I just can't thank them enough.

Table of Contents

Part I

China

Chapter One
Guilin: The Beauty of China

A WONDERFUL THING happens when I am in an airplane: I feel suspended in space, where possibilities are endless. For a time, I have left the bustling world behind; the excitement of what lies ahead becomes almost overwhelming. Travel has always been one of my main passions, one I have had to ignore for many years, mainly due to physical problems. Finally, I have left my comfortable home for four months of adventure, circumnavigating the world, initially by myself; later, meeting my sister Judi to explore parts of the world together.

It's a strange thing—when I travel, I seem to leave fatigue behind. There always seems to be a surge of energy for adventures. When at home, all my energy seems to go into existing, but traveling brings me a kind of freedom I can't find doing anything else.

As I sit suspended in the atmosphere ensconced in a metal bird, my mind travels. For over a quarter of a century, I worked as a family physician, putting in long hours seven days a week. I also traveled a lot, rationalizing that hard work allowed for hard play and I enjoyed both. I sip my lukewarm airline tea and ponder what new adventures lay ahead—what will happen? What could I make happen? Whom will I meet? What might add meaning to my existence?

A MOUNTAIN OF white appeared ahead of us as we drove down the highway into Guilin, China. The amorphous white blob was moving and blowing in the wind. It was too low to be cloud. I was fascinated and could not pull my eyes away. I couldn't possibly imagine what it could be.

As we overtook the moving white mass, it morphed into a man on a motorcycle encased by about forty live geese whose elegant long white necks were undulating in the wind. The man's head was almost hidden from sight by the geese heads towering above him. With their necks waving in the wind, the geese seemed as though they were thoroughly enjoying the ride, which was most likely their last. I was so impressed by this sight, I was rendered speechless, and spent the next day looking for goose man or a relative, all to no avail.

When I attended school in China in the 'eighties, I heard a lot about Guilin, especially about the beauty of traveling by boat down the Li River. We had wanted to take that boat trip at the time, but it didn't work out. Even though we were adult medical doctors, we were instructed to ask permission to do anything or go anywhere other than medical class and work. Being respectful of our host country, we did just that. JoAnne and I requested that we be allowed to make arrangements to go to Guilin for the week-end.

"Of course you can go," Director Wong smiled, "but first you need to apply for this form at an office."

He quickly wrote something down for us on a scrap of paper. Off we went, stood in line for hours, received the form, only to be told we needed something else from another office. Each time we were encouraged and told we could go to Guilin. To make a very tedious story less so, the travel week-end came and went, and our paperwork was still not complete. Director Wong, the head of the school, nodded sadly, as though to say if our paperwork were finished, then of course we would have been able to go. After several months, we realized that the authorities were loath to say "no" to anything, and therefore just made it impossible for "yes" to happen. It would have been much easier on us if they would have just said "no" to begin with—we would not have wasted so much time waiting in lines, and most likely would have rebelled and gone anyway. So Guilin passed us by on that China stay.

BUT NOW I could experience it—this amazing city of Guilin. By Chinese standards, it is very small. The core of the city is only about seven hundred thousand people, but together with the outlying areas, there are about four million (still small by Chinese standards). It has many, many parks, four lakes, and the Li River runs through the city. Streets are lined with large boulevards with full-leafed trees in the middle and on both sides, and many streets look out over water. And, of course, there are the lights, multi-coloured, even psychedelic at times, which are fun and beautiful. The city is a marvelous blend of ancient and space age. The architecture is varied with modern buildings of assorted shapes alongside the old style buildings and pagodas. One can be driving down a very modern boulevard, with cars and motorcycles zipping about, and then have to swerve for a water buffalo sauntering along with its owner. Some signs are in English but by no means half yet, although I fear that is coming. Sculpture and artwork abound and the city has a holiday feel to it.

FOR OVER TWENTY years, I have wanted to experience that trip down the Li River from Guilin. I had heard it was one of the most beautiful areas in China, if not the world, and that particular boat trip was known for its intense beauty. Many of the wonderful Chinese water paintings of mountains and water have used the Li River and Guilin environs as inspiration. Guilin was thought of as a city for honeymooners because its beauty was romantic and lyrical. However, this was now not the idyllic "old days," but the consumer-driven twenty-first century, and it was with a certain amount of trepidation that I followed Joanna down the stone dock and onto the waiting boat.

Joanna was a twenty-seven-year-old guide dressed in designer jeans and trendy clothes who was going to show us her city. Off we headed down the Li River, also joined by an American, June.

We were ushered inside a long, air-conditioned cabin. The outside walls were all windows. Two leather benches faced each other with a low table between, just high enough for bruising one's knees at the slightest bump. There were about eight such booth and table setups per side in this lounge, with a small bar towards the back. As was typical in China, doilies covered the backs of the seats and tea pots and cups sat on the table.

Just after we left the dock, I looked out to see many, many other boats. We were on our boat, and hundreds of other folks were on their boats, all heading down the Li River, all the boats in a row, guides talking, horns tooting, just like the African Adventure Ride at Disneyland. The Li River Cruise Ride. The boats all followed the same path in the river, just like at Disneyland. For all I know, there could have been a little railing underwater, and all the boats were attached to the railing and there was really no captain at all, just some Disneylandesque worker of the levers. It was comical, actually, and distracted from what I thought would be a meditative morning.

I went exploring to the top of the boat, where there was an outside deck. No chairs, no benches, just the deck, because it was apparently inconceivable that a person would want to be outdoors in the fresh air surrounded by nature and beauty, when that same person could be sitting inside, on a doilied leather bench in air-conditioned splendor. For a good part of the trip I chose the outside deck, even though it rained for most of the day.

The eighty-kilometer trip took seven hours, starting out at the docks in downtown Guilin and ending up in the town of Yangshuo. The trip was pretty much the same as it would have been thirty years ago, except for the ubiquitous cell phones.

The mist and rain surrounded the boat, but I loved the trip just the same. Water buffalo grazed along the edges of rice paddies. Somehow, seeing them brought home the fact that I really was in China. On my first visit to this country in the 1970s, I had actually ridden a water buffalo through a rice paddy to the amazement and amusement of both my traveling companions and the local Chinese. It was almost other worldly, yet of this world. I could have been in any century—I felt linked to eons of people and their land. I have always had an affinity for these animals, these *shui niu*. It was one of the first words I ever learned in Chinese.

At times, from my perch on the outer deck, it was as though I were inside a Chinese water painting. Many differently shaped peaks showed through the mist, each with its own descriptive name, like Crown Cave (*Guanyan*), Half-Side Ferry (*Ban Bian Du*), and Mural Hill. One of the main landmarks in Guilin is Elephant Trunk Hill because the hill resembles an elephant drinking in the water, so they say. I could see the crown of Crown Cave, and thought I could see the half-side ferry. Mural Hill was very appropriately named with its bursts of colours. But back in Guilin, when I tried to see the "elephant drinking water" in Elephant Trunk Hill, no matter how I maneuvered my head and my eyes, I still saw an oddly shaped rock that to my mind resembled a doughnut more than any pachyderm slacking its thirst.

BEFORE WE LEFT, I had asked Joanna if there were toilets on board. Since she answered affirmatively, I embarked with confidence. I hadn't traveled for a very long time and forgot that there are toilets and *there are toilets*. It was, of course, a squatter: a hole with the river beneath it surrounded by a slippery wall and nothing on which to hang one's hands, or anything else. I won't regale you with the details of the deed, but trust me, it was not a pretty sight.

Back in the main cabin, the coiled up poisonous snake seemed to call to me. *She-jiu* is a special wine which the farmers drink and the tourists avoid. The huge snake, presumably dead, lay in the jar, and one drinks from it—kind of like the worm in the tequila thing, but macho-ier. Big jar, huge snake. The wine is supposed to make one strong.

Of course I decided to try it, much to the absolute shock and delight of the locals. Joanna giggled and all the other tourists gathered around to watch me imbibe and see if I would drop dead from the poison. Or the snake. The wine tasted like wood alcohol, but it must have worked as I felt great all day!

Soon it was lunch time. I had been watching all the folks in little fishing boats who were catching crabs and fish and handing them directly to the boat kitchens, which were just woks set up at the back of the boats. I ordered river crabs for lunch. They were tasty but June said they reminded her too much of spiders. Never mind—more for me to enjoy as I devoured the teeny delicacies, shells and all.

Throughout the day, we passed many mountains in the mist, like those depicted in so many traditional Chinese landscape paintings. We sailed by rice paddies, more water buffalo, fisherpeople, and bamboo forests. It rained, or at least misted, the entire trip, but that wasn't necessarily a detraction. It was as though the artist chose to depict the mountains and rivers on a rainy day.

THE RAIN WAS pouring down when we docked in Yangshou, from where we were going to drive back to Guilin. Because it was raining so hard, everyone wanted to sell us umbrellas, even though we all had them.

"Umblellaaas, missy, umblellaas."

"Umblellee, missy, missy umblellee here."

Hearing hundreds of non-English-speaking-people pronounce the word "umbrella" can be a very interesting experience. I had no desire to laugh, especially at anyone trying to speak a foreign language, but I could not contain my giggles as we limped into the market, doubled over from hearing the various mangled ways of saying that one word: umbrella. We were trying to be supportive of strangers attempting to speak our language. We all failed.

We walked through the "Hello-hello Market," so called because the vendors all approach the tourists saying "Hello, hello" and shove their wares in your face. This reminded me of The Womens' Market in Hong Kong where my friend James had been interpreting for me. One woman said something to me and I asked James what she said.

"What's the matter—you don't understand English?" James asked. What she had said was, "Hey, lookie, missy." And here we were in Yangshou, walking down the streets to "hello hello" and "lookie missy" a thousand times over.

The vendors were much more aggressive than when I was last in China—and much more numerous. The T-shirts were the typical tourist stuff, like "I climbed the Great Wall" and things like that, T-shirts that were never seen in this country twenty years ago, but there were also shirts that said "I survived SARS" and "Disinfected." Scary stuff.

We stopped at an art gallery to buy art and to use the bathroom. The proprietor kept trying to tell me something as I was the first to use it. I finally figured out what she said. "Be careful of the bathroom cat." Now I am not overly comfortable with cats at the best of time, so it was with some trepidation that I entered the bathroom. What would happen? Why was the cat in the bathroom?

Were there rats and was it a guard cat? Would the cat attack me? Eat me? I had seen some pretty skinny animals around. I carefully poked my head through the door and looked around. What else was lurking in that squatter? Sure enough, there, behind a half wall, sitting in the darkness, tied up to a metal rod not far from the squatter, was this terrified little black and white fluff clearly more frightened of me and my activities than I was of her. Her tiny head peered carefully over the peeling half-wall. Skinny? Yes. Hungry? Probably. Dangerous? I didn't know if it was an attack cat or exactly of what I was to be aware. It is hard enough for me to use those squatters without having to beware of the cat at the same time; I talked soothingly to the cat while I was trying to do my business (squatting), the entire process being akin to rubbing one's stomach and patting one's head at the same time.

A LOCAL FISHERMAN with his cormorants was standing in the square at the end of the market. Our fisherman friend was right out of a picture book—small stringy white goatee with a white mustache framing his mouth and running down his face below his chin, his tan weathered face covered with a large, round bamboo hat. He wore a long black coat ragged at the edges. A long bamboo stick slung across his shoulders, with two large, black cormorants on each side. In this area, the birds fish for the fishermen, mostly at night.

They dive into the water, catch the fish, and bring them back to the fisherman. I later learned that the reason the birds don't eat the fish is that the fishermen tie a cord around the cormorant's neck and so the bird then becomes dependent upon the fisherman for food. The birds live with the fishermen, and are apparently like family members. This man had four cormorants on a bamboo pole, and they fished for him daily. The birds were currently happily sitting on the bamboo pole laying across the old man's shoulders, no cords around their necks now; the birds seem to look up to the old man as the benevolent head of the family. This tableau made a very striking picture. For money, one could pose with the cormorants and the fisherman. One did.

DRIVING BACK TO Guilin we saw lots of "brick factories"—large fields with little A-frame roofs about two feet off the ground, under which the bricks dry for two months before being used for building. We also saw pomelos everywhere, on the roadside, on the back of trucks, on makeshift tables. Pomelos had always arrived at my house in someone's hand—every year, at Chinese New Year, my adopted Chinese family in Victoria always brought these big yellow fruits for us to enjoy at our celebration. Now for the first time, I am seeing them in their natural environment. I remember when I had initially tried one. After peeling off the thick skin, we ate the sections of pomelo, which are not unlike large grapefruit sections, yet they have no sourness or acidity to them. Now I understand why my friends are so excited to have them—the pomelos are very numerous around here, this is close to where my friends are from and pomelos remind them of home.

The first time I was shown how to eat a pomelo, in return I taught my Chinese friends how to eat artichokes. It was a gustatory cultural exchange, full of laughter and new tastes.

I had met their mother at the hospice where I worked. During her terminal illness, I helped arranged for two of her daughters and her only grandson to come from China to Victoria to see their dying mother. She already had one son, one daughter, and her husband with her in Victoria. Once the family was reunited, they wanted to stay together, and so began applying for immigrant status. After their mother died, we stayed connected, growing closer and closer. Ultimately, they were able to move out of the tiny, grungy apartment in which they lived, and were able to purchase a house. The following year, they bought their own restaurant. They are third generation restauranteurs. We watch out for each other and I am privileged to have them in my life which has become enriched with their presence.

AT THE GUILIN Tea Scientific Research Institute, a research and tea growing facility at the outskirts of the city, I learned a huge amount about tea in a few hours, more than I ever thought possible. We were met by Tea Master Nico, who had studied in University six years to become a Tea Master. I was amazed that any human being could learn that much about tea, but apparently Nico had, as he never ran out of information for us. He was a pleasant-looking young man, dressed in a striped purple, blue and red long shirt, wearing a large, conical bamboo hat. After we were introduced, he summoned us over to a shed where we were similarly outfitted with the large head coverings. We learned that the large conical hats were used not only for keeping the sun off of heads, but for holding the harvested tea. We followed Nico into the fields of green, listening intently as he explained that the tea plant, *Camellia sinensis*, produces green, oolong, and black tea. The difference is in the oxidation and age of the plant. I looked around the field of green at these beautiful plants, standing chest high. The leaves were about five to fifteen centimeters long and two to five centimeters wide, and what I found interesting were all the many different shades of the color green. We watched harvesters off in the distance as Nico explained that the young leaves were preferred for the harvesting; they are the light green leaves, while the older leaves are a darker green. The different ages produce the different tea qualities. Nico plucked a leaf from the bush and rolled it between his fingers as he talked. He told us that the fresh leaves contain four per cent caffeine. He passed the tea leave around for us to smell and touch.

We followed Nico into the drying sheds where various pans of different sizes leaned against the wooden walls, each one containing leaves in different stages of dryness. In the centre of the shed were two women dressed in blue shirt and blue pants, red patterned kerchiefs on their heads. As Nico explained the drying process, the two women shook large shallow metal baskets several feet in diameter over a warming oven, turning the bright green leaves into a darker mixture. The women worked steadily as Nico showed us the contents of the pans.

From there he led us under a stone archway covered with ivy, up one flight of stairs to the right, down a hall and into a room for a ceremonial tea tasting. We sat around Nico on stools made of lacquered tree trunks; he sat on a stool in front of a lacquered table which had also been a tree, glistening light brown and beautiful. On the table were a heated tray and apparently a hidden sink, as Nico poured a lot of water onto a tray, and the floor remained dry. Around all the tea paraphernalia were delicately patterned porcelain cups for us to use in our tasting.

Nico explained the Chinese tea ceremony. Men and women hold their cups differently, and a person has to take not one, not two, but three sips of the little cup, and hold it with the fingers just so in each hand. There are both formal and informal ways of holding one's teacup, and one can say so much by the proper or improper placement of the fingers. I wondered how many times in life I inadvertently gave inappropriate signals by holding my tea cup in such a fashion that might mean "screw you" or maybe "good health to your third uncle."

Nico poured the hot water into the pots with a flourish, all the while regaling us with tea knowledge and history, while he poured tea with a flair. First we smelled everything. Then we tasted yellow tea, green tea, oolong tea, black tea, and more. In the twenty-first century, tea is still the most widely consumed beverage in the world after water, and after that experience, I could understand the allure more than ever before.

We returned to the hotel for only one hour's rest before dinner which would be followed by an Acrobatic show. As we walked into the restaurant, we passed by dozens of cages lined up outside against the wall, filled with live animals where one could shop for dinner. Sitting at our table, aware of these cages just on the other side of the wall, I experienced an intense discomfort, an urge to release all the food animals and take them home as pets. However, by sheer will and an acute awareness that Canadiana is not the only culture in the world, I was able to overcome this discomfort and my North American sensibilities, and allow myself to participate in this culture.

I find it difficult to be accepting of others when it comes to animals and their welfare—I don't believe in animal testing for any reasons and I certainly have trouble with little critters, even snakes who are not my favourites, sitting in their cages waiting for some hungry diner to claim them as food. If I were boss of the world, I would definitely outlaw such things, but I am not, and as I tend to be a guest in other countries often, in order to spend my time peacefully, I need to be accepting of cultures so variant from my own. But there is nothing easy about that. I hope that in time, attitudes will change, and I certainly will do whatever I can to help that along. No doubt those experiences contributed to my becoming a vegan following that trip.

SITTING IN THE restaurant with June and her friend, I opened the menu and started to chuckle. The food and menus here fascinated me, partly because of the content and partly because of the creative translations. (My last morning in Hong Kong, Eric and I had lunch together, and on the menu was "Braised osseous coco with red wine sauce in homemade mushrooms bread." I opted for the squid-ink noodles instead.) This restaurant had some very interesting items on the menu (creative spelling theirs, not mine): long-noded pit viper cooked in three tastes, fride masked civet, fried bamboo rat, soft-fried bee pupae, fied bull's sexual organs with ginko, stir fried duck's offals, fried ducks tongues with different vegetables, boars sexual organs with spicy salt. What to have, what to have . . . I just couldn't decide. We opted for long-bone fish which Joanna helped us order, a local fish which is supposed to have only one long bone and therefore would be easy to eat. This was decidedly not true—the long-bone fish had more little bones in it than a sardine convention. We also ordered some shrimp, which were even smaller than the spider crabs at lunch. All in all, it was not my favourite dining experience.

Then we went to the theatre, where a huge neon sign announced: Dream Like Lijiang, New Ballet Circus. I thought it was going to be a typical Chinese Acrobat show. Was I mistaken! Streaming up the stairs with the excited crowd, I felt the electric excitement in the air. We took our seats on the main floor of the theatre, about two-thirds of the way back. All around me, different languages bounced off each other in excited patter. I turned my ticket over. On the back were instructions for theatre goers, like latecomer info, no smoking or cellphones in theatre, etc, but my favourite of all was: "All viewers should be neatly dressed." A little late to be telling folks, don't you think?

The New Ballet Circus was the only company of its kind in China, a mix of ballet and acrobatics—but the overall effect was definitely Cirque du Soleil-ish with an Asian twist. From the second it started, I knew we were watching something incredible—the theatre was pulsating with music and lighting and movement. The performance was enthralling and extremely avant-garde and hip and sexy, although there was nothing lascivious about it. It started with a bunch of almost naked beautiful boys and then fairies (women) and dancers costumed as animals, moving in such a way that they captured and portrayed the essence of the creatures, some real, some fantasy, all brought into a larger than life reality. The human/animal performers moved in a way that made me forget they were human, as they captured so precisely the sense and movement of their creatures. I was surprised that the lighting and staging were so effectively computerized, because the last time I had been in China, the concerts, although very well staged, were certainly not state of the art like this one.

The costumes were Cirque du Soleil at their best. The music was eclectic as well—Enya, Loreena McKennitt, The Moody Blues, ragtime and the Charleston, kumba-kumba-kumba-kumba-chero, some Asian music, some very contemporary world fusion stuff, just an incredible mixture. The performances— how can I describe someone flying through the air, in time to music and gracefully landing in the arms of another swinging in from somewhere unseen? It's as though they were a different species—soaring through the air, leaping and tumbling and balancing. I can barely walk and I watched a man leap in the air and catch hold of a pole mid-air with his toe. We are all born with the same bones and muscles and yet it's so amazing what some people can do with theirs. We would barely be over one incredible scene when another one took place. There were no pauses, no down times, throughout the entire performance. The overall effect—lighting, music, staging, costumes, dancing—everything that emanated from that stage filled every human sense. The performance was a cross between Cirque du Soleil, Classical Ballet, and an LSD hallucination. It was one of the most enjoyable times I have spent in a theatre. I didn't want it to be over, and when it was, I didn't want to leave.

THE NEXT MORNING started by our visiting Reed Flute Cave, an amazing horseshoe-shaped network of caves in the middle of a mountain. They were named after the reeds at the mouth of the cave, which were used to make flutes. Of course, the entire entrance to the cave was littered with vendors selling souvenir flutes. During WWII, the Japanese hid out in these huge caves. The caves are living and grow one to twenty centimeters every one hundred years. It is truly amazing to think of rocks growing, but the rainwater, which has calcium carbonate, seeps through the rocks on the hill, and the limestone is dissolved. This water seeps through the ceiling and drips down, causing the stalagmites (growing up from the floor) and stalactites (growing down from the ceiling) to grow. As long as water drips, there is rock growth.

First we had to climb the stairs which wound half way up the mountain. Just before we entered, while we paused to catch our breath, there were instructions for visitors. My favourite: "Please observe social ethics." We then entered a wonderland full of stalagmites and stalactites, all wonderfully lit up in an artistic manner. Each "scene" was given a name like, "A Centipede Frightened by a Magic Mirror," "A Lion Sees Off Guests," or "Pines in the Snow." One grotto, called "Crystal Palace of the Dragon King," was large enough to hold a banquet for one thousand people, in between the naturally occurring pools of water. I could just envision the banquet tables set along the inner still dark pool of water, the chatter of the invited guests reaching up to the icicle stalactites and the waiters weaving through the stalagmites carrying tureens and steaming platters full of delicious foods. In my mind, the smells of the banquet dishes were quickly displacing the dank smell of the caves. My reverie was shattered by June's calling me to continue with them though the dripping caves. However, I would have enjoyed attending my pretend banquet a little longer.

We made our way through spaces so narrow our hands touched both sides of the wall, and then we would enter larger caverns, and then again walk through narrow weaving pathways. All around us, the rocks were lit up in creative ways as we made our way through the two-hundred-and-forty-meter long cave. We were inside the cave at least an hour, inside this natural phenomenon which the Chinese call 'The Palace of Natural Arts'. It is said that a visiting scholar wanted to write a poem about the beauty of the cave. It took him so long to find the right words that he turned to stone. We left before we began to harden.

Driving back from the caves, I saw Goose Man's cousin and finally understood how he had the geese on his bike. This guy had six wooden crates lashed behind his seat, two high and three across, and each bamboo crate had at least four to six geese in it. These particular geese were multi-coloured and only a few had their necks out, and so overall were nowhere near as impressive as the imposing amorphous white blob of the other day. But at least I now understood how they could have been riding, because with the white mountain of geese, the crates had not even been visible with all the necks sticking out.

OUR NEXT STOP was South China Sea Pearl Institute, where Guide Number Eight took us around and explained all about sea pearls. We stood in a large anteroom, with photos of oysters and the stages of pearl-making on the walls, while she demonstrated with a real oyster and pearl. The pearls come from He Pu, a small town right on the South China Sea just three hundred kilometers from Guilin. He Pu is very famous worldwide for its pearls. It was very informative for anyone wanting to know how pearls started, and what became of them. The South China Sea Pearl Institute was extremely proud of the fact that Bill and Hillary Clinton had visited the place, and had the photos everywhere to prove it. The 'Institute' was really a very beautiful and modern pearl store, with long aisles of gleaming display cases, artfully arranged with every kind of pearl jewelry you could imagine—rows of rings, earrings, money holders, bracelets, individual pearls to put on whatever you might desire. The room was cool, and there were comfortable seats for those who were not actively shopping.

Chapter Two
Guilin Impresses

A BIG CHANGE on this trip from previous travels was the ubiquitous presence of cell phones altering the travel experience. Whenever we were finishing doing something, Joanna just called our driver (for some inexplicable reason, June had dubbed him Mr. Dragon Man) and he pulled up just as we were exiting.

But the cell phones were not always positive—they insinuated themselves everywhere, as if people could not be in the moment, or enjoy an experience without phoning someone to tell them about it, or else sending a photo which they have just taken and then talking about it on the phone. Whatever happened to looking, feeling, experiencing with one's whole body and mind, and then later, after it is over, sharing it with friends? Today it seems that nothing is real unless we can send a photo of it through our cell phones and then discuss what we are seeing and feeling as it happens. This new way of experiencing things saddens me no end. Of course, the cell phones do come in handy when needed to summon a driver, or call for help or other necessities. I suppose I must conclude that they are both good news and bad news.

ON THE ROAD back to Guilin we passed many fishing farms—large pools of water where folks from the city come to catch a fish and then cook and eat it. They are not allowed to fish in the Li River. Only specially licensed fishers can do that. There are fish farms where people fish for recreation and gustation.

We ended up having lunch at a terrific place in downtown Guilin. Our driver dropped us off at a corner in front of a large McDonalds sign. At first, my heart sank when I had a brief thought that it might be our place of dining for the day. I had totally underestimated wonderful Joanna. She led us up a flight of stairs, leaving the McDonalds sign down in the street, as we entered a gustatory and olfactory heaven.

The food was displayed all throughout the restaurant on long tables with blue velvet skirts down to the floor. There were dozens of bowls of noodles, and one long table full of colourful hotpots. Bowls of noodles and fish were lined up in front of a white-hatted chef cooking behind a big wok. The sights and smells and noise—well, I was home.

When we arrived at the restaurant, we were each given a card. We walked about pointing to what we wanted, and waiters wrote it down on our little card. When we were done deciding, not an easy task, we handed in our cards, and eventually the food showed up at our table. It was sort of like dim sum, except we did all the wheeling around and picking. We seemed to be the only non-locals in the place. I loved it because it was dim sum-y and right up my taste bud alley.

AS WE DESCENDED the stairs of the restaurant, Joanna had just finished phoning the driver and there he was, pulling up right under the McDonalds sign. Big Mac or dim sum for lunch? I think we made the right decision. After a short ride through the modern city, our driver dropped us off beside the water while Joanna went into her office to arrange for tickets for our afternoon boat excursion. June, her friend Annie, and I walked along the water's edge. We were happy and content in the warm sun, our tummies full, as we strolled along the concrete abutment by the water. We took photos of the large pagodas across the water and the intricately tiled rooftops on our side.

We boarded a boat for a ride through the waterways of the city. There were dancing water fountains and many beautiful pagodas on the shore.

From the very beginning of our boat cruise, I had decided to stay outside as opposed to sitting in the cabin on doilies in quasi-air-conditioned splendor. I much preferred the open sky, the bright sun, and an unobstructed view of the sights. A sailor had tried to coax me into the inner cabin, but when that failed, he gallantly opened up a chair on the rear deck where I sat like a queen for the rest of the tour. It's interesting to me that the preferred seating, by the tourists and locals alike, is inside the boat on doilied benches with stuffy not-quite-adequate air conditioning, rather than being outside in the real air, under the sun and sky, with nothing at all obstructing one's views of the vistas.

At the very back of that boat, I pretended I was a queen sailing on the water, as the red and gold starred Chinese flag flapped in the breeze beside me. I might even have raised my hand in a subtle queenly salute to the passers-by. I sat there in the back, my Tilley crown shading me from the hot sun, grinning around me in my queendom. I regally looked out upon all the activities on the shorelines—the fishermen, the people sitting and talking, people walking along the water's edge, looking at the brightly coloured flowers, all in spring bloom. I felt the fresh air on my face, the warm sun on my body, I smelled the flowers on the shore—okay, I was beside the motor with its gaseous fumes, but I aimed my nose skyward as we sailed along and could *almost* smell the beautiful flower fragrances wafting across the water. We passed by fisherpeople in flat little bamboo boats—really they were just four sticks of bamboo lashed together and they sat flat on the water and seemed to stay afloat. And we saw swimmers and washers, washing everything from veggies to clothing to bodies (live) in the Li River.

The boat tour ended at a dock beside a magnificent bronze sculpture of wild horses, larger than life, galloping along the water's edge. I wanted to stay and play with them, or perhaps hook them up to my royal carriage. Their golden manes blew in the wind, their nostrils flared; the lead stallion had one hoof raised as he surveyed his realm, not unlike my own.

By now it was mid-afternoon, getting hotter, and we weren't done our sightseeing yet. Joanne made a quick cellphone call, and lo and behold, there was Mr. Dragon Man, pulling up to load us just as we walked by the stone sculptures of the geese scattered on the walkway.

Just a short drive to the Xiongsheng Bears and Tigers Mountain Villa in Guilin, where they have over eighty tigers, more than two hundred bears, as well as lions, leopards, birds, and other wild animals. The guide told us it was a research institute and they have been breeding white Siberian tigers. Every year they release tigers into a natural protected park, but after walking around a bit, and not being shown any research facilities, I wasn't so sure how 'research' oriented it was, and wondered whether or not it was just a big zoo. Hard to tell.

After walking around with the guide for over an hour, watching the tigers play in their large compounds, and commiserating over those who were in small cages, we came to a rest area. The guide could not tell us why some animals were still in very small cages, while other animals were in very large and well appointed (for tigers) areas, with swimming pools, large lounging areas, the odd tree for shade, and of course, high fences.

At the rest area, over to the left, was a large arena with an animal "show," which some of us chose not to watch. While Annie walked over to the arena, Joanna, June, and I sat on a concrete bench beside a white plastic table, sipping lukewarm orangeade and talking. Apparently, the show had trick riders, both humans and bears, who rode horses. There were other shows as well—tigers catching live pigs, and lions fighting bulls. There was no way we were going to participate in such a spectacle. Instead, we turned to the right to watch a huge field in which there were many dozens of bears playing. What is research oriented about performing animals?

I angrily slapped the table as the noises from the arena filled my ears. June and Joanna commiserated with me completely. We had a long discussion about zoos, animal shows, animal rights, and our frustration at being helpless to change things for these animals today. As we talked, our eyes never left the field in front of us. We were fascinated by a black bear who, at first, we thought was 'dancing' to the music emanating from the arena, but the more we watched him (or her), the more we thought he was exhibiting neurotic behaviour. Here was a huge enclave, with dozens of other black bears, many of whom were playing with friends, swimming in the bear pool, or snoozing in the sun, and yet this bear was all alone, under a tree, frantically swaying to and fro, to and fro, to and fro. I so wanted to be able to hop the fence, go into bear talk mode, and find out what was on his/her mind. Happily, most of the other bears and other animals in their large enclosures seemed well-adjusted, as much as a non-animal psychologist could apprise.

I was so tired by this point, I could barely stand upright and walking was questionable even with the aid of my cane, and yet we still had a long way to go to get back to the entrance and our van. I fortified myself with the knowledge of all the wonderful animals I would meet along the way. And I was so right— including a whole slew of newly born bear cubs. The way they played with each other brought smiles to our faces, and I wanted to crawl right in there with them. But of course, that would be neither research oriented nor prudent.

The weather was so hot and muggy, and I got a bit dehydrated because I didn't like to drink too much when I was out. I would rather not attempt toilet ministrations away from the hotel if I didn't have to. Earlier that day, I went into a washroom that had one side all stalls of Western toilets and the other side all stalls of Eastern squatters, and as I made a mad dash for the Western side, most of the women (all Asian) choose the opposite side. I was amazed. I guess it comes down to what one is used to.

THAT EVENING, MY last night in Guilin, I thought I would rest and catch up with email and phoned down to the main desk for an internet connection. Soon there was a knock on the door. A tall, young woman, smartly dressed in a uniformed blue suit, entered. She saw that I had an Apple MacIntosh computer, smiled, turned on her heels, and walked out, then returned after a short time. In her hand was a page of instructions that were half English, half Chinese, and half numbers. I know that is more than two halves, but it was very complicated and confusing. After spending some time trying to get an internet connection and failing, she went down for assistance.

Another woman came up to my room. Soon after, the first one returned, and then a man entered the melee. It only took about two and a half hours to hook up, all the while with people coming and going and the phone ringing every two minutes. I thought that it was not a good thing that I had an Apple computer. In the end, the problem was that the original connection from the hotel was not good; ultimately the man came back, changed it, and things were fine. My Mac computer's name remained unsullied.

At one point, the first woman I had met wanted to see my photos, so I showed her a little slide show from Hong Kong while we were waiting for the next person to show up. I was tempted to order potato chips and have a party, as we were chatting and laughing. She later told me she was upset because the hotel was not as up to date on modern things, like internet connections, as Beijing. She said, "In my next life, I want to come back as a foreigner." I thought that incredibly sad, and I encouraged her to travel a bit in this life. I hope she comes to see her strengths and beauty without wishing to be someone else.

AIRPORTS DO NOT seem to be my forte on this trip. After checking in at Guilin airport for my flight to Shanghai (transferring at Guangzhou), I was told I was overweight (my luggage too) and had to pay—okay, it was less than twenty dollars. But then we discovered the agent had ticketed everything to Guangzhou and I was going to Shanghai, so poor Joanna kept running up and back from the check-in counter to the cashier, paying money and trying to make sure the luggage was properly ticketed. This took over thirty minutes. The agent would not see anyone else until she was completely finished with me. There was a huge line forming behind me. I couldn't understand the mumbles in Chinese, but if looks could kill . . . I was not a popular person.

I kept insisting the agent had not put my luggage back on the conveyor belt. Joanna kept insisting that these people were professionals and she had talked to the agent three times about the luggage. Joanna told me not to worry as she kept pushing me towards security while I glumly eyed my luggage sitting in a pile by itself off in a corner. Joanna said she was sure my luggage would arrive in Shanghai. I was equally sure it wouldn't. Joanna pushed me forward toward the security entrance. I kept glancing balefully over at my poor abandoned luggage. Joanna kept gently pushing me towards security; I kept pointing toward my forlorn luggage. She pushed me forward a bit more. I dug my heels in and pointed to the luggage. Ultimately, between all the pushing and pointing, with one last loving look at my luggage, I managed to enter into the security area.

It was a short flight to Guangzhou. The airport was extremely modern, with a modern gangway from the plane to the terminal. I expected a simple walk down the gangway into the terminal, which I could see just ahead, but I forgot I was in China. Instead of entering the terminal via the gangway, we exited the plane onto the gangway and then immediately had to walk down several flights of stairs from the gangway onto the tarmac and into an awaiting bus! The bus drove us all the way around and outside the airport and let us off at the front, where we went back into the terminal, checked in again, went through security again, all for a connecting flight. Even though the airport appeared very modern and beautiful, some aspects, like the boarding process, might have made sense to the Chinese powers that be, but to my Western mind seemed a bit disorganized and chaotic.

Sitting on the plane, anxiously awaiting my arrival in Shanghai, I thought about how the airport experience typified a lot of China today. There is a huge effort to do all things the "Western" way, except everything just missed, things just weren't quite right, they didn't quite work. This was another big difference from my trips here previously—now, if it was Western, it was by definition, preferable, whether or not it was appropriate or functional. It saddened me to think of the Chinese throwing away so many of the "old ways" for the Western ways instead of keeping things that work as well as things that define them as a people.

In the early 1980s, I had studied in China for four months. That was before the days of computers and emails. Even phone calls were tricky and extremely expensive, but out of desperation, I allowed myself one call home a month. I hungered for words from home and wrote a lot of letters, achingly awaiting answers. In fact, I even wrote letters to then Prime Minister Pierre Trudeau and author Kurt Vonnegut. Amazingly, both answered.

Over twenty-five years earlier, the experience was equally difficult for my family. My parents would go weeks without hearing from me, even though I wrote regularly. They had to rely on and trust the fact that I was able to take care of myself.

During that time, I had a personal problem with a friend. Had I been at home, I could have discussed it with those close to me and solicited their advice. Alone in my boarding room in Shanghai, I was flying solo. I felt isolated, out of touch and all alone. It was certainly very different from today when I have such easy access to all my support systems. I managed to resolve the problem well on my own, and although it was painful and difficult, I think I matured from the experience. Today I suppose it would be easy to start a blog and have problems discussed in cyberspace by whomever was interested.

There is something to be said for just going away and being incommunicado for some time; it certainly adds a different dimension to traveling and being in a distant land. On this trip, I hear news from home almost daily, which was very reassuring—one never feels away or out of touch. Of course, all I had to do was not turn on my computer, but it was too tempting to use, so I did. It was a lifeline across the ocean. Using computers and telephones takes away a lot of the uncertainty and isolation that added excitement to traveling in the past. In the old days, traveling was like flying from trapeze to trapeze without a net.

I believe that today people don't experience the same kind of growth when traveling, because they have such easy access and instant communication with friends and family and don't have to make important decisions without input from those who care.

Technology does make living easier, but does it make it better? Or more exciting? Does it give us a chance to prove ourselves, to have adventures on our own, and make decisions that impact ourselves and others without constant consultation with those far away? I always felt more "away" when isolated, of course, and painful as that was at times, I think it magnified the allure of traveling. Plus that very isolation allowed me to grow in ways that differ from the growth of today's trips, where everyone I know travels with me via my computer.

My thoughts were distracted by the lights of Shanghai, where I was to meet my dear friend Hu Ping who was meeting me at the airport.

Chapter Three
Shanghai: Reflections upon Returning

IN THE MID-1970S, a group of my friends and family wanted to go to China. In those days, the only way one could get a VISA was to be part of a recognized group, for example, teachers or doctors. These groups often had waiting lists of over three years. We just wanted to go to China for the travel experiences and adventures, but we needed an identifiable group so that we could accurately fill out the necessary forms. So I simply invented the Calgary Women's Tour Group, and explained on the application that our group wanted to study the women and children of China. It sounded good to me, and it must have sounded good to the Chinese authorities because in no time at all, we got our permission to visit China to study the women and children of that country. There must have been a dearth of Women's Groups applying to visit China in those days. And that was how twenty of my friends and relatives and I got to experience China before the borders were open to individual tourism.

It became apparent, once there, that all Western visitors, so it seemed, got to see exactly the same things, no matter what one might write on the application in terms of our specific interests. We all stayed at the same hotels, went on the same tours, saw the same nursery schools, the same hospitals. But we were thrilled to be there, and we eagerly absorbed everything we could about this interesting country.

While there, my mother had an attack of bursitis, and this was immediately cured by acupuncture. Initially I ridiculed her for trying it, but I changed my tune after I saw how effective it was, and decided to learn a bit about the practice of acupuncture when I could.

So some five years after my first trip to China, in the early 1980s, I attended the preeminent place in the world to study acupuncture—the Shanghai College of Traditional Chinese Medicine, in Shanghai, People's Republic of China. The course I took was a graduate course for physicians and other health care workers and resulted with the blessings of the College of Physicians and Surgeons, in my becoming the first licensed physician to incorporate acupuncture into medical practice in Alberta.

I had not been back to China since I had finished that course many years ago. I looked forward to seeing my friend Hu Ping, who had been in my class at the Shanghai College where we had become close friends and remained in contact with each other.

When I first met Hu Ping a quarter of a century earlier, she could not speak a word of English, and I could not speak any Chinese, but we became instant friends. Hu Ping's husband, Jin Jie, was already in California, and she was anxious to be able to join him. She was taking the acupuncture course because it was sanctioned by the World Health Organization and recognized in the US, and once graduated, she would emigrate and hopefully be able to practice acupuncture in California.

The course was a very intense one. For the first month, we met all day in the classroom, six days and one evening a week. The second month found us in the classroom only during the mornings, and the afternoon sessions were spent working in our assigned hospitals. The next few months, we worked all day at the hospital. But no matter at what stage we were in our training, we always had a two-and-a-half hour lunch "break," which the Chinese insisted we Westerners needed so we could rest. Even when we were working at the hospital all day, the school sent a van to bring us "home" for the lunch break so we could sleep. The van then dropped everyone off at their respective hospitals after their afternoon naps. I had no intention of having a nap during the day while I was living in China—how weird would that be! Sleeping when I could be learning or exploring!

Hu Ping and I were each assigned to different hospitals to do our work. We received special permission from the school for us to spend the mid-day rest period together, so that I could ostensibly teach English to Hu-Ping. She would in turn teach me Chinese, but the school was not aware of our reciprocal pact.

So Hu Ping taught me how to take the bus from Shanghai Hospital Number Six to her aunt's place where we spent hours each day talking, eating, laughing, and sometimes crying together. We stayed in touch after Hu Ping, and her young son Jun, immigrated to the United States and joined her husband in Glendora (a suburb of Los Angeles) and we try to see each other as often as possible.

Jin Jie had become an architect and built up a very successful practice in California. Hu Ping did become licensed to practice acupuncture, but ended up helping Jin Jie in his architecture business. In the early 1990s, they were visiting China when an old friend told them about a government architectural competition. They entered it and won. Since then they had been working more and more in China and ultimately moved back to Shanghai, where they built up a large, wildly successful architectural firm.

I HAD NOT seen them for many years, as the last few times I was in California, they were in China. As my plane bumped down onto the runway I was filled with the anticipation of seeing my old friend again. As I walked out of the baggage claim into the main terminal, I immediately heard my name, and there was Hu Ping, arms open for a welcoming hug.

I slowly moved out of her embrace and held her at arms length to look her over—she hardly looked any different from the last time I saw her. She was smiling and laughing, as I was, both of us absolutely delighted at our reunion in the city where first we met.

She introduced me to Xiao Li (pronounced shee-ow lee), her cousin and driver. Xiao means "little" in Chinese. I remembered when I was at school in China, most everyone was Xiao (young or little) Someone or Lao (old) Someone. A tall, handsome face with bright, clear eyes smiled down on me. I liked him immediately. There was nothing "Xiao" about him except his name. We set about to gather my copious luggage, which I was sure did not follow me to Shanghai.

Oh me of little faith—there was my luggage—all intact, in the right place. It had triumphed over snarky agents, incorrectly filled out baggage tickets, and late connections. I was thrilled that Joanna had proven me wrong.

Xiao Li carried all my luggage to the car and drove us home while Hu Ping and I chatted in the backseat. Sitting in the car, looking through the window, I was astounded at the changes that had occurred in the city over the past quarter of a century. Freeways were everywhere, crossing one over the other, full of cars. Freeways! When I was last in China, there were barely any cars on the streets at all. Bicycles and buses, yes, but cars—hardly a one, except the odd car bearing diplomats or other functionaries. Now, there were thousands, tens of thousands of cars, zipping along and over and under and around freeways which blanketed the city.

China has 1.3 billion people. Shanghai alone has 16 million people. If you think about it, Shanghai and Beijing contain one-third again more people than the entire country of Canada. And we North Americans tend to be so arrogant at times, when we are really such a minority in terms of the people in the world.

Jin Jie and Hu Ping have a wonderful life and home here—a spacious, elegant penthouse on the twentieth floor, with every modern convenience. When Jin Jie won the competition for a thirty-seven story building, The Future's Exchange Building, the highest building he had previously designed was a three story apartment building. He said he did a lot of studying after winning that competition! Since then, they have designed hundreds of buildings in Shanghai, and we saw many of the impressive edifices. Now the highest he had designed was fifty-two stories (the highest in Shanghai was eighty-eight, but they were building one that was to be ninety-five stories).

Both Jin Jie and Hu Ping grew up in incredibly poor households after the Cultural Revolution. Before the revolution, many families had their own homes, but afterward, they were all confined to a tiny room, with multiple people sharing one kitchen, if one could even call it that. Hu Ping and Jin Jie had some very rough times, first in China, later in the US, and now both are flourishing.

Hu Ping and I had a long talk about all of this after we got back to her apartment, and I guess the maxim is true: What goes around comes around. They were good people (still are) and now they are in a position to help others and they do. They have done incredibly well and I am so proud to know them and call them my friends.

I STAYED AT Hu Ping's for over three weeks. I used her house as my base camp, going off on several expeditions and always returning. I have never had a better hostess! I felt completely at home, staking out my own corner on the large living room sofa, between Jin Jie in his lounger and Hu Ping in her couch corner. In fact, months after my return, I had arranged for a Canadian friend of mine to visit Hu Ping and Jin Jie. She had kindly sent me a picture of her from their home. There she was—sitting in *my* corner! I must admit to feeling somewhat displaced after seeing that photo.

Hu Ping and Jin Jie created an environment where I could feel completely comfortable, in every respect, physically, mentally, and emotionally. I had my own room in the apartment, with my own bath, but best of all, I had my own air conditioning with a remote control. How cool was that! I had lived through Shanghai in the summer twice already, and to return to Hu Ping's after an exhausting day of touring and eating and talking and laughing and walking and plop down on my large bed and crank up the coolness that soothed me and my aching feet and full belly—well, I was home, and could easily have stayed there for a very, very long time.

Most days would find us talking about all the changes that I noticed in the country. We usually talked as we strolled down the street to the store, or through the back alleys to the tailors, or around the corner to buy the brightly coloured small cacti which Hu Ping loved and enjoyed having on her kitchen windowsill. This sharing of the daily errands of the household showed me a part of the culture I wouldn't have seen had I been just a tourist.

Over the next several weeks, as we went about doing our errands and sightseeing and eating, I noticed many more changes, which we enjoyed discussing. We loved talking about all the differences between then and now, and simultaneously marveling and despairing at them.

Traffic was beyond description. When I was in Shanghai before, I was so amazed at the traffic and commotion in the streets that I made a short film just of traffic alone; I thought seeing was believing and I couldn't possibly have described what I saw. There were what I called accordion buses—really two buses hooked together with an accordion type connection. They used to be so packed that when they were full up, people on the streets would literally push their feet against the boarding peoples' backsides to help squash them into the buses. The first time I saw that, I was amused and amazed, but it was not a solitary event.

Now, some twenty-three years later, it was the same as before except many thousands of speeding cars and many more motorcycles were added into the mix. The street signs meant nothing—a sign saying "don't enter" apparently was there just to look pretty. Red lights, green lights, flashing lights didn't matter. People went, cars went, whenever and where ever. Cars were passed on both the right and the left, sometimes at the same time. One day, our cab driver was traveling along a big divided boulevard and wanted to change directions, so he turned right around and drove against the one-way traffic, dodging the cars coming at us, until we came to a big intersection and he could cross over. No one seemed to mind. No one was honking. It was a normal everyday occurrence.

The big corners have traffic assistants, people who stand around futilely blowing their whistles while about twenty thousand people, on foot, bike, motorcycle, and non-describable vehicular contraptions try to cross the street in all directions. It really does defy description.

It seemed as though many people wore a uniform of some sort. Of course, the traffic assistants had uniforms, complete with fringes and epaulets, some bright yellow and red. Walking down the street, I saw people who work in restaurants, trying to bring in customers. They all wore these very fancy sashes over their shoulders and down to their hips. Colorful tassels dangled off them as they waved their customers into the eating establishments.

When I was in China in the 1980s, most everybody wore blue or grey slacks, and white or light blue shirts. That was about the extent of sartorial China. On this trip, there were the most modern of fashions seen walking down the street, including bare midriffs and chic hairdos.

Clothing had changed, traffic had changed, but I chuckled when I saw that the rubber stamping industry was still going strong and the stamping in China had remained unchanged—everything had to be stamped, often much more than once. Each piece of paper had multiple stamps on it. Even bills in the restaurants were stamped. I have no idea why.

One big difference on this trip to China from previous visits was photography. Now, I go around with my digital camera, taking pictures and often emailing them to people. I remember what we used to do. The first time we were China, our big bus pulled into a small village. We were the first Westerners many of the locals had seen. We went into a field and took a Polaroid photo of an elderly woman, thoroughly enjoying her and others' reactions, all two hundred of them surrounding us, as they watched the photo develop on the paper. They had never seen anything like that, and when we presented her with the photo, her eyes almost bulged out of her head; she started laughing and chattering away gleefully. I did not understand a word, but it was clear that she was delighted with the process.

Today, Polaroids no more. People, even in small villages, have become accustomed to digital cameras and cell phones. Although the new way is certainly easy and convenient, it lacks the interpersonal interactions which I had previously valued.

On most streets, all the signs are in Chinese. One day we were walking along Nanjing Lu (*Lu* means "street") and there, over Chinese signage, was the unmistakable visage of Colonel Sanders. I actually did a real double take as I found that white goateed face quite jarring looking out at me from a place that I considered extremely out of context with the colonel's face. Yet KFC is quite popular around here. In one downtown block alone I saw a KFC, Pizza Hut, and Subway, and I wasn't even looking hard.

Outside the apartment complex where we lived we came across a young man selling DVDs. He had a small table set up on the sidewalk just outside our gate. On the table were many wooden bins of DVDs, mostly English ones, and fewer Chinese. He had many that just came out—the very newest of the DVDs. I was amazed to see titles I had not been able to get just three weeks earlier in Canada or the US.

While I was buying thirteen DVDs—the total price for all thirteen came to 85 yuan, which is $12.86 CDN ($10.27 USD)—I could just see the small garage somewhere with tables full of electronic equipment and many young men running around making their illicit DVDs. I laughed because he had DVDs that my friends at home were anxiously waiting for! And even though I was getting them quite cheaply by Canadian standards, Hu Ping always made sure that I got a better deal as she negotiated with the young man.

The quality of the knock-offs was excellent overall—we watched a movie at home. When they worked, they were good; but they didn't always take. Still, at \$0.98 a DVD with English entertainment on the packaging, who could complain—the packaging alone was worth the price. They were in packages with both Chinese and English, but the English was mostly gibberish because the DVD was a knock-off. The writing was mostly in Chinese, with photos from the movie, and there was also a little English blurb. Here are some examples, quoted verbatim:

> From Queen Latifah's *Beauty Shop*:
> "The (the boon. Pulls the method of) is a well-known hair style designer her There is a "haircare" of party of many distinguished friends regardless employee or customers are all pleased the reveals to her the endocentric secret . . ."

> My personal favourite is *Sideways*:
> "Exceeding the (protect the second inlifts the) is writer dream that a lamentable failed do can't and. He is still don't from it get away from out in pain and sufferings of the divorce, looking at the old friend right bower (give the horse sea ascend the strange) Will s can be living to step into The grave of the love.Exceed the have the research to the wine, before the wedding of the right bower, he decide to take the old friend to travel togetherTravel, go to the wine of California produce the base, borrowing the wine to release the mood."

I can hardly wait to see these films!

WHEN I WAS at school here, I had a teacher, Wang Yisheng (pronounced wong-y-shung; Wang is her last name, and *yisheng* is the Chinese word for doctor, so Wang Yisheng means Dr. Wang). Wang Yisheng was a superb physician and teacher. In fact, many Chinese would use up their two weeks annual holiday to travel to Shanghai just to be seen by Wang Yisheng for whatever ailed them at the time.

Near the end of my acupuncture course in Shanghai, I was asked by Wang Yisheng if there was anything I could do to help their oldest daughter go to America. She wanted to study psychology (not an option at that time in China) plus she wanted to experience and make her way in the US. Since I was not a US citizen, I prevailed upon my sister, Judi, who had been part of the Calgary Women's Tour Group to China, and who was currently living in California. Judi signed the papers as we sponsored Wang Yisheng's daughter in the US. This was in the 1980s. The daughter is now happily married with a young daughter, living a contented existence in Austin, Texas. Every year without fail, I receive a Christmas card from her addressed to Auntie Ruth. *Ai-ee* is the Chinese word for Aunt, and is a title of respect. When we visited schools in China, all the little children referred to us as *Ai-ee*. I must admit to being very touched and always looking forward to receiving those letters addressed to Auntie Ruth.

I had only met Weizhen through photographs until 2010, more than a quarter of a century after sponsoring her to come to North America. I was then on a book tour and made a point of going to Austin so we could meet. And to my utter delight, her mother, Wang Yisheng, was visiting at the time. I cannot begin to explain my absolute pleasure at finally meeting her and seeing Wang Yisheng again. My sister Judi was with me as well, and we spent several wonderful days all getting to know each other.

THE CHINESE ATTITUDE toward gratitude and respect is strong. Hu Ping, Wang Yisheng, and many others all seemed to want to thank me in many different ways for things I barely remember doing over the past three decades. To my repeated embarrassment, this gratitude didn't stop with a dinner party or exchanging presents. It went on and on, with many dinners and many expressions of thanks, both verbal and material. The first day I was at Hu Ping's home, she walked into my room with a huge stack of fresh 100 *Yuan* bills. "Here," she said, "spending money for Shanghai." Of course, I couldn't accept that. But she insisted on buying me a little digital camera after mine died from the rain in Yangshou. I tried to say no to that, but she prevailed. Not only did she provide a Chinese home for me, but she kept doing things for me, making me feel as though I were the Queen of Shanghai!

ONE DAY, HU Ping and I went to visit Wang Yisheng. Normally Xiao Li had been driving us everywhere, but that day we grabbed a cab.

The area where Hu Ping lived was very New York-ish. We lived in a large complex behind shrubbery walls, and guarded gates—very quiet and peaceful with lanes meandering through tennis courts, children's parks, little lakes with fish, rock gardens, and lots of trees and gardens. But once outside, we were in the busy, concrete streets of Shanghai with their speeding drivers. Hu Ping just hailed a cab as though she were in New York City. The car screeched to a stop in front of us, we hopped in, and peeled away, all in a Shanghai second. We drove to Wang Yisheng's home, and then, when the cab driver left us off in front of an entry to a street, all of a sudden, we were in a very different environment.

The street led into a residential area. There was a street, but no vehicular traffic. There were no trees, no plants that were visible. A sense of age prevailed. The red bricks of the buildings looked old. The paving stones upon which we walked looked old. The wooden doors opening into the apartments looked old. The people looked old. Laundry was hanging out of the windows, left to dry in the warm sun. There, over against the wall, sitting on the stones were two old women, a blanket spread out before them on the ground, a meager selection of vegetables, old vegetables, sitting on the ragged, red blanket and offered for sale. I looked up and there, walking towards us, was Wang Yishang. Her wise eyes crinkled up into a smile and her mouth followed. I was so excited to see her; it was the first time in almost twenty-five years. She seemed not to have changed hardly at all, although I later found out she had recently broken a hip. She was a tiny woman, hovering around five feet, and very, very slim. Her black hair had only a smattering of grey in it. We exchanged long, emotional hugs and then Hu Ping and I followed Wang Yisheng down a street that had a lot of narrow alleyways going off of it. Most of the people we saw there were elderly. I wondered if they had decided to stay where things were familiar, rather than move into more modern areas of the city.

Wang Yisheng led us through a doorway. Over the step was a small kitchen—really, a counter with two hot plates, a few woks, and one sink. That was the kitchen for everyone living in that building. Then we went up an extremely steep and narrow flight of stairs into the one-room apartment of Wang Yisheng and her husband Shen Laoshe (*Laoshe* means teacher—he taught mathematics and physics at the University). Wang Yisheng told us that years ago, before the Cultural Revolution, her family owned and lived in the entire building.

Wang Yisheng was a young girl when Mao came into power. The 1950s, under Mao, was a time of great hope for the people of China. If you had nothing, you got something; but if you had something, you lost it. Wang Yisheng's family lost the building, of course; so many other families similarly lost their homes. Shen's family had also been very wealthy. Now Wang Yisheng and Shen Laoshe lived in only one small room. They had thought about getting a newer apartment some years ago, but missed the time when they could afford it, and now all the prices were too high. The paint was peeling off the walls and ceiling. A double bed stood in one corner, a small square table occupied the middle of the floor, covered with glass over doilies. A very small desk sat against one wall, and a bureau stood alongside a window. There was not a whole lot more. Everything was extremely clean and neat. Out the door, down the hall just a bit, was a very modest bathroom.

They have two daughters, one in Paris and one in Texas. A few years ago, they went to Austin to visit their daughter Weizhen. It sounded as though the daughter lived in a suburb, both she and her husband have cars and went off to work every day, and on the week-ends, they would golf, and otherwise amuse themselves. After two months, the parents missed Shanghai and so came home. Since then, I have had the opportunity of visiting Weizhen's home, and it was very different than I initially thought. Weizhen and her husband Xue Jun have made a wonderful home for themselves and daughter Leah, and live very fulfilled and busy lives. It was a privilege and honour to ultimately meet them.

Wang Yisheng was sent to Sweden for two years in 2001 because she is so well-regarded as a physician. She was terribly lonely when there and hated the food. However, after she finished her work in Sweden, apparently acupuncture and Chinese medicine became completely acceptable as a medical modality in that country.

I think they are both very happy together. So they remain, both retired, two extremely intelligent, cultured, and wonderful people, in this building where they have carved out a life. How fortunate for the world that these two pre-eminent people managed to get through such a difficult time in Chinese history and emerge the way they did, positively influencing people all over the world.

We sat around the table at Wang Yisheng's apartment and presented gifts. Their customs are of the old days, and so the presentation was quite formal. I was not expecting quite that, but was able to hold my own. Wang Yisheng probably speaks English minimally better than I speak Chinese, which is to say, we really cannot communicate in words too well, but Hu Ping was right in there, and of course, there was lots of smiling and hugging. Much to my surprise, Wang Yisheng had two lovely gifts for me—a beautiful silk embroidery in a round frame depicting panda bears, which sat on a wooden stand, and a colourful Chinese porcelain mask. I was a little embarrassed with my maple syrup and Victoria tea towel, but she seemed very pleased with all the little gifts I brought for her, soaps and Canadiana knick-knacks, so I hope that was the case. I noticed that they had a glass cupboard with photos of their children and cards and other things set out. In it was prominently displayed a holographic card I had sent to Wang Yisheng in the 1980s! Was I surprised to see that card more than twenty years since I had sent it.

I asked Wang Yisheng what the biggest differences were over the past few decades, and she immediately said the quality of life was improved. Today, regular people can go out to eat at a restaurant (as we had done) and there is also a lot more freedom.

Wang Yisheng and Shen Laoshe then took us out to lunch. We walked the few blocks from their home. On the way, we walked by a beautiful building—very modern, just different enough to catch one's eye; it wasn't just a vertical box and it was clear that it had been designed not only for function but to please the eye as well. I admired it aloud. Imagine my delight when Hu Ping told me it was one of Jin Jie's earliest buildings in Shanghai. No wonder he is so successful.

We walked into the restaurant through two large glass doors. The tables were covered with light pink tablecloths and the red plush chairs looked inviting. The lightly coloured walls of gold held a variety of mixed artwork, a very eclectic exhibit—I was a bit taken aback to see Mona Lisa staring at me. This place, with its thirty or forty tables, was much cozier (and quieter) than one of the neighbourhood restaurants near Hu Ping's home where we had dined earlier, with its many hundreds of tables and attendant roar of satisfied diners.

We had a banquet for lunch—they ordered so many things, many of which I could not identify. Ordering a meal in China is a big production, with much consultation. How different it is, eating in a Chinese restaurant with my Chinese friends than in a North American restaurant with my North American friends. There, each of us would look at the menu, minimal discussion may or may not ensue as to what each one of us would order; we would tell the waiter what we each want, and that was the end of the ordering discussion. Not so in China. There is always a huge discussion as to what to order, and this involves everyone at and around the table, including waiters and chefs, with much gesticulating and lively discussion, as though this were the most important thing happening on earth that day. I have yet to have a meal, even with just two of us, where the discussion resulted in fewer than ten items. The table is usually loaded up with cold appetizers, main courses, soups, desserts, although frankly, it was hard for me to tell the difference. Still, I am getting fairly fluent with my Chinese culinary vocabulary and I continue to be fascinated with menus. Here are some of the latest (verbatim again): Fairy grass with honey, Pig's Bone and Water Melon, eel with medicine hot pot, spicy hoof cube. I'm not even mentioning the more common items like steamed water turtle and donkey meat.

Sitting at the table with Wang Yisheng, Shen Laoshe, and Hu Ping, I ate and ate, and just when I thought I was going to explode (one has to be polite and try everything at least once), they brought on dessert. I had thought we were finished the meal. A cake appeared—dessert again. Next came some meat dumplings—again dessert. And then came lily pod seed soup or something like that—again dessert. There were about ten more courses after the first dessert. It occurred to me that their expertise with new technologies has now extended to desserts as they are getting bigger and better! What ever happened to a piece of orange or watermelon after a meal?

WANG YISHENG IS probably one of the finest physicians in the entire world. Her influence has remained with me during my entire medical career. I was a much better physician after I met and worked with her. Over lunch, she told me she remembered me because of how I was with people, that I was a good doctor, clever and good with the patients. She did, in fact, remember a lot about my practicing medicine in her hospital.

That fact that she remembered me so well, even though she had taught many hundreds, maybe thousands, of people, was incredibly flattering to me. I had thought we students, all doing the same things, would just blend into a big blur for the teachers, but I was one of the few Wang Yisheng remembered. How thrilling for me to realize that our medical respect for each other was reciprocal—that she had similar feelings for me and my work as I had for her and her work.

I HAVE ALWAYS loved *Pesach* (Passover), and I really did want to attend a *Pesach Seder* (ritual meal) in China. Being a stranger in Shanghai did not leave me many options at Passover, and although I tried to find a private Jewish home that would invite me, all we could come up with was Chabad House. Now I have always thought of Chabad as the Jewish equivalent of the people who knock on your door with the Watch Tower, but more energetic, like Jewish evangelicals. They are everywhere in the world, it seems, which is a good thing if you are in a strange place and feel the need for something Jewish. Chabad House was welcoming, so I decided to introduce Hu Ping to this Jewish ritual evening.

We actually did most of the arrangements to go to the *seder* online. All I had was an address, and Hu Ping and I were dropped off in front of a large white house. We walked up the stairs into a large entryway and were warmly greeted by several women. Chabad House is part of the more orthodox movement of the Jewish religion. The men, it turned out, were downstairs in the synagogue part of the building, where men and women were separated for their prayers.

We walked through the entryway, and were shown into a large room where eight large tables were set, occupying most of the space in the room. We were seated at a table for six which was prepared for Passover, with ritual foods and prayer books at each setting. The *rebbitzin* (rabbi's wife), a friendly sort with bright red hair, came over to talk with us. She explained that they had planned one huge *seder* of over four hundred people but just the day before, the owner of the venue wanted more money under the table and the rabbi refused, so they lost their venue. They had one day to find an alternate venue, and did, but not one that would accommodate everyone. So one rabbi and three hundred and fifty others were elsewhere while Chabad House held the fifty leftover folks and the Australian rabbi and rebbizin. I've never been a huge Chabad fan, but I had to admit they were exceptionally nice, engaging, and interesting, and I thoroughly enjoyed meeting them.

When the prayer services were finished downstairs, Hu Ping and I were joined by four men: one from Sweden, and three Israelis. Hu Ping was the only Chinese person attending the *seder*. All the other Chinese were servers. I think this must have been difficult for her. That and the fact that the main language of the evening was Hebrew. Although most people spoke English and some spoke Chinese, Hebrew was probably the most common language spoken that evening. The four men at our table were all chatting in Hebrew and just assumed we didn't understand. In fact, they were being quite rude and acted as if we didn't exist. Hu Ping had never been to a *seder* before so, for all she knew, men were supposed to be rude! I reassured her this was not the case. We indulged in many surreptitious eye rolls between us over the bad behaviour and lack of manners. Finally, I blinked my eyes at one, and calmly asked, in Hebrew, *Beitzim, b'vakasha*, please pass the eggs. The men froze in mid-conversation, mouths agape, as silence blanketed the table. After they recovered from the knowledge that I could understand them, the conversation definitely changed to include us. They were much nicer to us after that, almost as if we were real people.

Some *seders* last three hours, some last eight or more; it depends upon who is running them, and how much discussion and eating and drinking take place. Although we arrived on time, about six in the evening, we left just after eleven. We couldn't stay all night, and they were just starting the third cup, so there were hours and hours left to go. I was happy to leave before it was completely over. Somehow, I was hoping for something a little more Chinese oriented, since we were in China, but sitting in that room in Chabad House, we could have been anywhere in the world, China, Canada, or Timbuktu. The services were all universally the same. I was happy to have attended a *seder*, but disappointed that it was no different than any *seder* anywhere else. However, on reflection, that is possibly a positive thing—that a Jew can go to a *seder* anywhere in the world and know exactly what to do and what is happening. As with most things in life, there are two conflicting sides to consider.

The *rebbitzin* had given me a box of matzo and so the next morning, for breakfast, I made fried matzo and eggs (a Passover treat at my house)—sans butter—with Chinese oil, in a wok. It turned out not too badly, but I thought one might have to develop a taste for it. I watched Jin Jie and Hu Ping turn the matzo over with their chopsticks, as though they were looking for something that might foretell savoury tastes. They didn't find it. They smiled bravely although I'm sure they were wishing for Shanghai breakfast buns. Jin Jie and Hu Ping were very polite and ate some, but their taste still had a bit of developing to do as I think they would have preferred congee (gruel)!

SUNDAY IN SHANGHAI. We went down memory lane. First we went to see the apartment where Jin Jie grew up, and where he lived with Hu Ping when they first were married. They lived with an aunt and uncle, and when Hu Ping's and Jin Jie's son came along, there were five of them living in the room. As we walked down an old alleyway, laundry wafting from the windows, children playing on the cobblestone, my friends pointed to a very dark, dank doorway. Inside, seven families shared a kitchen; there was no bathroom, just a pot in the corner of the room in which they lived, which was emptied daily. People mostly showered at work at the factories.

Then we drove to the place where Hu Ping grew up. Some of the older people on the street remembered her. We walked down an alley past the place where she used to buy hot water for a penny (okay, a *fen*). They had no hot water in the house, of course. Hu Ping's family had owned the whole house, just as Wang Yisheng's family had owned theirs, until the Cultural Revolution, and then like so many others, they were confined to one room. There was one community shower room on the street—a room so small I could barely fit in it, much less turn around. A tiny purple plastic tub lay on the floor and a hose attached to a water pipe dangled into it—this served many hundreds of people. I had to keep reminding myself of the difference in numbers—where we in North America might refer to hundreds *or* thousands, here in China they have hundreds *of* thousands, or millions.

We drove through Pu Dong, a new suburb, across the Wangpu River from downtown Shanghai. Geographically, Pu Dong is to Shanghai kind of like Kowloon is to Hong Kong. Fifteen years ago it was all farmland and old shacks. Today it is about as modern a suburb as you could imagine—wide treed boulevards, freeways, and bridges all wind around high rises and shopping centres. Most of the buildings are less than ten years old.

We went to visit Jin Jie's first building—the one for which he won the competition. It is called The Future's Exchange Building, only thirty-seven stories, which is a baby in the Shanghai skyline, but impressive—unique and pleasing to the eyes. Another building of his is the Civil Defense Building, the only building in downtown Shanghai with a rooftop helicopter pad.

We walked around Xing Tian Di (new sky, new earth), which is about as trendy a complex as I've ever seen. Greeting people with Vidal Sassoon signs, it could have been anywhere in the world. They had Lido-like cabaret shows with girlie girls, Starbucks, McDonalds (here it's considered a plus), and very elegant shops. Outdoor kiosks sold wares from everywhere in the world. It was the kind of place where the "beautiful people" go, very pretty to look at, was universally trendy, and not particularly Chinese in character. I wanted to return to the back alleys myself, into what I consider the real character of China. But who knows— maybe Euro-chic has become part of China's new character!

Apartments are very expensive in Shanghai and the prices keep rising. For apartments that are around two thousand square feet, the cost is something like half a million US dollars. There is no way the average person can afford that. The government is actively tearing down all the old streets and rebuilding with modern high-rise giants. Jin Jie told me it is common for the government to tear down a large section of housing, and build, for example, four high rise apartments, and use one building for public housing for the people who were displaced. It is more expensive for them to live there, but the government provides loans, and it is way cheaper than what the apartments in the other three buildings would go for. If the people didn't want to do that, they would then be relocated to other public housing about fifty miles out. Luckily, there was a very good subway system there as well.

We went to the tallest building in Shanghai, eighty-eight stories, which is part Hyatt Hotel. It is an amazing architectural feat—the Hyatt starts at the fifty-fourth floor—below that are office buildings. On the fifty-sixth floor is a wonderful lounge open to all the rest of the stories above so one can sit in the lounge and look up at this curve of thirty-two gleaming golden floors spiraling upward, culminating in the acme of the eighty-eighth floor lookout. I sat in the lounge, drinking a tasty latte, and craned my neck at all angles as I looked at the coiling mass of walls all around us. It was awe-inspiring.

Jin Jie and Hu Ping like to bring their relatives to the lounge—most local Chinese have no idea that such a thing exists in Shanghai—they just can't imagine it. This reminded me of the African tribes who couldn't see ships in the harbour because they couldn't dream of their existence or others who couldn't see their first airplane because they couldn't conceive of its possibility.

MUCH LATER ON in the day, we went to Heng Shan, where I had lived when I studied in China. It has been totally remodeled, and is now a four star hotel, but let me tell you, it wasn't even a two star or a one star building when I lived there. Back then, the building was shabby, genteel in a forgotten sort of way, as though it might have been elegant at one point a very long time ago. Traces of this remained in the size of the rooms, but not much else as the hallways and front lobby were dark and musty. We paid forty *yuan* a night then, which we thought was very cheap, but it was more than Hu Ping paid for rent for the entire month. Hu Ping told me when she first visited me twenty-three years ago at Heng Shan, it was the first time in her life she ever saw wall-to-wall carpet. And now, taking the place of the old red carpets was gleaming white marble and wide open spaces. The man in the elegant suit behind the desk was a far cry from the raggedy red-jacketed old man shuffling down the hall and who only sometimes appeared by the front door to greet us.

Back then, I never really thought of the building as being run down—it was just where we lived in China. Looking at its transformation made me realize how shabby it really had been back then.

Shanghai is a city of contrasts. On one side of the street you might see the most modern building, fifty or more stories high, and across the street are little alleyways lined with broken down houses full of multiple families crowded into single rooms. Huge freeways and bridges span little roads where one car can't even fit (twenty-five years ago there were no cars, except for the odd government official). I find this juxtaposition of the very modern and the very old, the most interesting aspect of Shanghai. It is everywhere one looks. A limousine passes a bike, wooden crate attached to the back which is full of something or other; bikes zigging in and out of unbelievable car traffic; little elderly Chinese slowly doing tai chi while younger Chinese walk their leashed cocker spaniels through the park; old shacks serving as the backdrop for modern giants. It's truly fascinating.

We then returned to my home away from home, so I could get ready to spend a few days exploring Xian. Hu Ping was going to use the time to catch up on business in Shanghai. Armed with much travel advice, I bade them farewell and headed out.

Chapter Four
Xian: Tour Guides and Terracotta Warriors

AS THE PLANE circled Xian, I fidgeted with anticipation. Xian, home of the Terra-cotta Warriors, Eighth Wonder of the World. Sheee-aaan, even the name has a magical and exotic sound to it. Get this plane down!

At the Xian Airport I looked for my guide. I could not see anyone. All over the airport, guides were holding aloft signs with names prominently displayed. The other passengers were all being met, and I was standing alone in the middle of the airport, desperately looking for someone who might have my name on a sign or sheet of paper. Finally I saw a tall, stringy woman, with short brown hair and shorter skirt, who was holding a large sheet of paper folded over. I walked up to her and pointed to the paper; she lazily opened it up, and sure enough, there was my name.

I held out my hand and smiled.

"Hi. My name is Ruth."

"Hello," she said, "my name is Peegee,"

"Peegee?"

"No, Pee-gee."

"Pee-gee?"

"No. Peegee. Peegee!" She was shuffling her feet in frustration.

"Spell it please."

"P-E-G-G-Y."

"Oh, *Peg*-gy?"

"Yes! Peegee."

"What is your Chinese name?"

"Wu Pei Kwan."

"Why don't you use your Chinese name?"

"Because foreigners cannot pronounce it or remember it." She then gazed upon me with a look that could only mean she thought I was the stupidest person in the world.

"I see."

And that was my introduction to Xian.

Xian is the capital of Shaanxi Province, a small city of six million. Xian was the start of the Silk Road, back in the second century B.C.E. when the city was still called Chang'an. This trade route connected East and West, bringing the desired silk and other materials, and also ideas, concepts, and news of the world, from the corner of Xian in China all the way through India, Russia, the Mediterranean, and on to Rome. It wasn't called "The Silk Road" until the 1800s, when the German scholar, Baron Ferdinand von Richthofen, named this greatest of the East-West trade routes. Over the time of the silk-laden caravans, a city sprang up that needed protection by strong stone walls. The walls from the Tang Dynasty (618-907 AD) that had been built for this purpose were fortified and enlarged by the Ming Dynasty (1368-1644 AD), leaving the city of Xian with the most complete and complex city wall system surviving today in China.

My guide expectations were high because of the excellent experiences with Joanna from Guilin. I had no reason to expect differently in Xian; well, after the sign in the airport, perhaps a little reason; well, okay, some significant reason, but still, I had expected Peggy to be at least adequate as a guide.

Peggy, or Wu Pei Kwan as I secretly and stubbornly referred to her in my mind, led the way up the stairs winding to the top of the walls of the city. That was about the extent of her guiding, as she wandered off somewhere and left me to contemplate the scenery. The walls surrounding the old city were built of stone twelve meters or forty feet high, almost fourteen meters or forty-six feet wide at the top, and even thicker at the bottom. They were almost fourteen kilometers (just under nine miles) in length and the walls were encircled by a large moat. The four main gates of the walls face in each direction, standing as sentries, and from my vantage point above the city, standing beneath the ramparts, it was easy to see how this wall system rendered these stones impervious to outsiders. The city sprawled on both sides of the moat. These walls restrained the invaders of centuries past, but they could not restrain urban sprawl, as they now sit in the middle of a thriving metropolis.

There was a stillness up on the walls, despite the bustling city down below. It was as if the walls imparted a protection, not only from invaders but from extraneous sounds and sights, from smells and from dust, so that I felt the walls and I were alone under the massive blue sky.

Strolling slowly along the ancient stones on top of the wall, so wide and so thick, I could easily imagine chariots galloping down its length. I liked being there because I could truly imagine the old days—I could feel the oldness in the stones, it just oozed out recounting sagas of long ago.

PEGGY HAD SUGGESTED that I attend a concert my first night in Xian—a show about the Tang Dynasty, with traditional music, dancing, and costumes. She explained that maybe my view wouldn't be so good because she really had to fight for a seat as it was very crowded, it was heavy tourist season, and although she had done her best, I shouldn't expect much. When I got there, I had a table for eight all to myself, third row from the stage. And the place was about one-third empty. Peggy did not want to sit with me though, because she said the place was too crowded. However, once I offered to buy her a drink and feed her some chips, she settled in for a spell.

The costumes and performances originated over a thousand years ago, in Chang'an, during the Tang Dynasty. I thoroughly enjoyed the ancient instruments, stringed and otherwise, such as the *Pai Xiao*, a three thousand year old instrument, somewhat reminiscent of panpipes. It is said that the Tang emperor was so impressed by a flock of orioles flying overhead that he ordered his musicians to compose music on the *Pai Xiao*, to imitate the sound of the orioles. We heard this music recreated by Gao Ming, internationally acclaimed as a *Pai Xiao* musician. The performances varied from drummers dancing and leaping over massive taiko drums to elaborately and brightly clad maidens waving long ribbons of silk in complicated patterns, to all-women orchestras of ancient stringed instruments.

Part of the ticket price included a post-concert traditional banquet, so Peggy sat me down for the Feng Wei Banquet Specialty meal. This is what the menu said (verbatim):

Appetizer assortment, steamed dumplings, fried dumplings, baked dumplings, dumplings in soup, sweetened dumplings, traditional homemade dumplings, seasonal fruit plate.

For dinner, I was first served ten little dumplings in a big steamer, then another five dumplings, then another five which were homemade, although I couldn't tell the difference, then some more dumplings, then dessert dumplings, then dessert soup, and then yet more dumplings. As much as I have always loved dumplings, I was plumb dumplinged out!

A free cocktail was included—I ordered the champagne cocktail. I chuckled over the fact that on the menu, a bottle of Perrier cost 35 *yuan* ($5.30 CDN) and a champagne cocktail cost 20 *yuan* ($3.03 CDN). The champagne wasn't half bad, either.

THE NEXT DAY—my first full day in Xian, I was picked up by Peggy and Driver Li. I had opted for a private car with Peggy and Driver Li as opposed to a huge tour bus—I'm not so great being in the middle of crowds of tourists and I had a list of specific things I wanted to see while in Xian. What I wasn't counting on was Peggy's English, or lack of it. She could spout out the odd memorized tour guide facts as though someone were pressing a "speak" button, but she had no idea what I was saying. I am better than most at deciphering fractured languages, but her English was very difficult to understand. At first, the Peggy puzzle was kind of fun and a challenge, but as the day wore on, I just got quieter and quieter. It would have been preferable had she just said to me at times, "I don't understand you." Instead she would say "yes" or "no" or something else which later on would turn out not to be true anyway. But at the start of the day, at our first stop, the Big Wild Goose Pagoda Buddhist Temple, I was still enjoying her.

She kept right on talking about Buddah's "disemples," even though I repeated the correct word for her countless times. She simply could not remember the word "disciple," no matter how many times I pronounced it. She then began telling me a mostly indecipherable story from long ago about a town that was bloody. I tried to clarify why it was bloody, and Peggy got more and more impatient with me, stamping her feet and waving her long, skinny arms. I couldn't imagine which great battle would have rendered the town bloody. It took me forever to figure out that *bloody* really was *flooded*.

The Big Wild Goose Pagoda Buddhist Temple was originally built in the Tang Dynasty in 652 CE. I found it intriguing that although the temple was full of tourists, many other people had come to worship and pray.

According to legend, there once were two branches of Buddhists, meat-eating and non-meat-eating. One day, the meat eaters could not find any food. One monk looked up at some wild geese flying overhead and said, "Today we have no meat. I hope the merciful Bodhisattva will give us some." And just then, the lead goose broke its wings and fell to the ground. The monks felt that this was a signal ordering them to be more pious. They established this pagoda on the spot where the goose fell and desisted from eating meat thereafter. And that it why it is called Big Wild Goose Pagoda.

The Pagoda houses the multitudinous materials and artifacts brought back from India by the hierarch Xuanzang, who, after seventeen years and one hundred countries, returned to China with Buddha figures, artifacts, and sutras (dialogues of Buddha), many of which were translated into Chinese, as well as tomes of great importance to scholars.

Next, Driver Li chauffeured us to the Jade Factory. On our way, we passed a lumber yard—Peggy called it the wooden factory. When we were in the car, Peggy kept asking me what animals I liked. I told her about my dog at home, and how much I missed her. I thought it was nice of her to ask.

Once we got to the Jade Factory, Peggy handed me over to the local guide, Amy, and after whispering a few words to her in Chinese, left me with her to do the touring.

There was a small area near the entrance, behind a large observation window, where people worked with the stone, and a huge area, which was called a gallery, except every item had a price tag. After a time in China, I learned that a "factory" really meant a small area where the craft was practiced and a large area where sales were made, or at least strongly urged. I decided that the definition of a factory was a place where the tourists were supposed to go to spend their money.

Amy greeted me and immediately walked me over to a shelf of jade dogs. They were nice, but I was interested in observing the jade carvers on the other side of the observation windows. Amy left me by the windows watching the carvers and returned shortly with a handful of jade dogs.

"Amy, why do you keep showing me dogs?" I asked.

"You do not like them?"

"Of course, I like them, but I want to see everything here, not just jade dogs."

"You will not buy a jade dog?" she asked incredulously. "Your guide told me you wanted to buy a jade dog."

Peggy arrived. "You buy dog?" she asked.

"No, I did not buy a dog."

"But you tell me you like dog!" Peggy frowned at me. "I do like dogs, but that doesn't necessarily mean I want to buy a jade one."

"Why you no buy dog? I tell guide you buy dog," Peggy muttered as she sulked off towards the door.

By now, Peggy/Wu Pei Kwan was starting to irritate me just a bit.

WE DROVE BY a number of buildings set in a park-like area. I asked what it was. Peggy said it used to be a *dsood*.

"A what?" I asked, peering out the window.

"A *dsood*. A *dsood!*" She leaned forward, pounding her fists on the armrest, shouting at me as though I were cretinous, "Dsood, dsood—zed oh, oh, *dsood!*"

Oh, of course.

We continued our touring at the terra-cotta factory. Again, there was a small room with a couple of workers making headless terra-cotta figures, then a huge upstairs and downstairs full of display stores. Presumably, the terra cotta head factory was elsewhere. On display (and for sale) were silk rugs, embroidered and silk clothing, jewelry, many terra-cotta figures of course, and jade sculptures.

A young man with a gentle demeanor and earnest looking eyes, wearing a crisp suit, approached me.

"Please, to try this on. It will look beautifully on you." "Please," he continued, "to feel this. What a wonderful souvenir for you."

He worked so hard, and was so nice about it that I felt I let him down when I didn't buy anything. However, on the way out, I did see a souvenir that I liked a lot. I asked Peggy if we would have a chance to see more like that, as it was not cheap.

"Oh no," she said, "only here."

"Are you sure?" I asked. It was a 3D depiction of the terra cotta warriors set in an acrylic slab, and it seemed to me that this type of souvenir would likely be available at the museum where we were going later that day.

"Yes," she answered. "I'm sure. Only get here."

Needless to say, I bought the souvenir, and saw it many times over during the day for less than half of what I paid for it. I was miffed more than a little bit.

On we drove, chatting away in the car about the emperor. Our conversations sounded like this:

Me: "How did the emperor die?"

Peggy: "Fifty years old."

Me: "Why did the emperor bury the terracotta warriors?"

Peggy (emphatically): "Yes!"

TALKING WITH PEGGY reminded me of an incident I remembered from when I lived in China in the 1980s. An Australian friend, Pam, had needed some writing paper. She walked into a shop.

Pam: "Do you have some paper?"

Shop lady: "Some paper?"

Pam: "Yes, I need some writing paper."

Shop lady: "Writing paper?"

Pam: "Yes."

Shop lady: "Do you speak English?"

I laughed with Pam when we talked about it. She teased me because often when I was trying to increase my Chinese vocabulary, I would ask a local, "Say it in Chinese please" and the response would invariably be, "It in Chinese please."

WE FINALLY ARRIVED at my reason for coming to Xian—the Museum of Qin Terra-cotta Warriors and Horses. In 1974, some local farmers were digging a well, and they found some pottery shards. Originally, the local farmers were upset, because they thought finding pottery pieces of people, like fingers, etc., was, as Peggy put it, *bad lucky*. They alerted the officials, and the archeologists arrived en masse. They unearthed thousands and thousands of life-size terra-cotta warriors and horses that the emperor had buried. The site has now been named the Eighth Wonder of the World.

When we got to the museum, I made a particularly clumsy dismount from the van. Immediately, I was surrounded by at least a dozen guys pushing wheelchairs. "Madam, madam, wheelchair, wheelchair." I shook my head politely but they kept following me, willing me to fall into the seat of their particular wheeled chariot. I ended up having to shout at them in Chinese, "*Bu yao, bu yao*! (I don't want it, I don't want it)." Only then did they disperse. Peggy, of course, did nothing to help me emerge from the wheelers and dealers, and I had to hurry to catch up with her.

The terra cotta warriors were ordered to be built by Qin Shi Huang (Chin Shee Whong), the first Emperor of China, in the second century, BC. Although his legacy was very complex, he was thought to have unified all of China and began construction of the precursor of the Great Wall of China. Qin Shi Huang wanted to be immortal, and while his physicians were searching the world for products that would extend his longevity, he ingested mercury as a stopgap measure. He ultimately died from mercury poisoning, ironic since the only reason he took it was to live longer. In his later years, he did not want to be alone in the afterlife, should it come to that, and so he had constructed a huge underground mausoleum with thousands of soldiers and horses who would protect him as they stood in their ceramically inert forms in and around the underground rivers of mercury their emperor had designed. The enormity of this project and Qin Shi Huang's concepts, twisted though they may have been, were absolutely unbelievable, all the more so when I thought about the fact that this happened thousands of years ago, before modern tools and conveniences.

When the warriors were dug up, they were all in pieces because some rebels thousands of years ago had ransacked the tombs and burned all the warriors. So, as a sign by one of the archaeological pits states: "The pottery warriors and horses were stick together from hundreds of broken pieces." The archaeologists did a lot of sticking, and the results and sites were amazing, truly.

There was a long driveway from the parking lot to the main museum area, which we traversed by tram. Once in the main area, I looked around the plaza: a large central square surrounded by five or six large buildings. The ground was concrete, the buildings were concrete, very modern and very clean looking, both in look and actuality. There were flowers planted along the outside of the buildings, which looked inviting.

The museum had three main pits. Pit 1 was the largest and was the first to be opened. In Pit 1, there were over two thousand unearthed warriors and horses, with another four thousand yet to be dug up, all standing ready for battle. Every one was different. It was an awesome site—gave me shivers to see it. Impressive also was the edifice over Pit 1—a huge dome, with the ceiling spanning the entire distance across the archaeological site with no support except on the sides. It was a stunning architectural achievement—sloping sides leading up to a massive curved dome of a ceiling, covering six thousand terra cotta warriors and horses. The modern and the ancient blended together into a unified whole. I couldn't get enough of Pit 1 and wanted to stay there for a long time.

Since I could not rely upon Peggy for any kind of accurate information, I had taken to reading the signs that were displayed all through Pit 1. After each sign, Peggy would suggest that we go for lunch, and I would suggest that we continue reading the signs.

After we concluded the tour of Pit 1, Peggy dug in her heels and damn near insisted we go for lunch. So we left and walked through the plaza, under a group of tall, leafy trees and into another building which housed the restaurant, even though I personally could have foregone lunch and stayed with the terracotta warriors. Once we got there we were told there were no seats, yet half the place was empty.

After a lot of yelling (in Chinese) between Peggy and the hostess, I agreed to go upstairs to another restaurant and have a quick lunch.

Peggy said: "I pick you up at 1:50."

Me: "No, 1:30."

Peggy: "1:50."

Me: "1:40."

Peggy: "1:50."

Me: "No, 1:40."

Lunch was what Chinese think Westerners want in a Chinese lunch, fork and all. I have to keep remembering that I am making assumptions about the Chinese as well; it's not only them making assumptions about me. I'm sure I'm just as wrong in my assumptions about them as they most certainly are in theirs about me.

Peggy showed up perhaps a bit closer to 1:40 than to 1:50 and took me over to see the 360° movie, depicting a brief history of the site, prior to heading over to Pit 2. While looking at the archers and chariots ready for battle in their terracotta armour, Peggy kept trying to tell me something. She said the warriors were the *maxid*. She was very angry at me for not understanding her.

"Why you not understand English?" she yelled. "They are maxid!"

I had been very patient up until now, but the last two days' frustrations finally got to me. "Peggy, there is no such English word as *maxid*," I yelled back. I don't think she believed me.

"The *maxid*, the *maxid*," she yelled, stomping her foot heavily, and then spelling it out for stupid me. Then with her index finger, she wrote the English letters on her palm, but it still took me about fifteen more minutes to realize she was talking about the "mixture" of warriors, horses, and archers.

In Pit 2, there were some display cases. In one was a sword found during excavation. After two thousand years, this sword was still sharp! It contained chromium. The Germans discovered chrome-plating in 1937, but the Chinese used it over 2200 years ago. The ancient Chinese also had mastered using alloys, and their weapons were very scientifically crafted. For example, an arrowhead might contain a higher percentage of lead for greater killing power. Combinations of copper and tin were recorded for different types of bronze ware and many of these were displayed.

On the way to Pit 3, we passed though the gift shop. Sure enough, there was my souvenir, many of them, all significantly cheaper than I had paid earlier that day. Peggy pretended that she didn't see them, which was quite a feat, since they were everywhere.

Pit 3, the latest dig to be discovered, was thought to contain the command centre or headquarters for the other two pits. The Multi-Exhibition Hall Museum, which displayed many special exhibits behind glass, complete with printed explanations, was our last stop. The entire complex was an impressive site, and well worth the trip to Xian. In spite of the aggravation of Peggy, seeing those terracotta warriors affected my life; even the thought of the site still gives me shivers.

A long road led back to the parking lot where Driver Li awaited. It was very, very hot, and we were tired after spending the day walking around the museum site. It was as though in order to get to the car, we had to walk the gauntlet of loud, overbearing and overeager vendors.

The vendors surrounded us, grasping at our arms, shoving their wares in our faces, and shouting, "Lady, lady, ten dollars, ten dollars, too much, okay five dollars, five dollars, look lady, one dollar, one dollar, lady, lady look one dollar, one dollar." And there were hundreds of them, fighting with each tourist and with each other. I wish I could say Peggy came to the rescue, but she did not. Looking bored and distinctly untroubled, she slowly meandered ahead while I battled to keep a modicum of space around me into which the vendors were determined to insinuate themselves.

Capitalism has captured China with a vengeance. There are places I didn't even want to go to because of the vendors. Peggy wanted to take me to a silk "factory." Although I truly would have loved to see the silk making process, I put it off for another time. I didn't want to fight off a bunch of people trying to sell me something I didn't want. Everything cost money—not a lot, mind you, but one still has to pay. At lunch, a young woman came around with a decanter and glasses, very tiny glasses, and asked if I would like to try some pomegranate wine.

Free samples, I thought.

"Sure," I said. She poured a thimbleful of wine. I smiled and drank.

"That will be five *yuan*," she said. So I paid.

After the warriors, we went to Huaqing Hot Springs, a lovely area ranked among the Hundred Famous Gardens in China. It was developed around 600 CE for the Emperor Xuanzong (685-762) and the beautiful Lady Yang Guifei to take a bath. They had pools for the lady, pools for the emperor and pools for the princes, and pools for the officials, and I was starting to get just a bit bored looking at all the different pools. We walked over to a wonderful area with spigots and mineral water coming out—it is supposed to be healing water, it was a very hot day and the water looked so inviting. Peggy asked me if I wanted to wash with the water.

"Sure," I said, "I would love to." So I did.

"Half a *yuan*," she said.

I paid.

On the way back, we were supposed to go back to the old wall—my request, because I truly loved the old wall, although I was pretty tuckered after nine hours of walking. However, after Peggy and Driver Li chatted a bit, Peggy said that it would cost more money to go to the wall; not part of our original deal. I snapped. That was the last straw. I told them to take me home. I felt as though they didn't see me, but just saw one large *yuan*. It made me very sad for this country which I love. But then I came back to the hotel, tired, grumpy, disillusioned, lugging my stuff behind me. As I got off the elevator, a housekeeping person saw me, immediately came over, took my packages, and led me to my room and opened the door for me. This was a large hotel, yet she knew which room was mine and she was incredibly helpful and kind. My spirits and enthusiasm for the country revived instantly.

Later on that evening, I walked into the gift shop to buy a post card. A group of young girls were chattering away in Chinese and Sarah McLaughlin was singing about angels in the background. I love all these strange juxtapositions.

THE NEXT MORNING, I got picked up by Peggy and Driver Li at six a.m. to go to the airport and back to Shanghai. Driver Li had a pet cricket, *Guo-guo*, in a jar in his car. He'd had him for two weeks. Their life expectancy is about four months. He fed him corn. Driver Li would sing to the cricket and the cricket would sing to Driver Li.

On the way to the airport, the conversation went like this:

Peggy: "I want ask you something."

Ruth: "Sure, go ahead. Ask."

Peggy: "What means 'duck'?"

Ruth: "Duck?"

Peggy: "Yes, duck."

Ruth: "Duck? Duck???"

Peggy: "Yes, duck. At airport, you tell me you were duck."

Ruth: "Duck? No, I don't think so. Duck? Oh, you mean doctor?"

Peggy: "No doctor. Duck. You tell me you duck. I later ask my husband what means duck and he not know. What means duck?"

Ruth: "Duck? Duck is *ya* (I translated for her into Chinese—duck)."

Peggy: "No *ya*. Duck. Sometime people who not married . . ."

Ruth: "You mean people who are not married are duck?"

Peggy: (enthusiastically) "Yes!"

Ruth: "No. There is no duck."

Peggy: "Yes. Duck, duck." Her voice was implying that I didn't know of the existence of the very word I was purported to have spoken.

Ruth: "Duck . . . duck . . . You mean divorced?"

Peggy: "No." After a time, she said very softly, "Maybe I make mistake."

That was the first, and only, time that Peggy/Wu Pei Kwan ever admitted to having made a mistake. I never did figure out what she meant.

At the airport in Xian:

Peggy: "How you see friend? You friend meet you at airport?"

Ruth: "No. I'm taking the train and she'll meet me at the train."

Peggy: (shocked) "By yourself?"

Ruth: "Of course, by myself."

Peggy: "No. You no want people to meet you? You can't go by yourself."

Ruth: "No. I can take the train by myself."

Peggy: "I tell people to meet you."

Ruth: "I don't *want* people to meet me."

Peggy: (shaking her head in despair at this stubborn foreigner who thought she could travel alone in China): "How you go by yourself?"

Peggy then took it upon herself to tell everyone, or so it seemed, at the Xian airport, to take care of me. I don't know what she said, but I literally wasn't allowed to move an inch without someone grabbing my arm and my luggage (which was just carry-on and very easy to manage). I was glad to leave Xian.

The Museum of Qin Terra-cotta Warriors and Horses was outstanding and well worth the visit, but the vendors and especially the fallacious assumptions about foreigners had become an effrontery. Finally alone, I walked through the departure gate, one confident and happy foreigner, much to the chagrin of Peggy, my less-than-perfect guide who was so positive I would not survive alone in her country. I walked forward, leaving her shaking her head in dismay at my perceived ignorance. Yet I knew that through that gate lay many more wonderful adventures in China. And I was right.

Chapter Five
Return to Shanghai: Inside the City

THE PLANE FROM Xian arrived back in Shanghai at Pu Dong Airport. As we taxied to a complete stop, the music in the plane came on, loudly playing "The Mexican Hat Dance," followed by "Vaya Con Dios." It was perhaps my fallacious assumption that "The Mexican Hat Dance" and "Vaya Con Dios" would only be played in North and South America and not in China. I didn't know why I felt like that, but by the time "Vaya Con Dios" came on, I could barely contain myself. I could not understand why people were not convulsed with laughter while standing in the aisle, as I was. Nobody else even appeared to notice the music or at least seemed to think it unusual. Perhaps it was I who was out of place.

In the airport, I asked directions twice, and then, walking past KFC, followed the signs to the MagLev, an electric train faster than the Bullet Train of Japan. I had no trouble making my way at all. The MagLev had big comfy seats of golden plush leather, which really shouldn't have mattered as the ride only took seven minutes to traverse a distance that would have taken one hour by car. We reached a speed of 431 km/hr. The ride was smooth and fascinating. Each car had a little sign above the doorway stating what the speed was at that moment. I really enjoyed that ride (and it saved Hu Ping and Xiao Li hours in the car) and barely had time to feel smug about Peggy's insistence that I could not navigate Chinese planes and trains on my own.

WHEN I GOT back home to Hu Ping's, there was her son Jun, who had just arrived from California. I first met him in China when he was four years old. He was now twenty-seven. He had graduated from Berkeley, and now had another one and a half years to finish his architecture degree. He was spending a few months in Shanghai working with his dad. That night, we went out for dinner: Hu Ping, Jin Jie, Jun, his girlfriend, and me.

Before dinner, we went to visit Jin Jie's and Hu Ping's offices. I wanted to see where they worked, and I think they wished to show me the offices of which they were so proud. They have the whole twenty-fifth floor of a large office building and employ over forty people there. In the ten to twelve years prior to my trip, they had done one hundred and eighty-six projects in China. Some projects have thousands of buildings, such as large residential complexes. Their largest was almost nine square kilometers, with over eight thousand units. I remember when my family was involved in building in California, and each section of our project was two hundred units, which we then though was huge. I guess everything is relative, so to speak.

We got off the elevator and were faced with a beautiful sign announcing the architectural company. Inside the reception area were two smiling young women, just cleaning up and getting ready to leave work for the day. Everything was very modern and clean and elegant. We walked around a corner and there, facing us on the wall, was the "Employee of the Month" chart, full of happy faces beaming out at us. An easiness prevailed; I did not feel stilted or uncomfortable at all, but rather, excited somehow by the surroundings. I was tempted to get a ping pong game going once I saw the table in the staff room, but was lured away to see the main office, via a large board room—I could see Jin Jie sitting at the head of the oval wooden table, his calm intelligent voice ringing out. My reverie was interrupted by Hu Ping pulling me into the large office where two desks sat, one for Jin Jie and one for her. A large shelving unit along one wall held many trophies and awards that they had won. There were wonderful renditions of projects they had worked on hanging everywhere on the walls. I felt such a burst of pride for my friends. Jin Jie explained that they are only the twelfth largest firm in Shanghai, although they are one of the largest International or "out of China" firms. This was a long way from our tour the week before of their humble beginnings.

I sat on the cream-coloured leather sofa in their office and laughed with Jun and Xiao Li, while Jin Jie and Hu Ping attended to business. When they were done, we all went down to the Green Dragonfly Restaurant, which had been newly renovated and was located on the second floor of their office building. It was the night before the official opening to the public, and the restaurant had invited special guests for a private run-through. Because of Jin Jie's status, we were VIP guests.

The restaurant was amazing. We walked up a wide flight of wooden stairs, covered by a canopy lit by little coloured lights. It was very tastefully done, with images of green dragonflies projected onto the steps. At the top of the landing was a large Buddha, with incense burning in front of him.

Inside were many waterfalls and streams full of happily swimming fish, ostensibly happy because they were not going to be eaten. The chandeliers had crystals hanging from them, with rainbow light shimmering off the crystals, glistening in the air. For some reason, I seemed to have become enthralled with the lighting chandeliers on this trip to China, and in this restaurant were some of the finest I'd seen—artistic and original shapes, prisms reflecting rainbows, yet none of them were ostentatious. Everywhere we went I was always surprised at how beautiful and original the lighting chandeliers were, mostly a luscious gold or silver metal with wonderful prisms and lights entangled in the structure. I have a personal affinity to lights and prisms and rainbows. In fact, I opened a hologram gallery in Calgary in the 1980s. It was one of the first in Canada. I never tired of looking at the holograms and prisms of lights.

We were taken down a curved walkway and shown into our dining area. Each dining area in this section was separated from the others by curtains of metal filaments or panels, all very beautiful. We had a sofa and chairs and many, many pillows in front of which was an elegantly set table, as though the royalty of the world were expected for dinner. The sofa was set up high, so that we walked up a step or two to sit down. Then we were at just the right height for the dining table, yet we could recline into the masses of subdued coloured pillows all around us. A little silver bell, like our teachers used to have on their desks at school, discreetly sat on the table, should we wish to summon a server. Even though the restaurant was huge, we felt completely private. In our own little room, the sounds around us were muted. There must have been hundreds of other people dining there that evening, yet we were alone in our little nest—protected from sounds and stares of the other diners as we lounged in our hedonistic urban chic alcove.

The deputy manager came to welcome us, introduced himself as "English name David" and apologized personally to me that their English menus weren't available until the next day. "Have a rest," he said, "have a rest."

And we did, reclining amongst the pillows in our Baccanalian luxury. I ordered the house special cocktail to start, which was milk, mint, and wine. I couldn't conceive of a drink with that mixture, and curiosity compelled me to try it. Although it sounded appalling, I have to say it was truly delicious—the kind of drink that could serve equally as a before dinner cocktail or an after dinner cocktail. It was really, really good! Even now, some time later, when the memory of that drink hits my taste buds, I smile at the unlikely combination of ingredients, knowing that I will never come close to making it on my own. So I guess I will have to return to the Green Dragonfly for an encore.

Then the food started coming. It was the first meal we had without a huge discussion as to what to order—we were just brought one delicacy after another. Jun and I decided the style was Asian fusion. We had coffee and bean paste served on Pringles. That's one thing that hasn't changed in the past quarter century—Pringles potato chips were as ubiquitous then as they still are now—

all the hotels have them in the mini-bars—they are everywhere! We had real fois gras, served with strips of bread crusts, shrimp with caviar, smoked duck, and on and on it came. They brought a huge ice bowl to the table full of Chinese vegetables served with a wasabi sauce. We had a delicious curried crab and little dumplings folded into shapes like tiny chickens, or maybe they were meant to be crabs, it was hard to tell.

At one point, the owner and manager came into our little dining room to toast us. There is a special way of holding a glass with each hand which is meant to show honour—it was very formal, and was very sweet as the gentleman toasted our table.

The food service went on and on. And much to my delight, after the last of many desserts, they brought watermelon. Hu Ping and I looked at each other and giggled. When I lived in China a quarter of a century ago, many folks called me *Aiyi Shi Gua* (Ah-yee shee gua, which means Auntie Watermelon) because I loved watermelon and ate it so often. It was a perfect end to a perfect meal and evening.

The next day, Wang Yisheng and Shen Laoshe came to our place. As a gift, they brought me watermelon. She remembered! Hu Ping and our guests reminisced before going for lunch.

I learned that while Hu Ping was dating Jin Jie she worked at a fabric factory. The boss of the fabric factory warned her against dating Jin Jie, telling her he was a very dangerous man, ostensibly because his parents were in Taiwan. She didn't stop seeing him but the price she had to pay for that was no advancement and no pay raises. I think in the long run, she is very happy to have stayed with Jin Jie!

After sharing mostly sad memories of experiences and losses during the cultural revolution, the four of us walked to the restaurant where I had been with Jin Jie and Hu Ping the first night I was here—the Tang Dynasty Palace Restaurant (*Tang Kong Fandien*). This is one of my favourite all-time restaurants because the food is exceptionally fresh and delicious. I loved coming here. This restaurant seats about four hundred people and always seems to be very full and very loud. In Shanghai, people don't have *dim sum* the way we are used to it— which is the Cantonese Way. Back home, the little carts are wheeled around the dining room, they stop at each table, the server lifts the lids and the diner points to what delicacy should be placed on the table. One never needs to know the names of the items, as point and eat works very well. Luckily for me however, I had learned the names of my favourite dishes, because in Shanghai, things were done differently.

Here it was called *Dien Shien*, and instead of carts coming around, we wrote on a piece of paper what we wanted. Even though I couldn't write Chinese, I attempted to speak culinary Chinese, and usually Hu Ping translated my mangled Chinese and wrote it down on the order sheet. The food was still the same—I could still order *jiaotze, ha gow, ham soi go, mi fen* just like at home.

We had a large meal, again with a lot of consultation as to the dishes. I kept urging Wang Yisheng to eat more. Although she did eat with enthusiasm, she didn't eat much. Wang Yisheng is a very tiny person. Over lunch, I learned that she weighed 35 kg, which meant that my dog, Reenie, a wolf-husky cross, weighed more than she did!

Several months hence, Wang Yisheng and Shen Laoshe were going to visit their daughter in Paris for two months. They would also be traveling to Italy. This dinner was my farewell to them. I was sad to say good-bye to them, but hope to see them again sometime.

WALKING HOME, HU Ping and I entered the complex where we lived, called *Hua Ming*. This was the first time we had actually walked through the entire complex, as we usually were just dropped off at the front door by the car. There were many tall buildings surrounding walkways, waterfalls, playgrounds, tennis courts, and gardens laid out between them. But what I liked the best was the sign at the entrance listing the rules, both in English and Chinese. Here is the English (verbatim):

1. All facility is designed for residents of community only.
2. Please don't shinny up trees, pick flowers, trample on the lawn — please cherish surrounding of whole community.
3. Children playing in courtyard using facilities shall company with the guardian, please regard safety.
4. Please don't discard rubbish, sundries at discretion, keep the tidiness of the community.
5. When the pet go outside, the retinue shall accompany around, please don't let it out at will.
6. Please obey above regulations conscientiously.
Definitely directions we should all follow.
I liked #5 the best. Hu Ping laughed. "What are they supposed to do? Push it back in?"

ANOTHER RESTAURANT, ANOTHER menu. We passed over (verbatim): the steamed meat balls in supine soup, the lamb chep Austrillia style, poached bamboo, and the double boiled snow frogger stuffed papayan. I smiled at marinated fish in "cotus leave"—I was pretty sure they meant lotus but with the menus we've been looking at lately, it could just as easily been coitus. It seemed to me that this restaurant really wanted to be Western—the first thing on the menu was Tiramisu highlighted with a big photo of it. Below the tiramisu was their feature dish—a photo of a meager plate, entitled baked potato skin. And there sat one lone potato skin on a large plate. The description followed: "it is used American potato, added unique sauce and baked with pozza cheese. It's scented and tasty." Yum!

Over dinner we talked about housekeepers/cleaning ladies who are the same the world over. Jun told us about Lu, Hu Ping's cleaning lady. He commented that maybe she did a little too much. One day Jin Jie had sorted out pictures from a trip into many piles, only to find that Lu mixed them all up and put them back into one neat pile. That morning, Hu Ping got out her clothes for our upcoming trip—five days worth of socks, underwear, pants, etc. All in five little piles. Lu put them all back in her drawers! I suddenly worried about the little plastic glass I traveled with and used for taking liquid vitamins. I had visions of it being safely stashed away somewhere never to be found again. Luckily, after lunch I had the presence of mind to ask where my little glass was before Lu left because otherwise I never would have found where she put it. It was standing very neatly at the far back end of a high cupboard, looking very forlorn indeed until I rescued it and it could resume its journey with me.

BACK IN THE 1980s when I first arrived in Shanghai, it was early in the year and was freezing cold, so much so that I was forced to buy a cashmere sweater. What a hardship that was! I loved that sweater. I wore it every day that Chinese winter and many times since and it still looks brand new. Sometimes, I just take it out of my closet and feel the softness of it and remember . . .

As the months passed, it grew very, very hot, and I was suffering in my Calgary summer clothes. I thought Calgary in the summer was pretty hot, but it paled in comparison to Shanghai in the summer. I spoke with one of the school interpreters who took me to a tailor. I explained what I wanted—a very simple pair of short pants (or long shorts, depending upon how one looked at it), with a draw-string waist. That was it. The tailor told us this was too easy and they would not make it. So the interpreter suggested I try the tailors who work on the streets.

By then I had been in China for some months, and was able to speak a bit and find my way around the city. I had purchased the lightest cotton material I could find in the store, and then had to take it home to wash and shrink it in the bathtub, which took several days. Once the material was ready, our bus, on the way to dropping us off at the hospital to work, made a quick stop at an "independent" tailor. This gentleman was known by my interpreters, and he had set up his work space on the street. He had three machines and was very successful. He did not need an office or a studio or any type of shelter, for that matter. He just worked from the street. So the bus stopped. The school interpreter hopped out with me and explained to the tailor what I wanted.

At first, this tailor said it was too difficult! We explained again, and I realized that the difficulty came from my being a Westerner. I implored him in broken Chinese to help me not suffer from heat prostration and to make me these pants. He finally said he would try. He then measured me while hundreds of onlookers all offering advice gathered around us, all marveling at my Western girth.

The next day, the bus stopped at the street tailor for my first pair of pants. I had gray material and blue material, so he had made a blue pair and a gray pair, but he had some material left over, so at my urging, he made another pair, blue on one side, grey on the other. Hu Ping remembered them well. She was amazed when I told her I still have them and I still wear them! Those pants were a lifesaver when we later went down the Yangtze River and when we were in Mongolia. I thanked that street tailor many times over on that trip.

On this trip, I found myself in a similar situation—again, the heat and humidity was more than I had anticipated, and the clothes which I thought would be light summer clothes all of a sudden seemed too many layers thick. And I was tired of doing laundry every second day. So off we went down the street, carrying some articles of my clothing to show for samples. We went into the fabric store, had a mini consultation with the owner and she took us around the corner to Xiao Yang (Little Yang, because he was only around thirty years old). Xiao Yang heard what Hu Ping had to say and nodded. As he was measuring me, he started to smile. He said he had never made clothes for anyone that big before!

Xiao Yang and his wife lived and worked in this structure—I would be loath to actually call it a building—maybe ten feet by ten feet, right off the alleyway. It was built out of sheet metal and old grey wood. Half of it consisted of a loft under a low wooden ceiling, which served as their bed at night. A wooden ladder which they used to go up to the "bedroom" was pushed out of the way during the day. There was a small fridge in one corner. There was no visible bathroom or running water. Their two year old son lived in the country with his grandmother. They both worked very hard. Most of the money they made went to their son, so that he could have a better future and be able to go to college and have a good job. They both seemed like such nice, personable folks; it was obvious they worked very diligently, and took their jobs seriously. Hu Ping said they were lucky to have these jobs, as many people cannot find work these days.

After over an hour of talking and gesticulating and measuring, we left, leaving several articles of my clothing for him to study—he returned them to Hu Ping's house at ten o'clock that night. After buying the material and consulting with Xiao Yang about the labour and design, the cost of an "outfit"— which consisted of cotton pants just below my knees with zippered pockets, and a cotton shirt with pockets—came to about ten dollars for everything. Needless to say, I ordered several such "outfits." The price had gone up though, because the pants I had made on the street in the 1980s were less than one dollar each!

I anxiously awaited these pants before heading off to the Yangtze Gorges, the hottest part of China. Hu Ping's apartment was very cool, so in the apartment, I was very comfortable. But outside it was pretty hot and humid and would only be worse on the water.

XIAO LI DROVE Hu Ping and myself out to a complex of single-family houses, which had been one of Jin Jie's projects. He had designed the complex, but the developer couldn't pay his fee, so he gave Jin Jie two houses. Now we were in the car, driving on four lane boulevards away from the frenetic freeways of downtown Shanghai. It still looked like the city, but the buildings were lower and there were only thousands of people instead of tens or hundreds of thousands. An occasional tree could be seen. We drove by low-rise buildings and even the odd field swooshed by the car windows. The farther we were outside of the downtown core, the more we would see vehicles other than cars, contraptions I could never have imagined, such as little bicycles loaded down with enough product to fill a semi-trailer. Scooters, rickshaws, buses, and motorcycles weaved in and out of cars, which were still the predominant mode of transportation.

On our way to the country house complex, we saw the Chinese equivalent of the squeegee people. They walked along cars stopped at traffic lights, their backs straining with the weight of their wares, trying to sell maps, back supports, sun screens for car windows, and car re-chargers for cell phones. A pink-shirted, middle-aged woman looked up and our eyes met. She wore a white floppy hat to keep the sun out of her eyes, and even though her cotton shirt was light, the heat of the day showed in her face and slow movements of her body. I felt very uncomfortable sitting in my air-conditioned vehicle watching her. My heart

ached for her. Once more I wondered at the luck of life, and how we each came
to be in our respective places. Dozens and dozens of these people stood on each
corner in this area outside of the downtown core, both men and women. Only
once all day did I see someone buy something.

Xiao Li drove into a beautiful area through a large adobe rock tunnel,
following the road which wound around a lane leading to the houses. Off to
the right was a large circular building still under construction, which was to
be the clubhouse, Hu Ping explained. We pulled into a driveway which was
on a lane of large houses, quite close to one another, all with very manicured
lawns, gardens, and walkways. I thought of the cultural differences of "country
houses"—my preference would have been to have many, many trees in a wild
or more natural kind of setting with lots of space and privacy. These country
houses were beautiful, it's true, but they sat on a regular, albeit upscale street,
almost looking as though it were a Hollywood set.

The houses in this complex were very different from the ones in downtown
Shanghai and I doubt that regular citizens could afford them. Basically, they
were houses for ex-pats, people who had left China and perhaps returned, but
were used to a more lavish way of living. This type of 'North-American rich"
style house was very popular. In Phase One, twenty-five houses were built; in
phase two, thirty-five. Two more phases were yet to come. All houses were sold.
These houses were huge—the smaller style was just under forty-five hundred
square feet, and the larger one just over seventy-five hundred square feet. The
average house in the complex was over four thousand square feet, with the
average cost being about one million dollars of our money. They had every
modern convenience, with fully equipped kitchens and bathrooms. Hu Ping's
smaller house was already partially furnished and they were planning to use it
as a model of sorts. She had done an excellent job on both the interior and the
gardens. The country house was decorated to my taste exactly with lots of wood
and glass and natural elements, subdued and lush at the same time.

They were going to move in there briefly and then move into the bigger one
when it was ready—it was still under construction.

The houses sat next to each other, just above a stream behind a large lawn
with multiple gardens. Hu Ping spent some time with the gardener, planning
for more flowers around the huge stone barbecue and fire pit area.

AFTER WE DROVE back to the city, Hu Ping took me to Yu Yuen. *Yuen*
means garden, *yu* translates as peace and health, and the gardens were designed
with tranquility in mind. The car dropped us off on a busy street.

"We're here," Hu Ping said.

"Where? Where are the gardens?" I asked, remembering my last time there, so many years ago. I had a day off from my studies and thought it would be nice to go to a garden and read a book. A vague memory of Yu Yuen filled my head, from when I was first in China in the 1970s. That would be perfect, I thought.

I took a taxi from my home, and the cab dropped me off on a busy street. This was nothing like what I remembered. I started walking, wondering exactly where the gardens were. I was in an old section of town, so I started walking the colourful streets, wondering exactly where Yu Yuen might be. I walked by people cleaning their chickens in the street, washing their laundry, doing their mending, all outside because their inside accommodations were so small. I saw little children waddling in front of their doorsteps, their bulky pants opening in the rear to reveal little white bums. I marveled at how differently cultures addressed infants, and the clothing thereof. The first time I was in China, our group was delighted with the clothes of the young: from the front, they looked like regular clothes; from the back, they were split open almost to the waist. That way, when the youngster needed to relieve her/him self, she would just squat, do the deed, get up, with no dirty diapers to be changed. Pretty clever—we all admired the ingeniousness of the clothes-makers.

I sauntered by five old women squatting in the street in front of their purple plastic tubs full of murky water, washboards sticking out over the top, rubbing clothes, chatting within their group, and minding the toddlers. I smiled and nodded at them, while they stared at me without missing even one downward rub on their washboards.

I continued walking by markets with rotten tomatoes proudly displayed, live eels being sliced open, fish flip-flopping, chickens dead and alive, and after about an hour of wandering, started asking people where the gardens were. In those days, I could speak Chinese minimally, and was quite proud of my ability to use the language. Everyone gave me different answers, and to this day I don't know if it was because of my defective language abilities or if they didn't know or if they wanted to have fun with the foreigner. At one point, two men were both so sure of the way—except they each pointed in opposite directions. I wandered around for another hour until I spotted two Western people with a Chinese guide. I asked them for directions and was told to follow them. They were in a hurry, so I ran behind them for a quarter of an hour, and we came to exactly the spot where the cab had first left me off. They pointed at a wall of buildings and doors and walked off.

I stood there scratching my head, wondering where a famous garden could be hidden among the wall of edifices that looked back at me. I had apparently found the gardens but didn't know how to get in. Small wonder—I barely managed to notice the gate. It was just a carved wooden door along a wall of other doors and buildings. I could not see the gardens from the street. A young Chinese man who wanted to practice English walked by and decided to help me in exchange for an English conversation. Together we found a door to the garden which had a sign announcing it was locked until one o'clock. Another door had a notice saying to try still a third door. On my way to the fourth door leading to the gardens, I bumped into some of my fellow students, got distracted, and went for lunch.

After lunch, four hours after my initial attempt to enter the gardens, I went to the one o'clock door and walked into the gardens. I had forgotten what Sundays in China were like. What seemed like zillions of people abounded, emitting a low contented hum. I walked along the graveled paths, over bridges, under trees, looking around for a quiet place to read my book. I walked over the lovely wooden bridges, set at right angles to each other zig-zagging across the water and leading to the wooden pagoda-style temple which rose from the lake. Somehow I managed to find a rock off the path, under a leafy tree near a pond with a fountain spurting a cool mist, and sat down in the shade to read my book. I was sitting there quietly, leaning against my rock, focused on my book, and when I looked up, saw that a crowd of people had gathered around me. They were looking over my shoulders at the book or just standing in a semi-circle in front of me staring. I had been in China long enough to be used to this kind of attention, and after a quick nod in the crowd's direction, went back to reading my book. They would have talked with me had I tried to communicate, but I really wanted some alone time. Although they were all friendly, I didn't find this particular type of scrutiny very restful.

After an hour of feeling like a microbe under a microscope, my bladder and I had to move, so I stood up and started down the path. The crowd parted for me and after I left, they dispersed and went on with their business of relaxing in the gardens. I felt as though they were watching me as I might watch an animal in the zoo—everything about me was different to them and spoke of a different world, a different way of living.

I crossed back over the wooden bridges spanning the pond and went to what was then the traditional Chinese bathroom. It was a long trench where one just straddles and squats. There were partitions but they were only about two feet high. This meant that I could be "viewed" from either above or below the partition, depending upon the viewers' size. I supposed I must have been a sight worth watching: a large person who has not yet mastered the art of squatting, trying to do so over a trench, book tucked under my chin, trying not to fall, trying to keep my clothes dry, and especially, trying not to mind thousands of eyes viewing my every motion. I had an inordinately large number of women and children watch me do something I thought of as being rather personal.

I ended the day by deciding that the next time I had a day off, I would stay home and read.

Now, as I walked with Hu Ping through the same old streets and into the garden, I saw that nothing was the same except for some of the very old buildings. In addition to the zillion locals, many, many foreign tourists walked about.

Yu Yuen used to be just a big temple with a garden until several restaurants moved in. Then the local eateries, and places selling what Hu Ping called Chinese junk food came next. Then the stores moved in. Now it was a huge bazaar with stores on the street and in the old temple, selling Chinese wares and souvenirs, flanked by many nightclubs and restaurants. There were literally thousands of stores—I saw more tourists here than I saw in any one place since I started traveling. Yu Yuen was an exciting, loud, and bustling bazaar, full of everything anyone might want to see (or not see). The vendors here were not at all aggressive like in Xian, so we meandered around comfortably for a while, taking in the area. Hu Ping, Xiao Li, and I ate at a local eatery of the old style, where you spit your bones on the table. I liked that. No tourists there!

Back when I lived in China, I used to love going to the little restaurants where I could sit on a bench with other folks and spit bones to my heart's content. The first time I did that many years ago, I reveled in spitting my bones on the table, but before I could leave, some inner urge compelled me to put them in a neat little pile. One restaurant had a single bench which ran between two tables so as I was sitting there eating and spitting, a man sat down on the same bench with his back leaning against mine so he could eat and spit onto his table.

Immediately across from the garden's beautiful multi-angulated wooden bridges over the water, a Starbucks sign leaped out at me. Back home I love Starbucks. But when traveling, no matter how many times I saw Starbucks signs, I found it jarring. I was there for the China experience and tend to avoid patronizing North American conglomerates. But it was very hot and humid in the gardens, and I caved. I bought frappuccinos at Starbucks for Hu Ping and Xiao Li, who had never before tasted them. I have to say they tasted exactly the same as their North American counterparts. However, I don't think Hu Ping and Xiao Li were particularly impressed, as they very politely thanked me and then with little grimaces, took small sips from their frappuccinos which remained unfinished.

It seems strange to me that tourists come to China, stay in modern Western hotels, have North American breakfasts, eat as much North American food as possible or eat Chinese food with forks, go to tourist places, buy Chinese souvenirs, and then go home and expound on China-the-country when they really haven't seen the real folk or the way people actually live. It really is possible to travel and eat as if you haven't left home. I've met people bragging about how they can stay 'North American' no matter where they are. Personally, I like to try different things. Hu Ping was always asking me what I wanted to eat. I'd tell her that I didn't want to say because then I'd only get what I already knew—if she ordered, I would have what I didn't know even existed before. The same went for sightseeing.

Even if people have a very short time in a country, there are many wonderful things to do. I can't believe anyone could not be moved by standing on the Great Wall, then taking that experience home. After all, this is a human-made structure that can be seen from outer space; its enormity is staggering. There are many other wonderful things people could experience, but the Great Wall alone would be worth a trip to China.

There are many other types of things that people could do, whether they travel for a week, a month or a year. The first time I went to China, I went on a month-long tour, which convinced me I wanted to come back to learn more. Which I did—in the 1980s and then again twenty-five years after that.

My first trip was the tour with twenty women. The second, I lived on my own in the 1980s. Now on this trip, I was honoured to be part of a Chinese family (albeit a very privileged family now), living with them, eating with them, going to work with them. It showed me much more what the country was like and what the people were like, even though I didn't understand much of the language anymore.

DRIVING IN SHANGHAI continued to amaze me. It was always rush hour, twenty-four hours a day. The lines and lanes meant nothing, nor did all the "one way" and "do not enter" signs. People drove wherever. One day, a car came careening around a corner and almost smashed into us. The car was driving on our side of the road. A motorcycle policeman who was nearby shouted at the offending driver, but the driver shouted back so vociferously that the policeman slowly slunk down the road, red lights flashing impotently. The errant driver just continued driving errantly with no ticket and no accident much to Xiao Li's credit.

One day, as Xiao Li was driving us around the city, he expertly turned a corner onto a four lane street full of cars, buildings all attached one to the other, pedestrians filling up the sidewalks. And there on the corner was a large sign attached to a brick building: Shanghai Genetics and IVF (In Vitro Fertilization) Centre. It seemed so incongruous to see that sign on a corner amidst signs for furniture stores, restaurants, and other commoner types of businesses. IVF services are now readily available and yet it was only a short time ago that the one family/one child policy was rigidly adhered to. Were the times really changing that much? I wondered if it meant that families wanted their one baby *now* or wanted lots of babies to support them in their old age.

WE STOPPED BY to visit a friend of Jin Jie's and Hu Ping's. As they all sat in the living room chatting, I walked over to the windows to look out at another building. Many people were using their balconies as an additional room. I had seen this before and it seemed to be common—curtained-off balconies, balconies framed-in with greenhouse-type glass for extra privacy, balconies with clothes racks which function as large closets, balconies with washers/dryers. People had many inventive ways of "finishing" off the balcony space, and when I looked over at the large apartment building opposite me, the varied balconies did indeed present a colourful panorama.

WE ARRIVED BACK at Hu Ping's place to find that Xiao Yang, the tailor, did not let me down. Our trip down the Yangtze River was nearing, and my first outfit had just arrived. He did a stellar job—I now had a very lightweight pair of long shorts (or very short pants) in burnt orange, and a wonderful striped top— all one hundred percent cotton, cool, and fitting me perfectly! I know, I know— orange and stripes—but I liked them. The other outfits wouldn't be ready until just before I left for Japan and Russia, but if it was going to be as hot there as it was here, I would be grateful for my new apparel. Clothes at home that I thought were so lightweight seemed to weigh a ton in China. The humidity was worse than the heat, because it seemed to sap all my energy; heat alone could be healing and felt good, but combined with the humidity, everything in me that allowed me to function just oozed out with the perspiration. Anyway, I was very pleased with the new clothes. Such a deal for ten dollars! Xiao Yang wanted me to refer some customers to him—better yet, go into business with him, and I was so sorry that I was not younger and more entrepreneurial.

DRIVING TO SHANGHAI'S Pu Dong airport, the start of our adventure down the Yangtze River which would begin in Chongqing (pronounced chong-ching), we passed hundreds of cars stopped along the side of the road as we approached the terminal, or as the signs said, the "waiting house." Hu Ping explained that these people didn't want to pay for parking, so they pulled over to the side of the road and waited for their cell phones to ring, alerting them that their arriving passenger had deplaned, and then they just drove around for the pick up. Of course, if they were to get a ticket, they would pay much more than the parking fee.

Hu Ping and I chatted excitedly in the plane on the two and a half hour flight to Chongqing. We both had been there previously and wondered what changes we would notice but we especially wondered what our ship would be like. I had taken care to arrange a very nice room for Hu Ping as a way of thanking her for her hospitality and I could hardly wait to see the elegant stateroom I was sure awaited our arrival. As we dropped down through the mountains that surrounded the city, I peered out the window and eagerly anticipated another wonderful Chongqing experience. I had not been there for well over twenty-five years and looked forward to what lay ahead.

Chapter Six
Chongqing: Furnace of the Yangtze

CHONGQING SITS ON a peninsula at the convergence of the Jialing and Yangtze rivers, in the Southwestern part of China. Chongqing used to be the capital of Szechuan Province, but in 1997, the government changed that in an effort to make it a hub, a centre of mid-Western China, and now it is its own "province," containing thirty-two million people. It is the largest of China's four provincial-level municipalities.

We were met at the airport by our guide Mary, so-called only because we foreigners were obviously not able to remember real Chinese names, like *Nan*. Thankfully, Mary's English was excellent, if a bit stilted.

As we were driving to the hotel, she pointed out the window of the van. "It's busy, we encounter traffic."

She asked Hu Ping about the length of time she spent somewhere. "You did not linger?" she asked, surprised.

But at least she understood us, was bright, and her English was delightful. I hoped Peggy would be a one-time only experience.

Because the city was so hilly, there were very few bicycles here in Chongqing, and the city's main industry was manufacturing motorcycles.

Driving to the hotel, Mary told us that there were five "hearts" or main points to Chongqing city:

1. It is very hot. It is nicknamed "stove city." (Indeed, when we landed, after eight o'clock at night, it was still 31 degrees centigrade.)
2. It has many hot springs, second only in the world to Budapest.
3. The food is very spicy, and is known for the Szechuan hot pot.
4. The people are very hot-tempered but, she was quick to point out, are really good people, honest, open-minded and they make good friends.
5. Hot girls.

As we were driving to the hotel, I asked Mary where the hot girls were. "In the bars" she said. Oh, that I were forty years younger!

Mary continued talking about the city. "There are many 'mixed breeds' here." She explained that Chongqing is a melting pot of people immigrating from all over China; indeed, each of Mary's four grandparents came from a completely different area and background. Chongqing was the wartime capital during the Second Chinese-Japanese War (1937-45). It holds the dubious distinction of being the most bombed city in history.

After that, Chiang Kai Shek and the Kuomintang were stationed there, but following their defeat by the Communist Party and Mao Tse Dung, the city became headquarters for the Communist Party.

One of the main reasons Chongqing is such a popular tourist destination is that it has traditionally been the start of the Three Gorges Yangtze River cruises, which we were to take later the next day. As the little blurb on the pamphlet had said: "See one of the world's natural wonders before it is dammed." Damned, indeed.

THE FOLLOWING MORNING, Mary picked us up for a day of touring before taking us to the ship for our Yangtze journey. Her odd colloquialisms continued to charm me.

"Good morning, Mary, how are you?"

"Not so good," she replied, "my monthly friend has come."

"Oh," I said, somewhat abashed, not knowing whether the correct response was "I'm sorry it came" or, rather, "I'm glad it has come."

Because it was a week-long labour holiday, the streets were more packed than usual. Hu Ping was telling me that all the folk go out to buy Chinese junk food.

"Chinese junk food." Mary laughed. "Oh, that's vivid."

We drove around *Jiefangbei*, a municipality in the city where the streets were absolutely packed. Think the "crowdedest" you could ever imagine a mall or street or fair and then quadruple that ten times, and maybe it will approach the sight we saw. We couldn't see the streets or sidewalks because of the number of people. A happy rumble came from the crowd as the van crept down the road at a snail's pace. The air conditioning was on in the van, but I insisted on keeping my window down, because I loved to see and smell and hear the holiday celebrations surrounding us. People were everywhere, coming and going and sitting and standing and eating and talking, holding red balloons and filling up all available space with a joyful celebratory sound.

Mary and Hu Ping discussed how most areas in China have their own dialect. There is *Putonghua*, or Mandarin, the national language, but there is a Shanghai language and a Chongqing language, and so on, and most people cannot understand local dialects other than their own.

As we passed a large Chinese flag, Mary pointed out that it covered a Japanese advertisement. I had seen similar flags in Shanghai, and was told they also covered up Japanese ads. At the time, I didn't think much about it, but now Mary began telling us about the prevalent anti-Japanese feelings. There seemed to be considerable antipathy of the Chongqing population to the Japanese, according to Mary. I supposed the antipathy was particularly strong here since the city was so crucially involved in the many years of war between the Chinese and the Japanese in the 1930s and 1940s.

Mary pointed out the van window to the Jiangli River, which was essentially a dry river bed. River? All I could see was a very dry, flat area of brown scrub brush. I wouldn't realize until later how significant that would be for us.

It seemed to be a thousand degrees outside and Chongqing was showing us why one of its nicknames was "furnace of the Yangtze." Mary, however, did not seem to mind in the least the heat and humidity.

"We will go to Northern Hot Springs Park now," she announced.

"Okay," we answered, assuming we were going someplace in the city. "Where is it?"

"Oh," Mary answered, "only fifty kilometers away."

"Fifty kilometers! Mary, I don't want to drive fifty kilometers in this heat," I whined.

"You will love this park. You really do want to go. You will not be disappointed," she reassured us, and turned to the driver with some instructions I did not understand.

Mary became considerably more animated as the van started to ease out of the city. "You will not be disappointed," she reiterated.

Hu Ping and I were not overly keen to go, and could care less about traveling outside the city to a park, especially in the heat. As the van pulled onto the on ramp and entered the Expressway, Mary was definitely not disappointed.

Now, I already had a couple of weeks to experience the roads in China, but I never completely adjusted to the traffic. The van was our mini roller-coaster as we navigated the hills on the way to the park.

The far lane was labeled "overtaking lane," the middle one "carriage way" and the far right one "emergency stop area." These labels didn't make any difference because people just drove mostly straddling lines and paying no attention to traffic signs whatsoever. There were signs wishing us "Happy Trail," and "Have a good journey." There were also signs that said "Don't drive when tired," "Fasitn seat belts (sic)," and "Control Speed." Even so, it was just like a big Dodge-Em Cars ride at the fair, with cars coming at us in all directions. Heck, to me the whole country was like a big Dodge-Em Cars ride.

We arrived at Northern Hot Springs Park, pulling up to the little wooden gate house under a copse of leafy green trees for our tickets. I rolled down the window, letting in the fresh smell of green. This was a park the locals used, and there were many there. Indoor and outdoor swimming pools were available for our use, there were ten hot springs with paths linking them and the temple buildings, ponds, caves, and gardens. And, of course, we read and enjoyed many notices such as this one on the gatehouse (verbatim):

> "No admission to those with heart disease, hypertension,
> mental disease, epilepsy, VD, eye disease and infectious
> disease (I just shut up as I struck out on several counts).
> For the sake of your safety, please do not swim in the case
> of after-meal, after drink and being hungry tired and unwell.
> (Again, I would have struck out).
> Each body should treasure the facilities and pay attention
> to the hygiene in the swimming poos (sic).
> No towel, gasswear (sic again), balls and food are allowed
> to bring into the pool and no smoking inside.
> All the responsibilities and losses caused by violating the
> above regulations should be bored by the violator."

From the gatehouse, a road led to the parking lot, and then many walking paths, some concrete, some wooden, a very few natural dirt, meandered off through the green fields, weaving in and out between the trees and rocky overgrowths.

This park did not seem to be on the route of the Western tourists; I believe I was the only Western person there all day. It was nice to step out of the car and be accosted only by the sight of the beautiful trees and nature paths winding over the hills. No aggressive vendors here.

I could smell the fresh spring growth, hear the calliope-type music from the children's playground over the faint sound of drums off in the distance, which later we found to be a parade of sorts, with green-clad people walking and softly drumming their way through the park.

But it was hot, and almost from the beginning that was a detraction, at least for me. Mary, on the other hand, seemed quite happy and was determined that we were going to enjoy ourselves.

Like Chongqing, the park was very hilly, so we went up and down and up and down and up and down. It was well over 30 degrees, which was mild here as summer temperatures normally range over 40 degrees.

I didn't want to use up all my energy walking through a park in very hot and humid weather, but Mary was determined that this was a good park and I should enjoy it. I sat on a stone fence by the children's playground, the humidity draining the energy out of me by the second. Forty years ago I would have been running up and down those hills but, today, I felt twice my age. I kept readjusting my sunglasses which persisted in sliding down my face from all the perspiration. My sun hat was soaked. Hu Ping had gamely been following Mary up and down the hills while I rested swelteringly in the heat beside the children's playground. We were tired, hot, and bored and both of us really wanted to go to Old Town and see more of the people. Finally, Hu Ping convinced Mary that it would not be in any of our best interests to keep walking around this park if I were to collapse of heat prostration, so Mary reluctantly summoned the van, and we finally left Northern Hot Springs Park and roller-coastered and Dodge-Em Car'd our way back to the centre of the city.

THE VAN LET us out at Old Town. Mary told us it was called "Porcelain Town," at least in Chinese. This was the best part of the day. We were instantly transposed into a time hundreds of years ago. People walked on cobblestone streets past peddlers selling food, books, tools, toys, clothes, everything you can imagine, but particularly food of the Chinese Junk Food variety.

First we tasted sweet sticky rice on a stick, then deep fried dough. Next we approached the sugar candy booth, where music was playing from a crackly loudspeaker and a middle-aged woman sat at a table on which was a roulette-type wheel with, instead of numbers or colours, many different shapes of animals. I spun the wheel—round and round and round it went, with all of us eagerly watching as slowly it came to a stop—at a dragon.

"A dragon!" Mary yelled. "How precious. What good luck for you!"

I smiled, very proud of myself for having spun a dragon.

The woman then took her liquid candy and fashioned an intricate dragon which hardened immediately. She attached the candy dragon to a stick and handed it to me. The three of us stood there, me holding this dragon that was at least a foot and a half high, all of us taking some licks and bites of the delicious candy, as the candy woman prepared another shape for another spinner.

Next we had some tangy peanuts, and then I wanted to taste the fried crabs, so we got some of those. I have always loved crabs, and used to eat them with Hu Ping all the time when I lived there in the 1980s. But these crabs looked a bit different—they were small, less than two inches wide, dunked in some type of coating and then deep fried, coming out a burnt orange colour. They actually looked delicious. Unfortunately, they looked much better than they tasted.

Every kind of food you could imagine was for sale, and some you could not imagine. The narrow lanes were packed with people celebrating the holiday, everyone in a festive mood, eating, singing, and playing. The big difference between this place and Yu Yuen was the virtual absence of tourists here. Everything was for the people.

The cobblestone streets were very uneven. The actual act of walking was an adventure in itself. I was happy that I have never been a high-heeled person and smiled at the younger women tottering along on their spikes. I loved wandering in these streets, and could have done so for much longer than we did. Grazing in this old town was like being at a fair, and we loved it.

Although we had been eating pretty steadily for the past few hours, Mary insisted we go for the famous hot pot dinner at what she said was the top restaurant of the city. "You will not be disappointed," she said yet once more. This expression had become her mantra of the day which had taken on a contradictory meaning for Hu Ping and me. It should have been Mary who paid us to accompany her to the sites of her choice and not the reverse; ironic that we pay for a guide who goes to all her favourite places, whether or not they hold any interest for us.

So after walking around Old Town for hours, still not enough for Hu Ping and myself, we went for the famous Chongqing hot pot dinner.

I remembered being in Chongqing in the 1980s and the meal we had then, on the eve of our departure down the Yangtze, was without question one of the finest culinary experiences I have ever enjoyed. Each dish was an artistic delight, tasting even better than it looked, which I did not think possible.

Mary's choice of restaurants had no tourists as far as I could tell and was packed—a large establishment with hundreds of diners cooking on their hot pots, and the tackiest of floor shows taking place on the stage. Semi-nude girlie girls with large fans pretending to be Lido maidens pranced around a sleazy emcee encouraging the "girls." Think of a Las Vegas strip show gone bad; the feather fans were larger than the women who swayed as they tried to stand upright. There were many families dining there and they didn't seem to mind the floor show—in fact, most seemed disinterested. I, however, was fascinated by whatever cultural imperatives would have overlayed a Chongqing hot pot dining experience with a pseudo-strip show.

Mary joined us for dinner. She was not disappointed. Most of the food we sampled was wheeled around to the tables on little trolleys, and one just took a plate of whatever looked good. More or less. Then we would cook that food in our little hot pot which sat sizzling in the centre of the table. I did not recognize one single item that came around. I did try two or three different things, but they all tasted the same to me and they all tasted yuck. The food was too spicy for me, but even the not-spicy parts didn't taste particularly good. It seemed as though everything tasted the same as everything else, even though on the menu they advertised such varied things as fish and gastrodia soup, turtle soup with Chinese caterpillar fungus, ox-throat, frozen horse-face fish, meat frog, pigs brains, liver mushrooms, and the like.

I asked Mary what she normally ate for breakfast.

"Oh," she replied, "I usually eat a Western breakfast—milk and oats."

We talked about the Buddhist temple we had seen earlier that day at the park.

Mary asked me what religion I was. I told her I was Jewish.

"What do you believe in, Mary?"

"Money," she replied.

Perhaps it was because I was not very hungry, perhaps it was because I found these particular show girls offensive, but that pseudo-night-club spicy non-distinct hot-pot production of a dinner that Mary had so wanted us to enjoy was not one of my favourite dining experiences. I hoped that Mary was incorrect when she said this was the top restaurant of the city.

After the restaurant, we got into the car for the ten minute ride to the ship. Sitting together in the back seat, Hu Ping and I discussed our trip.

"Hu Ping." I smiled. "I just cannot *wait* to stretch out in our beautiful first class cabin. I'm sure we will have a good one." I had entreated my travel agent to get the best cabin for us, as I wanted to repay Hu Ping for her exceptionally generous hospitality.

"I'm tired today, and that cabin will be so nice," Hu Ping replied. We wondered out loud for a few minutes about our ship, how nice it would be, how happy we were to be nearing the end of a long day when we could finally lay down in our super comfortable cabin beds and sleep.

"I can feel the breeze off the water on my face already," I said. "Just another few minutes to the boat."

Mary was uncharacteristically silent.

Hu Ping and I were exhausted after the full day, our bellies were full with the old town good food being covered over with the bad food of the hot pot experience, and we both felt we had about fifteen minutes of consciousness left before we would fall into a deep sleep.

As we were driving toward what we thought was the dock, Mary casually informed us that they were taking us to the People's Hall where we will board a bus.

"A bus! No, Mary, this is a mistake. We are supposed to get on a boat."

"This is just a small car trip to the bus," she reassured us.

"The bus! But, Mary, we are supposed to board a ship!" I repeated. "What are you talking about? A bus?" The relaxing image of shipboard comfort left my mind very quickly.

"There is no water in the riverbed here," Mary explained. "Do you remember when I showed you the dry Yangtze riverbed? The boat cannot come up here anymore." She smiled encouragingly at us as the car pulled to a stop in front of dozens of buses, with hundreds of passengers milling around them, all equally confused.

"Mary, you must have known about this all day." I looked inquiringly at her.

"Of course." She smiled smugly. "But I did not want to ruin your day." She herded us toward our assigned bus. "This will be just a short ride to the boat; it is waiting for you at Fengdu, only three and a half hours away."

The last thing I felt like at that time was boarding a very crowded bus. Mary pushed us onto the bus. I felt my feet which were gripping the pavement giving way to Mary's exertion.

"Good-bye. Enjoy your boat trip," Mary sang as she gave my body one final push up onto the bus.

The buses were huge and packed. Every seat was filled, so there was very little room for our carry-on luggage. It did indeed take three and a half hours. I kept checking the big clock at the front of the bus: 2001, 2020, 2104, 2107, 2117, 2209, 2236. Finally at 2328, we arrived at the dock at Fengdu, which was to have been our first stop on the ship.

Chapter Seven
The Yangtze Gorges

WE WERE EXHAUSTED after our long, hot day. The odour of an outhouse gone wrong assailed us as we alit from the bus and worsened as we approached the ship.

We stood on the dock; it was almost midnight. We were holding our carry-on luggage, the smell of urine overpowering all our senses, looking down at the one hundred concrete steps we had to descend to board the ship—the ship—wait a minute, this was not looking like a luxury ship! I turned to Hu Ping and raised my eyebrows in a question—do we go ahead, do we stay put? What to do?

Realistically, what could we do at midnight in a strange place? We walked towards the smell of urine and the ship. The one hundred stairs were hard, uneven, and difficult to descend. It did not help that we were all exhausted.

The smell of urine increased significantly once aboard the ship. It really was terrible. Of course, there was no elevator on the ship and we were several floors up. We were shown to our room, which was about as small as a room could possibly be without its walls meeting. We found out about the possibility of upgrading to a suite about ten minutes after we saw our room, but by then, others had already beat us to it and there were no more vacancies. We were hot and tired, and returned to our room. We could not both sit on our respective ship beds facing each other at the same time as there was not enough room for our knees in between. We didn't waste a lot of time unpacking as there was a scarcity of space into which to unpack. We had a miniscule bathroom with a toilet, sink and shower, all-in-one really. There was no shower curtain because there was just a shower head coming out of the wall above the sink on top of the toilet. But at least we did have our own bathroom. My last trip down the Yangtze in the 1980s had not included a private bathroom. We did have a window, but it was dark outside so all we could see was black. I couldn't apologize enough to Hu Ping for the room. I had so wanted to present her with something comfortable and enjoyable. We sadly shook our heads, lay down, and both quickly fell asleep.

THE NEXT MORNING we awoke and staggered down the narrow halls with other grumpy tourists, all looking for the dining room where a Western breakfast was served. I learned that this boat trip would be 1100 kilometres long. We had traveled the 150 kilometers from Chongqing to Fengdu by bus, but there was still a whole lot of Yangtze to cover by boat. The ship we were on, called the Jeannie, held 280 (there were 276 of us on this trip); 120 were local Chinese and the other 156 were from all over the world.

After breakfast, we walked around the deck and looked landward. There, off in the distance, was a huge face carved into a white mountain. Below the face was a red temple gate that one presumably passed through to ascend. It looked intriguing and I awaited receiving information about Fengdu.

We were supposed to get off the ship for a land excursion at Fengdu. The ship hadn't moved, of course, and was right at the dock where we had embarked the night before. We were told nothing except just to be at the reception desk by nine-thirty that morning. All the expectant travelers crowded around the reception desk at nine-thirty, only to hear an announcement telling us that the tour off the ship had been delayed, and we should go back to our cabins and wait. So we did. After about half hour, we tried again. We got off the ship this time, walking through another "Hello, hello" market as we ascended the hundred steps.

Our ascent was greeted by many people shoving things in our faces:

"Hello, map, two *yuan*."

"Hello, water."

"Hello, hello!"

WE KNEW NOTHING about the off-ship tour until we were at the foot of the steps and the base of the mountain. I looked up. It was a very long climb to the ghost city of Fengdu. It was called a ghost city because of a clerical error. A long time ago, in the Han dynasty, two people lived in Pingdu Mountain, Yin Changsheng and Wang Fangping. The story got around that Yin Wang (King of Ghosts) also lived there. From that time on, the town, all two people of it then, and many more now, became associated with all things ghostly. They even sold the equivalent of ghoulish Halloween masks at the "Hello, hello" market at the base of the mountain. After climbing about a hundred and fifty steps of uneven rock stairs, we came to a suspension bridge with a sign (verbatim):

Notice to the travelers across the Hanging Bridge:

1. To ensure safety please do not stay on the bridge too long.
2. The kids must be taken good care handed by parents or relatives.
3. The old people and the persons suffering from heart disease and altitude-phobia must be company with the relative-and-friend entourages. If not, may request the staff to escort.
4. To avoid accident of safety, forbid anybody to run and jump on the bridge and to cross the bridge railings.

WE CROSSED OVER the suspension bridge and walked through a few temples. But because I was a bit slower than the younger folks, I would come up to the group just as the guide was finishing his explanation about what we were seeing. So all I knew was that we were at Fengdu, the City of Ghosts, that it had a suspension bridge and temples on high mountains, and that the vendors here were, unfortunately, as irritating as the ones at Xian.

I managed to go 345 steps up that mountain, which was about half way. Then I thought if I wanted to walk back down 345 steps, I had best desist going upwards.

We finally came back down the 345 steps to the Hello, Hello market, exhausted and wanting to get back on the bus. When we first got there, we had been told to come back to bus #10. So we got on bus #10. The driver asked us to get off. Yes, it was bus #10, and, yes, it was going back to our ship, and, yes, it was a shuttle bus, but it was taking another group back. Off went the not-full bus toward our ship, leaving Hu Ping and myself standing in the incredible heat after an exhausting climb, with nowhere to sit and no shade available. Except the market. I made use of the time by buying a ghost mask, which was what I believe had been intended all along. Then #10 bus came back and we tried again. Again, they asked us to leave and wait a bit longer in the heat. This time I bought a yo-yo, with which to amuse myself while waiting. Asking us to wait might have been a plan to have people do more shopping at the market—it certainly worked with me and, in retrospect, I shouldn't have encouraged it.

The third time they asked us to wait, we refused. We just sat on the bus until it got to the ship and then ran the gauntlet of the most annoying and pestiferous vendors since Xian.

I was tired, those one hundred uneven stone steps still had to be descended, and people were literally sticking maps in my face, yelling "Hello, map, hello, two *yuan*," until I just lost it and yelled at them in Chinese and English.

"*Bu yao, bu yao*, I don't want anything!"

That surprised them and they let us descend quietly after that.

That first morning, perhaps we were more used to the overwhelming smell of urine, for initially it did not seem as bad as the day before, but by three o'clock in the afternoon, I could smell it quite strongly again. The ship finally started moving about four in the afternoon. It was the first time it had moved so far. We had no idea what the next few days held in store.

The ship was incredibly disorganized. It was advertised as being "Five Stars" but if this was five stars, I would be a monkey's uncle. I wouldn't even call it one star. I had so wanted this to be an elegant, comfortable, super-special treat for Hu Ping. No one working on the ship seemed to know anything about what was happening. This whole part of the trip was a colossal disappointment.

About twenty years ago, when in Africa, I had awoken one day to find that there was no water at all coming from any of the taps in our little grass hut. Everything dripped dry dust. I walked over to the main hut for breakfast and was told this story by the proprietor: The Masai normally take their cattle to the river to water them. They learned that there were black tubes that carry "the river" in them, and so, on occasion, such as that morning because it was particularly hot, they poked their spears into the black tubes to water their cattle, thus saving a long dusty walk to the riverbed. Of course, when they were done watering, the holes remained.

"Oh well," she mused, "just another thread in the tapestry of life."

I told Hu Ping this story the day before on the bus, since we had no idea we would be in for such a long bus ride. It seemed that the next few days were going to hold lots of threads for this tapestry.

As the afternoon progressed into evening, things got a bit less unpleasant. I couldn't smell the disagreeable odour any more—perhaps I had become inured to it. And we were starting to know people and enjoy ourselves, sort of.

There was a most annoying American party—all my American friends and relatives, you should excuse me—but these guys were truly the epitome of Ugly Americans. Everyone on the ship was annoyed by them, and just our luck, they were seated at the table next to us. It was assigned seating. We were seated with a woman from Manitoba—small world, as that is where I was born and grew up—and her interesting Englishman of a husband. They were very nice, Tom and Edith, and that first night at dinner, we had been enjoying their company. We sat at a nicely set table, white tablecloth, red napkins, while young Chinese servers brought us soup and beverages. Tom and Edith were telling us some very amusing stories, but we had difficulty hearing them because the people at the table next to us were incredibly loud and raucous.

Tom said something to me.

"What?" I cupped my hand to my ear.

Tom turned to the offending table. "Could you please keep it down just a bit, folks. We're having trouble hearing here." He turned back, continued with his story, and I realized that the adjacent table had just ignored him and if anything, were even louder.

After my third "What?" Tom turned again. "Look folks, we just want to enjoy our conversation. Please keep it down just a bit." And he turned back to our table.

Now there was a loud rumbling of discontent from the American table. I heard one of the women advise one of the men, "Leave him. Just ignore him. Here, drink your beer."

They got louder and louder and we could not hear a thing. Finally, Tom stood up, all six feet three of him, and firmly asked, "Please keep the noise down at this table."

The beer drinker immediately shot up and took a step around the table, brandishing high his fist, shaking it and getting ready to take a punch at Tom. Immediately Hu Ping, Edith, and I stood up, palms held out placatingly, saying, "We don't want any trouble. We really don't. Please. Just go sit down." I did not want Tom to incur a punch on our account. It just wasn't worth it. Finally, Beer Drinker backed down and went back to his table, punchless. The four of us sat there and grumbled, but it didn't matter, because we couldn't hear each other anyway.

We wanted a table change, as these assignments were to last for the whole sailing. Later on that evening, I approached the maitre'd and his staff, but the ship's crew refused. When I persisted in asking why, I was told that foreign people were not smart enough to adjust after their initial assignments, and they didn't want diners getting confused. We were hoping that we would avoid fisticuffs the rest of the trip. Happily, Mr. Beer Drinker spent more time in the bar than in the dining room and we rarely saw his group after that first evening.

After the dinner that night, the staff put on the sweetest show of Chinese folk singing and dancing. The next day, we found out that the young women who worked in the dining room were all graduates of a dance school, and so they worked on the boat as both servers and entertainers.

The ship had given all the staff American names. Our tour director, whose real name was Chen, was called Howard. The servers/dancers we met were Vivian, Jenny, Vicky, and Summer. The young men who worked there were dancers also: Morgan, Gary, and Winston. How silly was that! And again the reason: foreigners couldn't pronounce or remember Chinese names.

I took some time out from viewing to go to the bar where Sherry and Morgan, two non-English speaking Chinese, prepared my drink (we won't go into that fiasco!). I hate to keep perseverating about these names, but it really seemed to irk me that the Chinese were not allowed their own names and had to be made over in the image of North Americans. I said Americans; it could also be British, but there were none of them called Carlos or Chiquita, or Hans or Ingrid.

These name changes are somewhat reminiscent of Ellis Island, where names were changed for the convenience of those already there. This seems like the reverse—the names are changed for the convenience of the tourists. Personally, I would rather call a Chinese man Chen than Howard, especially if Chen happened to be his name.

THE NEXT MORNING, we started going through the Gorges. That was the good news. The not so good news was that the passage began at six-thirty am, so at six that morning, they woke us up by playing music and then announcing the impeding vistas, while we quickly dressed and ran out on deck.

The Three Gorges, *Sanxia* in Chinese, were formed thirteen million years ago. The Yangtze, at more than six thousand kilometres long, is the third largest river in the world, after the Nile and the Amazon.

The first Gorge, Qutang Gorge, was the shortest of the three through which we were to pass. At only eight kilometres long, it had the distinction of being also the narrowest gorge, so for the twenty minutes it took to traverse it, we had mountains towering up on either side, sometimes as high as twelve hundred metres (four thousand feet). The mountains were stone and covered with foliage under the grey early morning skies. There was something quite surreal about passing through this gorge, as if we had entered another time in another world. It was very quiet and almost no one spoke (the Americans were no doubt sleeping off their latest bar visitation). We all gazed at the mountain walls surrounding us and up ahead at the Yangtze, narrow here leading us through the gorge, but no less mighty.

Naturally, this shortest gorge would be the one that we pass through at six-thirty in the morning. By seven that morning, it was time for breakfast and gorge was gone! The guide book describes this gorge thusly (verbatim): "the peak connects with the heaven and the boat sails in the earth ditch."

The Three Gorges Dam was built in 1997. One-point-three million people had to be relocated from the three gorges when they built the dam. Before that, there used to be white water rafting around the gorges, but now it is just like a big reservoir. The water was four hundred and fifty feet deeper before the reservoir—it was coming up and up and rising more every year. Chongqing is the end of the reservoir, which was why we needed the bus trip to Fengdu—Chongqing was all dried out. It's strange that for years, Chongqing was well-known as the start of the famous Yangtze Gorges River Cruises. Now they can't manage to get the boats there with the dried riverbed caused by the very damming of the gorges everyone is coming to Chongqing to see—or at least to start the trip there.

A NEAT THING happened at breakfast. It was open seating, and Hu Ping and I happened to sit with some people from Beijing. I noticed one Chinese woman eating with a fork, but using her chopsticks to get the food onto the fork, just like we Westerners use our forks to get the food onto our chopsticks. I, however, was discretely using my fingers to get the food onto my chopsticks as I was far too arrogant to be seen using a fork.

After breakfast we passed through Wuxia Gorge, the second gorge. It was forty-four kilometres long and went through two provinces. There were many limestone caves and working coal mines along the steep walls. This was pretty much the centre of China. In the summer, the temperature rises higher than 45 degrees. The water level was now seventy metres higher since the dam. That meant that half the sights to see were under water. It was already one hundred and thirty-five metres above sea level.

"Look" Howard said, the guide, aka Chen, "that used to be a town but it is all under water. There were two thousand people in that town."

"Oh look, we are now passing a coal mine under water."

"Oh look," he pointed, "there's a road that goes under water."

"There's a beautiful mountain just here, but it's under water."

"There's another village under water."

Actually, it's not that funny to think of the 1.3 million people who had to be displaced and relocated. Hu Ping told me that some of the older people did not want to leave, and so died on the land when it was flooded. They simply went into their homes, laid down on their beds, and waited. Five per cent of the 1.3 million people being relocated (65,000) have yet to move and the water is still rising.

LATER THAT MORNING, the ship stopped and we boarded a ferry.

"Ladies and gentlemen, Welcome to be here," came over the crackling loud speaker. We sailed about fifty minutes on the ferry, then alit and walked along a concrete dock where dozens of little wooden boats sat waiting for us. We climbed into our assigned vessel, fifteen tourists to one small boat.

Before we left the dock, a slight woman climbed aboard our boat. She was very pretty with dark ponytailed hair, and she was holding an orange life jacket.

"Lades and gentmen," she announced in a lovely high-pitched voice, "my Chinese name is Tan, Tan, T-A-N, Tan. Everybody, we must put on the life-jack and then tie up the lace-jack because it's safety for ourselves, yes, safety for ourselves." She demonstrated by donning the lifejacket.

As the boat eased away from the dock after Tan had ensured we were all suitably enclosed within our "lifejacks," she continued her safety spiel, "There are many wooden boats in this small river so watch your hands, watch your hands. Don't put your hand outside the boat. Maybe the other boat rub your hand. Thank you." She was delightful.

Tan continued: "Today we're enjoying the Bamboo Gorge by the small wooden boat. Small wooden boat. The local people call it peapod, peapod boat. There are six boatmen in each boat. Can you guess which one is our captain?"

We all correctly deduced that the sailor steering the vessel calling out orders was indeed the captain.

Tan explained that the local people, her people, were the Ba Minority people. The Ba Minority people were boat trackers, and were still considered to be a primitive culture, an indigenous people of China. They used to do their boat thing (paddle, then tow it uphill, turn around, and come down white water) stark naked, because they were poor and had rough clothes, and the rough clothes irritated their skin. But then civilization (and softer clothes) showed up in Badong County, and today they were clad, albeit minimally, in Speedo style swim suits and t-shirts.

The ten peapod boats slowed down after a time and the boat trackers hopped out of the peapod vessels holding long ropes, leaving only the guides, captains, and tourists in the boats. They formed a long line following a narrow path on the riverbed, and with the ropes looped over their shoulders, proceeded to pull us all upstream as they followed the path through the high green reeds growing by the water. There was much friendly yelling and order-calling among them, and they seemed to be having as much fun as we were.

As the boat trackers pulled us upstream, I marveled at how they could pull the boats attached to ropes which they hauled over their shoulders. Who were these people really? They were so like us and so different, all at the same time.

Tan's English was fairly impressive considering we were at a town that consisted of twenty families. I asked her how she learned English and she said through TV and books. As we sailed down Shennong Stream, off the *Chang Jiang*, as the Yangtze River is called in Chinese, Tan continued:

"Look in the water. The water is very clean and very shallow. Yes. No pollution. Water is very beautiful. You can wash your hands and face—if you wash your hands and face you will get young and beautiful." Needless to say, all fifteen in our boat felt the need for a refreshing wash. Just in case.

Above and around us were cave-filled mountains, towering over the clear stream. Tan pointed to a cave. "Before, the local people live in caves. The old men die—people put the coffin into high cave. That means they go to heaven." We all looked up the steep rock cliff to spot a cave, high, very high up, with the tip of what looked like a wooden coffin sticking out. I couldn't imagine anyone getting up there, much less carrying a coffin.

Tan looked up high to the cave, then down to the water. "Before," she continued, "water very shallow. Sometimes the boatmen put their hand in the water. They can catch a fish. Yeah."

The boatmen had pulled us upstream to the turn-around point. Now it was time to return.

We turned around and came down a tiny bit of white water, and I mean tiny bit. If one would blink, the white water would be gone, and that was as exciting as this rafting got.

On the way back, Tan asked, "Okay everybody, are you like a little song? If you like, I sing." And sing she did, in a high, pure voice. All of a sudden, the talking stopped, and only the musical lilt from Tan could be heard over the dipping of the oars. It was a magical moment—crystal clear voice filling the canyons, rhythmic sound of water moving, sun shining down on all the orange-jacketed folks, green all along the banks. Tan's voice rose and fell and lulled us each into our own private reveries.

In spite of the fact the "rafting" had lasted upwards of fifteen seconds, the scenery however, was truly special as it was untouched, green, with no evidence of tampering by humankind. As the postcard says: "Please come to Shennong Stream. Her clear stream and secluded paths will attract you not to leave there." It truly was very beautiful.

The ferry returned us to our boat. Every time we leave the boat we have to put around our necks a "boarding pass" which really says in Chinese: "Please take me to the Jeannie." And thusly the Westerners are able to return to their own boats.

I SAT IN my tiny cubicle of a room listening to Mozart over the ships intercom, quite enjoying it, when I heard a birdie choir singing along; in fact, it was the featured "instrument" of the musical piece. And then a wolf was howling to Chopin. I'm not joking, that was really coming in over the intercom. The birdies came back with Chopin as well, which was later accompanied by a rainstorm. And just when I thought I had heard it all, along came Tchaikovsky's

Swan Lake—accompanied by—a wind. And big waves. Only in China, I feared! The animal voices were the instruments. I imagined the actual recording: There sat an orchestra, dressed in formal black, and just next to the first violin, a bird house sat on a chair, where, on cue, several birdies popped out to sing their part. Next to the oboes sat a huge grey wolf, bushy tail keeping time, howling on cue along with Mozart. A Chinese magician sat behind the brass, and on command, conjured a rainstorm, or waves, in a little picture window of weather. The music CD was hysterical. I just could not stop laughing at it—rain, birdies, and Chopin, it was just too rich. I wanted to buy this CD that had brought happy tears to my eyes, but could not find one that was for sale.

THE LAST FULL day of the cruise, we were awakened at five-thirty am. Each morning started earlier and earlier. I'm glad the cruise was not a week long, or else we would have been getting up before we went to bed!

I wandered into the dining room for an early breakfast. Lansing came over to pour my coffee.

"Are you some more coffee?" she asked.

"Sure, thanks. Lansing," I asked, "how on earth did you get that name?"

"The ship give me," she replied. The ship has been giving out some pretty funky foreigner names.

WE LEFT THE ship at just after seven in the morning for a tour of Three Gorges Dam. Our tour guide, Cindy, introduced us to the area. We were in the town of Sandouping, where the dam is located on over fifteen square kilometers of land.

We all leaned against the massive stone wall overlooking the reservoir while Cindy told us about the project.

The whole thing was initially conceived of by Sun Yat Sen, considered to be the father of modern China. In the 1950s, he overthrew the old feudal system, and first came up with the idea of the dam.

The Three Gorges Dam was the largest water conservancy project in the world. Construction began in 1993, and was to be completed in 2009. The ship locks began operating in 1993. More than twenty thousand workers have laboured there. The major reason for this project was to control flooding as the last four large floods of the twentieth century have claimed over 320,000 lives.

The dam site was very crowded. Cindy told us that the previous day there were more than ten thousand visitors to the site. The walls were two hundred and eighty metres high and thirty-four metres wide. There were five lock chambers, but because the water level was so low now, the ships only used four. And it was free—there was no cost for using the locks. There were twelve generators ready, and two more being worked on; each unit provided seven hundred megawatts. There would be twelve more generators in operation by 2009. But the amazing thing is that all of this provided *only* one percent of China's power! The cost of the dam was twenty-two billion (American) dollars, ninety percent of which was provided by China. It was quite an amazing project.

One side was two hundred feet above sea level, the other five hundred feet. The whole project was built firstly to control flooding, secondly to improve irrigation, and thirdly, for power. Of course, there has been a negative impact as well, not to mention raising the water level five hundred and seventy-four feet (hence all the underwater sights of the other day). The famous Chinese sturgeon is now an endangered species because the dam has interrupted its spawning paths.

There was a huge park on the site, with a building containing an actual model of the dam—it was very detailed and fascinating to look at. But outside, it was difficult to see anything, because, as Cindy told us, "Today the misty is very thick."

Coming back to the ship, we ran the gauntlet of vendors—even worse than Xian, I think. It made me think of the 1959 movie *Suddenly, Last Summer,* starring Elizabeth Taylor, Katharine Hepburn and Montgomery Clift. Elizabeth Taylor, playing the part of Catherine, was recalling what happened to the character Sebastian, and in her memory, we see him disappearing beneath the feet of the "natives" where he ultimately died. Well, was eaten actually. I thought that might be my fate that day getting back onto the ship. I'd be just a bunch of footprints, left after I crumpled under the feet of the multitudinous vendors. There were *so* many, and they were *so* aggressive.

As I anxiously tried to glimpse the ship through the vendors, holding on to Hu Ping with one hand and using the other to keep a modicum of space between myself and anyone else, I heard a voice, and felt someone grab my shoulder, "This way, come with me, hurry."

I looked up to see a sailor from our ship, and beside him another sailor and another, all trying to encircle Hu Ping and myself, and once they did, like some sort of bizarre football scrimmage, they trotted through the vendors with the two of us inside the huddle, only occasionally feeling the thrusting hands of the vendors through our protectors.

After our team safely deposited us on board the Jeannie, they went back out for the others, and slowly brought back all the tourists onto the ship. We watched from the ship as tourists were encircled by the sailors cum linebackers, and waddled back to the ship with the vendors trying to infiltrate the circles. The noise was incredible, with the vendors screaming at the tourists to buy something, the sailors yelling at the tourists to come into their protective huddles, and the tourists just screaming in fear and/or frustration.

The ship cast off, and the noise of human yelling was replaced by the soft swoosh of the ships passing through the water. I stood on the deck, leaning against the railing, happy to have left the dock and the vendors. I looked waterward toward other ships, because the Yangtze River was in fact a busy waterway. I kept looking at the tourist ships wondering if they were the "first class" ships we had missed taking. Did the people on those ships appear to be any different than on ours? Not really. I did, however, enjoy watching all the different kinds of ships; there was one very large one built like a giant dragon, red tongue flaming out, tail high above the water.

We then sailed through XiLing Gorge, the longest of the gorges at sixty-six kilometres, and although the misty was still pretty thick, it was beautiful in a very monochromatic kind of way. It was a very pleasant morning, most of it outside in the misty, some of it in the bar drinking amaretto coffee with new friends.

Our ship eased into the large stone walls of a lock. Very quickly, the walls which had been almost at water level now loomed above us as the water level dropped twenty-five metres within ten minutes. Being in the lock was fun because there was a Chinese tour boat in the lock beside us, and people were communicating from boat to boat without speaking common languages, by playing rock, scissors, paper, and other such games. The lock systems have been fascinating with the water raising or falling huge distances in such short times, with everything working very smoothly. It was an impressive system.

Hu Ping and I had four days of Chinese foot massage on the ship. It was the only five star item on the ship—well, maybe four star, but very welcome nevertheless. My masseuse was Lili, whose English was as rudimentary as my Chinese. We could tell each other about our families, but when it came to philosophical discussions, there was just a lot of grinning, nodding, and gesticulating. However, there was nothing rudimentary about her Chinese foot massage technique as she was masterful and my feet were eternally grateful.

As the Yangtze trip was coming to an end, Hu Ping and I worried about getting back to Wuhan on time, as we had very little time to get the plane. We were told we would dock maybe twelve-thirty, maybe one in the afternoon (we had been scheduled to arrive at noon). It was similar to when I asked about our luggage.

"Oh," Willy said, "you can have it outside your room maybe at 9:30."

"Nine-thirty. Okay," I responded.

"Maybe seven-thirty, or maybe eight-thirty," from Willy.

"Okay, seven-thirty or eight-thirty."

"But maybe nine." Willy looked perplexed.

"Okay," I said, "luggage tomorrow morning outside."

He smiled gratefully.

We disembarked in Wuhan, walking past a band dressed in classy white uniforms, which consisted of more of the ships staff. These workers were talented indeed.

We were met by our Wuhan driver, Tony. From what we saw driving from the ship to the airport, Wuhan was a very beautiful city. Sycamore and palm trees lined the wide boulevards. There were nine million people in this city. Tony explained that there were more than one thousand lakes in this area, and the "vapour" from the lakes formed a blanket over the city, thus the city is nicknamed "furnace city." Like Chongqing. There are three furnace cities in China—Chongqing, Wuhan, and Nanjing. In the winter the temperature in Wuhan can go down to around minus 2 degrees with some snow. Wuhan makes all the Citroen cars for taxis.

I asked Tony about the people who were relocated—whether or not they had a difficult time, if there was any alcoholism or depression.

"No," he answered in typical Chinese-speak, "the people know they have no choice and have to adjust." So it appeared to me that they are not open yet to consider the difficulties some of the folks must be having, or at least not yet open to talking about it with foreigners.

Traveling with Hu Ping was fun for me but difficult for her as people kept assuming she was my interpreter. No matter what I did or what I said, I could not disabuse them of this notion. This saddened me somewhat. It was as though they could not wrap their heads around the fact that we were friends.

Chapter Eight
Good-Bye Shanghai: Good-bye to China

BACK IN SHANGHAI, I made use of Hu Ping's laundry room and packed up many boxes to ship home so I would go to Japan much lighter than I arrived in China. We had allotted one whole day to go to the post office for mailing packages home. It was interesting that one was not allowed to mail a sealed box—I had to pack the box in front of officials who examined everything, and then seal everything in front of them before they would accept it for mailing. But as long as I complied with the regulations, it really was not that difficult. I did have to know in advance, though, to come to the post office prepared with whatever I needed for wrapping and sealing.

THAT EVENING, JIN Jie and I were comfortably ensconced in the living room, talking about urban development. He told me that in the past ten years, over six thousand high-rise buildings have been built in Shanghai. But the problem was that there was very little care taken regarding environmental impact. I asked him about whether or not they had five or ten year plans.

"Sure," he said, "they are now on their eleventh five-year plan!" The problem was that the mayors and other public officials were usually only around for a few years, so they wanted to do many different large projects during their tenure, and let someone else worry about the impact. The sea level was lower than Shanghai, but with all the building coming up so quickly, the ground under the city was sinking, and soon it would be below sea level and there would be significant flooding. They had already built many retaining walls, but these were short-term Band-Aid solutions only. I thought of other cities where warnings had become realities, such as the flooding caused by Hurricane Katrina in New Orleans, and hoped that the solution for these problems would come in time to prevent a tragedy.

I wish my dad were still around—I'd love to discuss this with him as he was a flood and water control expert. I think he would find the situation here very interesting.

THERE ARE SO many more things about China that I found different and interesting. I was fascinated by the serving hierarchies in the restaurants. This was particularly noticeable in Hong Kong, but in Shanghai as well. There are certain people who can bring dishes to the table, but they cannot put them on the table. So they have to stand by the table with the steaming food on a tray, until another type of server comes up and takes the food off the tray and puts it on the table. There are people whose jobs are only pouring tea, and others who only clear the table. In Hong Kong, in many of the restaurants, the hierarchy was emphasized by different types of uniforms indicating each job. In Shanghai, it was a bit more casual, but still, some people stand by the table for quite a while, waiting for another type of server to take the food from the tray to the table. And every restaurant, no matter how grungy, has a wet towelette for each diner.

It is common in China for there not to be introductions. People were just not introduced to others as we were used to doing. Most people were called by their last names; one rarely would say "Mister someone," and there was no word for Ms. or Mrs. In a restaurant, when Hu Ping summoned a waitress, she'd call her *Xiao Jie*, which meant little sister.

Another thing about China I had noticed—I didn't know if it was because of the pollution, or the "misty" or some other cause, but it seemed as though many places were monochromatic. It was like when a film starts off in black and white and then dramatically turns into Technicolor—I kept waiting for the Technicolor but it just didn't come.

MY LAST AFTERNOON in China I went to the Bund with Xiao Li. The Bund was still a financial hub, but a far cry from its heyday as an international centre for the British, French, American, Russian, and Japanese banks and businesses. All of these different countries exerted their influence on the architecture, and there are many different styles of buildings along the Huangpu River. The famous Peace Hotel is located on the Bund as well, right next to the Nanjing Road Shopping Area. Formerly the Cathay Hotel built in 1929, it became the Peace Hotel in 1956 and was known as the "No. 1 Mansion in the Far East." The Bund was very interesting, but mostly for tourists. To me, the Peace Hotel has always been synonymous with Shanghai. The hotel is an elegant combination of east and west as it sits there in its majesty. What history its walls hold!

Being alone with Xiao Li was interesting, because when he said "No Eng-er-ish" he was serious. But still, we walked around the Bund and went through the tourist tunnel from the Bund under the water to Pu Dong. A long promenade followed along with the river, where one can look across the water to the high-rises of Pu Dong, which did not even exist when I was last here. The whole Bund area seemed to be much more of a tourist place than a place a historical significance—the Shanghainese really don't even go there.

"The tunnel" was this weird psychedelic little tram ride under the Huangpu River—very bizarre and very touristy. Hu Ping was born and raised in Shanghai and didn't even know this tunnel existed until I told her I had read about it in my tourist book.

IT HAD BEEN a very good stay here in China, but now I was happy to move on. My last morning there, my sister Judi called from Japan where I was going to meet her and I was *so* happy to hear her voice. It was time to continue on my travels.

China has always been one of my favourite places to visit, and has a very special place in my heart. I find it interesting how we seem to develop proclivities for certain places and not for others. I have certainly traveled to places where I never wanted to return, instantly feeling that antipathy in my heart. But China is not one of those places. I look forward to coming back again and again, each time noting the changes with interest and enjoying the wonderful parts of the country that remain the same, especially the Chinese people, for whom I have a great fondness.

But for now: Another day, another country.

Part II

Japan

Chapter Nine
Kuwana City: Everything is Little

KONNICHIWA, Y'ALL, I'M in Japan. It was nice to be back after more than a decade. Japan—where everyone is always so polite and quiet. I'm sure in Tokyo it was always crowded and noisy, but in Kuwana City, that was not the case. Even though Kuwana City was home to one hundred thousand people, it felt like a little toy city, with little roads, and little houses and little people, and little toilets and little rooms and I was so big, and felt even bigger there.

At Narita Airport in Tokyo, my sister Judi was waiting for me, along with Miwako and her daughter Shino. I had met Miwako at home in Victoria at my friend Angela's house, where she boarded while studying English. We had become friends and she invited me to visit her in Japan. Judi took a freighter from the US to Japan, arriving two days previously. When she was first checking through customs, a nice looking gentleman looked at her, inclined his head and said, "*Hai*."

She grinned a big smile at him. "Hi," she said. It wasn't until much later she realized he was saying *Hai*—yes and not hi—hi. Everyone here nods their head politely and says *Hai*, which means yes. But it is also what people say in agreement, and sometimes upon meeting.

Judi had four large bags with her, I had three, and the two of us with all our luggage made a very—how shall I say it?—gargantuan visage indeed.

I had told Miwako we might have a lot of luggage, but to her, that likely meant having a backpack plus a valise. She kept stealing glances at our pile of belongings, *tsk-tsking* and shaking her head in disbelief.

"So, Miwako, what's the plan?" I asked, wanting to get out of the airport and start seeing Japan.

"We are taking the train to Kuwana city, where I live," Miwako said.

"What about our luggage?" I nodded in the direction of the very large pile of commingled baggage.

"We take them on the train." Miwako looked to Shino. "That's why Shino came, to help us on the train."

I remembered the bullet train and how one has less than two minutes to board or disembark. "Wait a minute—we have to transfer, right?"

I looked over at this enormous pile of our belongings. I love my sister dearly, but she packs even more than I do; I have never mastered the art of packing lightly even though I am a worldly traveler. I cram in many things "just in case" and return home with virtually all of them unused, but at least I feel confident that, should I ever have an emergency where I might need an epipen to save someone's life, or an inordinate amount of gauze to staunch the bleeding of someone or other, or a plunger for somebody's toilet, I will always be prepared. It's like insurance—one hopes one never has to use it, but it's always good to have. Every time I set out again, I work on the minimization of packing and on each successive trip, my bulging bags are testimony to my failure. I know that my attitude does not exactly match traveling lightly in the world, and it is something I must work on with more diligence, but there we were, in the centre of Narita Airport, with seven pieces of clunky luggage.

The image of all our luggage and we four woman standing by the door of the bullet train getting ready to offload, run down the track and onload the luggage and ourselves onto another train in two minutes or less would just not play itself out in my mind without looking like a Three Stooges' recipe for disaster. I sighed deeply.

"We can ship all your luggage by train separately," Miwako suggested.

"Great, that sounds like a plan. When would we get our stuff?"

"Not for several days."

Judi and I looked at each other, shaking our heads. If we had known of Miwako's plans for us, we would have each brought a small overnight bag and shipped the rest. Miwako had the very best of intentions but we had to inform her gently that neither of us was wont to part with our beloved luggage.

"No, Miwako, I need my stuff. I can't ship it all off and not see if for a few days." This was a fairly simple statement but led to two hours of complex negotiations while better prepared travelers than we streamed around us.

Finally, we hired a private driver with a van large enough for three women and seven clunky bags.

It was late afternoon when we waved good-bye to Shino, who lived in Tokyo, crammed our belongings into the van, and headed off for Kuwana City.

"Miwako, where exactly is Kuwana City anyway?" I asked as the van pulled onto the freeway.

"Oh,"—she smiled—"not too far, just twenty minutes by car away from Nagoya, about six hours from here."

It had been a long day and a long flight, and now we were facing a protracted drive. This drive was the first non-little thing, but by no means the last, that I would encounter in Japan, as it involved sitting in a van for hours after a prolonged flight, not to mention attending the lengthy luggage summit meeting at Tokyo airport. However, all my luggage was safely in the back and I wasn't worried about losing any of the multitudinous things I would most likely never need anyway. So instead of fretting about the time spent on the freeway, I just relaxed back into my seat and enjoyed the time reconnecting with my sister and my friend.

I realized that we were driving on the right side again. In Hong Kong, the driver had been on the right, then in mainland China the driver was on the left. So when one drives from Hong Kong over the bridge to mainland China, that person has to switch on the other side of the bridge from driving on the left to driving on the right! And just when I'd got used to China, now in Japan, we were back on the right. I was glad I was not driving, that was certain.

Before long, I felt a bit peckish. Breakfast on the plane had been a long time ago—the flight attendant had been very surprised that I preferred a Japanese breakfast, but she brought it. I had no idea what it was—some pink things and some brown things and some white things—but most were fairly tasty for dry, unidentifiable finger food. Those multicoloured delicacies were all I had eaten all day.

"Miwako," I asked, "will we be eating dinner at your house? I'm getting a bit hungry."

"Yes," she replied, "we will be having cream stew and bread."

"Cream stew?" Judi and I looked at each other with raised eyebrows. I wondered if this meant we were having bowls of bread with cream poured on top. Or rice with bread or more unidentifiable pink and brown and white bits floating in cream.

"Yes, cream stew and bread. Is that all right?"

"Oh, I'm sure that's fine." I hesitantly smiled back at Miwako, as visions of unidentifiable multicoloured bits smothered in cream floated through my mind.

And of course, it was fine. It turned out to be creamed chicken and veggies and was delicious. The three of us sat on chairs around Miwako's table, not on the floor, much to our immense relief, while we dined on cream stew.

Miwako's home was very sweet, somewhat smaller than a Texas doll house and too little for all of us to stay there that night, so Judi spent the night in a hotel while Miwako very graciously gave up her little bed for me. I felt badly that she had given me her room and her bed but she was so hospitable and accommodating that all I could really do was smile at her and say *domo arigato gozaimas*—thank you very much.

The next day Judi and I both moved into another hotel in Kuwana City which Miwako assured us was the best in town. Our plan was to lay low for a day or two, do a little bit of touring and a lot of resting, before leaving for our next destination, Takayama. As I pulled out my credit card to pay for the room I realized that my first two days in Japan had cost me more than the last three weeks in China! There definitely is a price to be paid for "little and quiet."

The hotel was very . . . little. Everything was in Japanese, except for the first page of the information book which announced in big block English letters: "Information"—that was the only English in the whole book, except for one line on the page about food, where it listed (verbatim): "Break Fast, Launch and Dinner, at which you can snack on sea foof (sic) pilaf and drink Doraft beer."

Our room had two beds, seven large pieces of luggage, and two large women. To get to the bathroom from my bed, I had to run the obstacle course of sidestepping and jumping over and falling and tripping in order to arrive at my destination. Which was actually worth it, because our bathroom had one of those amazing toilets that apparently does everything to and for you. It had instructions on the seat and on the wall, complete with buttons and levers, and looked almost otherworldly. Maybe it's what the astronauts use in space, I mused. I was kind of scared to try it out at first, but it did have English instructions, which started like this:

"When you sit on the seat automatically the cold water flow. Wait for 'off' the lamp to wash. When you sit on the seat, STANDBY lamp starts flashing, if you press (picture of a symbol) upon seating you may have cold water spray."

It then went on to tell you how you could have front or back washes, and some things I really didn't want to know. I thought I might try it the next morning before my shower, because I was sure I would end up getting drenched. Judi told me that her toilet the previous night had little pictures explaining what to do, which would be much better, if not somewhat pornographic.

THAT FIRST DAY in Kuwana City, Miwako took us to a lovely park, Rokkaen, to explore the old residence of Seiroku Moroto, a local businessman in the late 1800s and early 1900s. From very humble beginnings, he successfully ran his family's rice business and became a most prominent citizen in Kuwana City. He commissioned a house designed by the British architect Josiah Condor, completed in 1913, that was half English Tudor and half Japanese, all surrounded by beautiful gardens and promenades. The maids worked in one part only—the maid who worked in the European part of the house did not go into the Japanese part and vice versa. I was fascinated by this split—two totally different styles of living. I could imagine Mr. Moroto deciding whether he would entertain in the British half or the Japanese half. Or perhaps he would sleep in a bed in the British part for several nights a week, and then move over to the futon on the floor in the Japanese bedroom. We toured this seemingly schizophrenic house which had become a museum, and then headed outdoors. In every direction, brightly coloured flowers waved their petals. We strolled over wooden bridges crossing streams, rambled along stone paths, and meandered through more gardens. With the bursts of colour everywhere, I felt my senses coming to life. After the greyness of China, life was technicolour again. Little, but nevertheless, technicolour.

We had lunch in a small café at the park. I said to Miwako, "I would like some more water. How do I call the server, please?"

On the table beside the window sat a little wooden box with a little wooden tower protruding. Miwako picked up this little contraption and pressed a small button on the top of the wooden tower and, sure enough, our server appeared, wearing a little receiver on her belt, responding to our electronic call. It seemed a bit strange to have such a high tech way of summoning one's server in the very park that held Mr. Moroto's historic artifacts because, walking through the house and gardens, we had been transported to a time long before the advent of electronic gadgetry.

PRESUMABLY BECAUSE KUWANA City was not a tourist destination, we so far had encountered only two English speaking people: Miwako and her other daughter, Aya. In China, even in the smaller places, virtually everyone I encountered spoke some sort of English, even if it was mangled like Peggy's. Here, even in the hotel, people did not speak English. But Judi was amazing— she went to the store for water and Coca-Cola (staples for us, to be sure) and returned from a most successful venture, arms laden with goodies. A smile and pointing goes a long way.

Everything seemed like an adventure in Kuwana City, even going for dinner. Beside our hotel was a wooden building, with wide steps leading up to a restaurant. Judi and I walked up the stairs and tried to get in, but there was a huge waiting line; it was packed inside and out, and the two guys behind the counter just shook their heads. So we went across the street to the Park Hotel to see if they had a restaurant. They did; unfortunately, it was a seafood restaurant and Judi is allergic to all things from the sea. Happily, a young woman there spoke minimal English and we asked her where we could dine. After a whole lot of nodding and talking and gesticulating, we were off, map in hand, to the Japanese Udon Noodle place, several blocks away. Unfortunately, the map was entirely in Japanese, including the name of the restaurant. Nowhere did it say Udon House of Noodles.

"Let's see the map." I grabbed it from Judi. "I see some Japanese characters on that building."

"No, we've not gone far enough to start looking," Judi countered. "Here, look," and she pointed to what was the Park Hotel on the map (we thought) and the Udon House of Noodles (we thought). They were several blocks apart.

We walked a few blocks further.

"Do you think the first three characters on the map look similar to those at that parking lot?" Judi asked.

"Gosh, I don't know." I peered at the piece of paper full of glyphs that carried no meaning for me whatsoever.

"Oh, wait, look at those." Judi leaned over my shoulder. "This little squiggle looks like that little squiggle." She indicated a sign across the street.

"Yeah, but look here," I pointed, "this cross thing doesn't match that cross thing."

Sooner or later, we were hoping for a match between the map and real life, and so we marched, from block to block, our heads going down to the piece of paper and back up to the signs on buildings, like two wayward chickens scratching our way down the road, comparing the markings, looking for a match. Judi was much better at matching than I.

We finally found a building whose characters matched those on the map, and walked into the building. The young woman from the Park Hotel had sent us to this restaurant because, although the menu was in Japanese, they also had pictures of the food.

We indicated we wanted dinner by pointing. Everyone spoke Japanese to us and we simply smiled in reply. We were seated, thankfully at a table, because I don't think either one of us could have gotten up if we were seated on the floor. Very quickly, the nicest waitress, dressed in traditional dark blue *kimono* and patterned *obi,* came over to help us.

Miwako had written down the Japanese characters for "pork" and "chicken" at our request, because of Judi's allergies. So first I pulled out my notebook and then said, "Chicken *kaarage.*"

The waitress smiled. "Aah, chee-ken *kaarage,*" and nodded her head.

Then I pointed to one of the pictures for my meal. The problem was that although we could see the pictures just fine, we had absolutely no idea what we were looking at. There were more little black things and pink things and green things.

"I would like *sake*, please."

"Aah, ohsahke-ay," she replied.

"A beer, please," Judi added.

"Grassah?" she asked.

"A glass would be fine," Judi said.

"Grassah beer?"

"Yes, a glass of beer."

"No." She frowned and started gesticulating. "Grassah?"

"Ah, draft beer. Yes, draft beer would be fine." Judi's command of Japanese was astounding!

"Arice-a?" she asked.

"Sure, rice is good."

"*Hachi?*" she asked tentatively.

"Yes," I answered, proud, that I understood, "Chopsticks are good." She looked doubtful, but smiled.

When she came back, I said, "*Watashiwa* Ruth," which means "my name is Ruth."

She nodded and said, "Aah, A-luth-a."

"Yes, Ruth." I was going to say *Watashiwa* Judi and point to Judi, but she beat me to it by pointing to Judi, and then introduced herself as Mica. Then the meal came.

Mica came over and explained everything in Japanese while pointing from this dish to that. I nodded. I had not understood one word.

Judi did indeed get chicken *kaarage*—Japanese fried chicken. And I got a bunch of pink stuff and brown stuff and black stuff, and some lobster tempura and a heavy round black cast-iron pot of thick udon noodles, simmering over an open flame.

"Wow, this looks really good, Judi." I armed myself with my chopsticks. I put them into the pot, stirred the noodles around, and with great dexterity, selected a few tasty morsels. I lifted them out of the boiling pot, and with great anticipation, widely opened my mouth as my nose became aware of the delicious aroma wafting upwards. I raised the chopsticks to my lips, and became puzzled when all I tasted was wood; the noodles had not arrived with the chopsticks and I looked up just in time to see them flying across the table and landing on Judi's delicious-looking chicken *kaarage*. Judi lifted off my noodles with a snicker and a sneer and held them aloft between her thumb and forefinger before delicately dropping them on my plate and starting to eat her chicken.

"It's not funny." But I couldn't help smiling. I sat up straight, readjusted my hold on the chopsticks, and picked several more noodles out of the pot. The noodles were very long, very hot, very thick and very, very slippery. As I was removing them from the steaming cauldron, in spite of my iron-clad grip on the chopsticks, those noodles slithered out of the pot and slid right down the side of the pot and onto the table. It was as though they were alive—long, white snakes, making their escape from the pot and from my chopsticks. I reached into the pot for some more, only to see them splatter all over the table.

Judi's smile had now turned into a giggle. "Stop it!" I commanded. She snickered. My frown turned into a guffaw and I joined her in laughter.

But I was now determined to eat those noodles. I grabbed some slippery snake-like undulating shapes with the chopsticks in my right hand, using the fingers of my left hand to hold them in place. The noodles slid down onto my shirt, down onto my slacks and onto the floor. I took another bunch from the pot with the chopsticks; they squished out and flew across the table landing on Judi's dinner. Two long noodles sat half in and half out of her glass of draft beer. Those noodles wanted to be everywhere!

Judi and I were still laughing. And the more we looked at what we had wrought, the more we laughed. In the middle of the table stood the black pot— it looked just liked the pots at the end of a rainbow, but instead of gold and other treasures overflowing, this one had steam burbling out the top and noodles writhing within. In front of Judi sat a very neat plate of chicken *kaarage,* with only the odd noodle lying across a chicken thigh. Beside Judi's plate of chicken, her glass of draft beer still had the remnants of noodles that had opted for a beer bath just moments earlier. Judi also had a salad plate, and I noticed two of my noodles hiding underneath the lettuce.

In front of me was an almost empty plate, but around it many noodles lay about, some still moving in the pools of broth which somehow just happened to be on the table. The other plates which surrounded my hot pot, which had once contained lobster tempura and pink stuff and brown stuff and black stuff, were now covered in bits and pieces of noodles. In fact, there was very little empty table or plate space, as most of it was covered with wayward noodles. Even my little *sake* cup was not spared. In shame, I lowered my eyes. Oh no—the floor had a carpeting of noodles which extended all around our table. Mica came over, looked at our disaster area of a table, smiled and went off. A few minutes later she came back with two forks and loads of napkins.

"No, *hachi*," I stubbornly responded, grabbing my chopsticks. And I did get a bit better at it—after the clean-up, only about half the noodles ended up on the table; most of the rest ended up in my stomach.

Throughout it all, an elderly couple across the way glared at us as though we were aliens from outer space as they daintily slurped their noodles. Not one noodle was out of place on their table—their noodles were only in their bowls and their bellies. But the young couple across from us equally had fun with their noodles and commiserated with us. We laughed a lot, ate a bit, and thoroughly enjoyed ourselves.

THE NEXT DAY we went to the Kuwana City Library to use the Internet. I thought we did very well: all the signs and instructions were in Japanese. And, of course, everything was very little. But we did accomplish our mission. We also managed well at the bank and post office, all without using any English, and were able to realize what we had set out to do. I learned how much we could accomplish without verbal language, while at the same time, realized how much we miss by not having the everyday human interchange of language. How I wished I were truly multilingual. These experiences showed me that most people are very willing to communicate by any means available to them. And since that is the case, it makes me wonder why there is so much general misunderstanding in the world. Certainly, everywhere we traveled, people only showed a willingness to communicate by any means possible.

LIKE MOST PEOPLE, when I thought of Japan, images of cherry blossoms, *geishas*, and *sushi* usually came to mind. Then, one day, while driving through Kuwana City with Miwako, we passed a tall, pink-bricked building. It looked like a nice place and I asked her what it was.

"Don't ask." She laughed, blushing a deep red.

I thought for a minute, and then, looking at Miwako's bright red face, asked, "Is it possible that it is . . . ?" I cocked an eyebrow at her.

"Yes," she answered sheepishly, "it is a Love Hotel." I knew that they existed in Japan and were places where people get rooms for a few hours. I would have thought that love hotels would be anything but classy, but this building was just that, and not dungy and grimy like our so-called "love hotels." It looked like the kind of place through whose doors anyone might enjoy walking.

The concept of a love hotel or *rabu hoteru* fascinated me. They are not just used for prostitution. Because so many Japanese young people still live with their parents, it also serves a purpose for these young couples who have not yet married. The entrances are very discrete and payment is usually by pneumatic tube or cash machines, so that discretion prevails. Some of the high-end love hotels have theme rooms, from cartoon characters all the way through heavy S & M. Although love hotel architecture can be garish with neon lighting and bizarre shapes, this Kuwana City love hotel seemed like a very decent building indeed, although the pink bricks were less subdued than the surrounding buildings.

Driving along, I realized we can now add to the cherry blossoms, *geishas,* and *sushi*, outlet malls. We passed one, a little one, to be sure, but an outlet mall nevertheless, with Tommy Hilfiger, Escada, Coach, etc. Just like a miniature California outlet mall, a little slice of Americana in little Kuwana City where no one speaks English.

Japan is cosmopolitan enough to have not only anomalous love hotels in most cities but also high fashion outlets malls. It all seemed very incongruous to me.

WE DROVE ON to Yoro Park, about an hour north of Kuwana City. Miwako had planned a picnic up the mountain, and after we'd parked the car, up we went. Walking straight up the mountain for some time was a truly lovely, albeit tiring, way to spend an afternoon. Surrounded by massive cherry and maple trees and greenery, rocks straight up on one side and straight down on the other, birds singing in the distance, we hiked vertically on. As we neared the top, I heard the sound of a waterfall, and then my eyes took in this wonderful steam of glistening pure water falling down the mountainside. A few minutes later we reached the top of the trail where the great waterfall about thirty meters high cascaded into a pool. A sign beside the pool told us that it was one of the top one hundred sights in Japan for beauty. We stood at the edge of the pool and watched the water drop from high up in the mountains, the droplets misting my cheek before the sun quickly dried them. I stood there for a while, enjoying the scene and finding myself agreeing with the Japanese beauty ratings. There is something mesmerizing about a waterfall and watching the water tumble down and hit the pond. The droplets disappear forever into the water pool, and yet the pool of water toward the shore is so still and quiet as though it is hiding a million secrets. I was most content to stand there for a long while contemplating this magical manifestation of nature, but Miwako moved over to a bench and began unwrapping her basket. As she pulled out a checkered cloth to lay upon the bench and proceeded to fill it with all sorts of Japanese goodies, I'm afraid the chicken *kaarage* and scrumptious-looking sandwiches called louder than the waterfall. We dined well beside this treasure of Japan, and then sat mostly in silence as we absorbed the scene and digested our delicious lunch. Afterwards, as we slowly sauntered down the mountain, Miwako told us the local legend of the area.

There was once a poor young woodcutter who supported his aged parents. He respected them and acted with great filial devotion, but they were quite poverty-stricken and he felt badly that he couldn't get good things for them. Every day he went up the mountain to cut wood and sell it. One day he went up a little higher than usual. He thought about the face of his father, and imagined him happily drinking *sake*, which he loved. He could not afford to buy sake for his father, and he so wanted to be able to do that. He wished the water would turn to sake. All of a sudden he lost consciousness and fell into the water. When he came around, he noticed that the water smelled like sake; he tasted it—it was sake! So he filled his *hyo-tan* (gourd) with the sake/water and took it to his father. At first, his father could not believe it was sake, but after the second sip, he was convinced, and happily clapped his hands as he, his wife, and the son rejoiced. And the father's hair, which had been white, turned black again.

Many little stores at the bottom of the mountain capitalized upon this legend, selling holy water from the mountain, sake, and *hyo-tans* of all sizes. I bought a bottle of holy water, as I truly do want to remain young forever, or at least not get so old that my life is over. So far, it's working, even though I've already drunk all the water.

After we descended the mountain, Miwako asked if we wanted to see another shrine on the way home, which had a holy horse.

"But perhaps you are overwalked?" she questioned.

"Well, perhaps, but I would like to see the holy horse."

So off we went to Tado Shrine, where a few days earlier they had a big harvest festival; the shrine itself is more than fifteen hundred years old. Every year on May 4 and 5, the Tado Shrine festival features *Age Uma Shinji*—the rising horse festival. While there are always horses at the shrine, they take centre stage during the festival. Young men dress in Samurai armour, mount their steeds and must jump their horses up and over a three-metre cliff. First the horse and rider gallop along a straight path, gathering speed, until they come to the slope which rises about thirty degrees. The horse must skitter up the slope and leap over the top, all the while bearing a rider in full armour.

This festival is traditionally believed to be an indicator of the harvest for the upcoming year. As much as I love the beauty of horses, and I'm sure we would have loved the costumes, I was secretly relieved we were not going to see the festival, as many animal-rights protestors attend for obvious reasons. Only about one quarter of the horses make it up and over the top and the rest of them fail quite disastrously, often finishing their lives during the effort of jumping the cliff. I was not interested in seeing the veterinarians and others care for those horses that had not succeeded in their implausible task of predicting the upcoming harvest.

By late afternoon, we were at Tado shrine, situated at the base of Tado Mountain. We walked up forty-eight stairs, but that only took us to the holy horse. From what I understand, he was a holy horse because of the fifteen-hundred year-old legend of a white horse who acted as a messenger from the local people to the *kami* (God) who lives on Mount Tado. The horse delivers the people's prayers to the gods who live in the water and rocks and trees, and the animals shared the power with them.

And there indeed stood the holy horse—what a beauty! He was immense; sleek as an Arabian yet taller than a Clydesdale. For one hundred *yen*, one could buy carrots to feed him, which, of course, we did. I marveled at the beauty of this magnificent animal as he gently nibbled the carrot in my hand; he stood so tall, with his unique grey mane falling over his sleek glistening, white hair; there was something very serene about him. And yet this holy horse stood in his serenity in a wooden stall like any other farm horse. I wondered if I felt he was special because he truly was or because we were told he was. I later found out that he lives in this stall for just a short period of time surrounding the festival; for the rest of the time, he has a large field at his disposal.

From the stall of the holy horse, we then meandered up the mountain to all the shrines there, praying and clapping twice as we went. Miwako showed us the appropriate way to pray: We would walk up to a shrine, which was a little wooden building with a small wooden trough in front of it, a slot having been cut into the trough.

First we would put some money in the slot, and then bow. We would then pray and when we were done, we each clapped twice. And after that, we moved on to the next one to repeat the sequence all over again.

I thought that since I found myself on a mountain in front of a shrine that accepts prayers, why not give it a shot? After all, when in Rome . . . With a little luck, the gods would answer my prayers. I did seriously offer up some personal prayers, which were a mixture of Shintoism, Judaism, Wiccan, and anything else that popped into my head. Why not hedge my bets, I thought. I remember when I was younger, I used to pray in as many languages as I could muster, just to increase the odds of God really getting the prayers. On that mountain, we did a lot of walking, praying, and clapping, and by the time we got back down the mountain, I was played out, prayed out, and seriously over-walked.

On the drive back to Kuwana City, we were mostly contentedly silent, fatigued from the day's climbing and touring. As Miwako drove, the three of us all comfortably leaned back and retreated into our own thoughts, which gave me a chance to do some thinking about the horses at Tado Shrine. I thought about all the protestors that come to the festival, who say, quite rightly I believe, that the festival fosters animal abuse. And then there are the traditionalists, who say that the festival goes back many hundreds of years, and needs to be kept intact for cultural reasons. Of course, if we used that thinking, I suppose we would still be doing live sacrifices. However, it does raise an interesting question regarding tradition and cultures, not just Japanese, but in general. I thought about my own Jewish culture, and what changes mean in such a rapidly changing world. If different traditions are continually altered to become politically correct for the times, then are they even valid after being changed? Are they what they set out to mean? Are they still authentic or merely puerile versions of something from a culture of long ago? Maybe keeping traditions the way they were is a way of humans trying to slow down time. No matter where my thoughts went, though, I still was on the side of the horses and wished them all safe, comfortable, and long lives.

I HAD BEEN away now for almost a month and a half, and I was missing my dog Reenie terribly. We were seeing lots of dogs in Japan, and this made it both easier and harder for me. I took comfort from petting the Japanese dogs I encountered on my early morning walks. There was the odd Beagle, Springer Spaniel, and Yorky, but mostly I crossed paths with the three main Japanese breeds: the powerful Akita, with which most of us are familiar, the medium-sized, muscular Kyushu, and the fuzzy Shiba Inu. The Kyushu is an ancient breed, intelligent and affectionate, but I was particularly partial to the Shibas who look a bit like Akitas, but are much smaller. They are medium-sized dogs, with a lovely thick reddish coat, and white/tan legs. They have such intelligent eyes. I later found out that both Kyushus and Shibas, two of the oldest dog breeds known, are so fastidious and go out of their way to keep clean, so that housebreaking is quite easy; in fact, they will, in most cases, housebreak themselves. These dogs brought me much pleasure as I passed them on the street, their all-knowing eyes communicating such love. When I petted them, I felt as though they were Reenie's foreign ambassadors, bringing loving canine greetings to me, a traveler bereft of her own dog.

MIWAKO HAD BEEN spending virtually all her time with us, and so we encouraged her to "take the night off" to be with her family, which is how Judi and I ended up going out for dinner again. We decided to give the restaurant next door another try, as it had been booked the last time we tried to eat there. We walked up the steps and into the building, and were in luck: there was one empty little dining room. The little rooms had either a pit with a table in the middle so that one sat on a bench with one's feet dangling in the pit, or just a small table off the floor, with no pit. It was a lovely restaurant, with lovely people, and, I think, a lovely menu, but I wouldn't know because it was all in Japanese and didn't have pictures.

Judi and I were seated in a pit room. Around the corner from us, was a group of eight spry young people sitting on the floor, their table laden with *sake* cups; they didn't need a pit. They glanced over at us as we awkwardly swung our legs up, over and around the bench and squeezed them down into the pit under the table.

Sitting on the table was a little dish of appetizer that resembled the Yiddish dish *zharkoya*, a kind of meat stew, and another little dish of short, dry white things that were not rice, not noodles, not anything I could identify. I tasted one, and didn't much want to know what it was after that.

Four people came to the small entrance to take our order. They did not speak English. We did not speak Japanese. So I just started naming Japanese culinary dishes with which I was familiar.

"*Yaki soba.*"

"Aah, *Yaki soba.*" The gentleman nodded.

"Chicken *kaarage.*"

"Aah, chicken *kaarage.*" Nodded the young woman nodded.

"*Sashimi,*" I said, "but just a little, an appetizer." I played charades, holding my fingers quite close together, indicating for them not to bring too much.

"Steak," Judi said.

"Aah, a-steak-a." They all nodded. "Cheecken a -steak-a, porko a-steak-a, or beef-eh a-steak-a?"

And so the ordering progressed.

And even though we tried to indicate that we did not want much, using our hands and grunting and pointing and measuring, the food started coming, and I am not exaggerating when I say that by the time they brought everything there was enough to feed maybe ten or twelve extremely hungry people, exceedingly well. A side dish of *tempura* turned out to be enough for a meal. A side of *yaki soba* was enough to feed at least six! And there was steak and chicken and noodles and rice and *zharkoya* and the white things and *sashimi* and beer and sake. And so on.

When we were finally finished, and had decided to take all the leftovers for Miwako to feed her family for the next week, we realized we had to get up and out. We were seated not really on the floor—well, yes, on the floor, with our feet in the little pit—but there was little room to maneuver and the two of us were not exactly svelte. First I swiveled and tried to lift my right foot up to the seat, but that wasn't going to erect me, so I swiveled the other way and lifted the left one. No, that wasn't working either. A titter came from an adjacent dining room. I lay down on the bench and swung both legs up along the seat and with my fists beside my thighs, scrunched up into a sitting position and folded my knees under me, ending up on all fours. Unfortunately, my hind end was sticking half way out the door to the room. The snickers became louder.

"How on earth are we ever going to get out of here?" I asked Judi, but I didn't think she heard me. She was lying on her back, rolling one leg onto the table trying to extricate herself.

I turned myself one hundred and eighty degrees until I was facing the door, but I was still on my hands and knees and still wasn't sure how I was going to get up and out. Judi was going through similar machinations. I crawled over to the entrance, but Judi had the same idea and we bumped heads in our efforts to get to the door. I leaned on her and, face first, half sitting on her, half falling out of the door, leading with my fists, I plopped onto the floor disentangling the rest of my body from Judi's body, and quickly plunked my bottom on the bench as though it were the most natural dismount a diner could make. Then I carefully put my shoes on, ignoring the titters that had become full-blown laughter. Easy for them to laugh at us, I thought. I looked over at them, all with their lithe bodies in contorted, seemingly comfortable positions. Wait until you are my age, I thought, and God forbid, my size—let's see you get out of a pit room then. With as much dignity as we could possibly muster, heads held high, we smiled at our laughing neighbours, gathered our many multiple bags of leftovers, and walked out.

OUR LAST DAY in Kuwana City before our trip to Takayama, I got up extra early, allowing at least half an hour to explore Japanese toilet culture. I walked into the bathroom and looked carefully at the instructions. Truly, they did not make much sense to me. I peered downward at the toilet and pushed a button. A spray of cold water hit me in the face. I quickly pushed another button and a stream of hot air buffeted my head. I realized I was actually presenting the wrong end to the toilet, so after studying the buttons again, I gingerly sat down and started pressing. I have to admit that I tried every button and fell completely in love with the "do everything" toilets! My thirty minutes sped by and I was having so much fun I was loathe to start my shower. I was hooked and would be back for another toilet session.

Chapter Ten
Takayama: Head to the Mountains

BY MID-MORNING, WE were in Miwako's car. We were on an adventure to Takayama, about a four hour drive from Kuwana City. The drive was mostly on a beautiful and clean expressway, passing through seemingly hundreds of tunnels winding around or through mountains. It was very scenic, green fields in the distance, lovely pastel landscapes becoming more mountainous, not like the craggy outgrowths of the Rocky Mountains, but rather many different shades of green in neatly organized patterns. There were geometrical shapes of land and rock—diamonds, triangles, squares—some outlines shaped by wire, some by foliage. Even the wild land looked neat, as though a master landscaper had planned the whole of outdoors. This tidiness appealed to me on some level even though I am a huge fan of the Canadian wilderness.

We stopped at a rest stop off the expressway. Almost everything inside was automated. Standing at attention, lights gleaming, was the coffee machine, where for 200 *yen,* one could purchase virtually any kind of coffee, latte, cappuccino, milky shakes (*sic*), cocoa, green tea au lait (really *sic*—I couldn't have even imagined that!), and more. I walked up to the coffee machine and deposited 200 *yen*. A small screen lit up on the front of the machine, and music started to play. My eyes bulged in amazement as I watched, on the small screen in front of me, an actual movie of what was presumably happening inside the machine play itself out on the screen. I giggled as I watched my cup move into place, then I heard and saw the coffee being ground, and the ground coffee being poured out. Milk poured from a tap, and all of it was combined in the cup. Then, on the screen, a top was placed on the cup and—poof!—the door opened just as the little movie ended. And there was my latte, waiting for me to pick it up and partake of its deliciousness.

There was lots of Japanese junk food available; Miwako bought these things called *dango* (I called them goo balls; that was what they looked and tasted like. I'd eaten them in China, too). They are made from rice powder and I think "goo balls" describes them perfectly. They tasted like a cross between a soft and savory gum drop and coconut-covered marshmallow and something else that was airy and sticky and incredibly tasty.

Ordering noodles was fun. I stood in front of the machine and studied the photos of the food. Underneath the photos were descriptions of the meal, but of course, they were in no language I understood. I watched other people order, and decided to do what they were doing. I deposited some money in the noodles machine, pressed a button of an inviting-looking bowl of noodles, and the machine spit out a little chit of paper which I took to the person behind the counter. I had no real idea of what was coming my way. The man behind the counter took the chit and disappeared, only to reappear later with a bowl of food that in no way resembled its photographic counterpart. Well, it was an experience. Once we had collected all our various machine buys of food, the three of us retreated to a bench outside and had a picnic on the side of the freeway before heading off again.

All the tunnels we passed through were bilingually named, but that was it— almost all of the other signs were in Japanese. I started to play a little game with the signs, interpreting them based on the pictures. Driving down the freeway, we would come across a sign, and I would announce stentoriously: "Crayons approaching," "Bumblebees ahead," or "Cartoon animals lurking," depending upon the pictures on the individual signs. Judi and Miwako chose to ignore me in this game, but I found it fascinating for I truly had no idea what the signs really meant! I entertained myself greatly and it was fascinating to realize that these signs actually meant something of relevance to drivers while they were a total source of amusement for me in my ignorance.

SHOES ON, SHOES off, shoes on, shoes off. Everywhere we went, shoes off, shoes on. I should have just worn flip flops the whole time I was in Japan. Arriving in Takayama, we checked into our *ryokan* (Japanese Inn), after we removed our shoes, of course. At first the three of us were going to share a Japanese style room—we had arranged for a large family-style room for three people. We opened the door to the room to see one floor covered with *tatami* mats and three rolled up single futons. That was about it. Okay, there was one small lamp on a tiny table in a little corner of the sleeping, living, and doing everything else room. Through a small door was another very small room which had a sink and a tiny shower. Off to the left was the toilet room, separated from the sink by a sliding door. I think it was the largest room in the whole inn. Judi took one look in the room and the idea of the three of us crowded on the floor with no room left over for tossing and turning did not sit well with her. No doubt the image made her head hurt. She didn't even get past the door of our quarters before hightailing it downstairs to beg for another room for herself. Which she got, and then had to lug her prodigious baggage up to the third floor. In our room, once the futons were down for sleeping, there was virtually no *tatami* mat space left. And the only place for me to sit other than the floor in the entire room was the toilet. The toilet sat in the toilet room, touching both sides of the wall, and as I later found out, when one sat on said device, ones knees would touch the far wall as well as ones elbows would lean up against the side walls. I could barely get in and I certainly couldn't turn around, unless I stood on my tiptoes and swirled in exactly the same place, all the while, banging my arms and other body parts against the narrow walls. It was a nice toilet though—when it was flushed, the tap over the sink attached to the back of the toilet automatically came on so one could wash one's hands. Japanese toilets are the best!

Luckily, our room was next to a lounge with Western-style chairs, and I found myself there often looking at people from different countries, trying to imagine what their lives were like. If I sat really still and watched, it seemed as though time stood still for a while. I imagined their travels and saw them living in their world, and I couldn't help but think that somehow I would be a better person for it.

I dreaded going to bed the first night, because of the difficulty of getting up from the floor every time I would have to go to the bathroom, which, for someone of my age and medical problems, is very often. There was nothing to hang onto—just floor, wall, and sleeping mat. Ah well, when in Rome . . . Or rather, Takayama . . .

That first night in the Japanese inn was interesting in a physical way. I watched Miwako gracefully sit down on her heels on her futon, and equally gracefully, lift herself up to her full height with what seemed to be no effort whatsoever. I developed a way of getting down onto the bed by elegantly bending my knees, putting my fists out in front, and flopping onto the futon on all fours. To stand, I would maneuver so that I was facing the corner of the wall. I would then get up on all fours with my head butting up against the corner of the wall, and "walk" up the wall with my head leading. When I needed to sit down, I sat on the toilet. As a large woman in a small environment, I felt like Gulliver in Lilliput. It was fun to try Japanese living, but I (and my knees) were glad it was only for a short time.

When traveling, anyone who likes to wear clean clothes most of the time has to consider laundry at some point. Because we'd read that this *ryokan* had laundry facilities, we saved up all our laundry for days prior to arriving. That first night, we went down to the laundry room—well, that was a misnomer: it was a washer and dryer at the bottom of a flight of stairs in a dank, dark little corner. Nevertheless, we brought down all our bags of laundry and waited in line until it was our turn.

The washing part went well. The drying part—suffice it to say that after three hours in the dryer, and hanging out all night over every surface in the room (there weren't many other surfaces than the floor), most of my clothing articles were still damp! What we had hoped to accomplish in just several hours actually took us several days!

TAKAYAMA IS A lovely city, with old and new sections divided by the Miyagawa River. It is in the mountainous region of Gifu Prefecture. The prefectures are akin to states and provinces; indeed, at one hotel, a young clerk asked me what prefecture I was from in Canada.

One night we went for local cuisine and were each brought a tiny little square hibachi cooker with a little grill on it, and miso paste stuff simmering on top. Then we were presented with beef; some we ate raw, and some we grilled on the little hibachi. We had local mountain vegetables and fish that looked and tasted like a very large sardine, and gooey white "sticky yam." It's called that, but I love yams and can't believe that it is at all related to the yams that I love. Now I have a reasonably educated palate, but this gooey white mess tasted like something that had been a reject from a dumpster. There were the usual black things and pink things as well. It was not a bad meal. It was not really a good meal either. However, I was looking forward to when we were going to try *shabu-shabu*.

EARLY THE NEXT morning we went to Miyagawa Market, the eponymous local market along said river. The market was on the "old town" side of the river, with market stalls backing onto the water, and wonderful old buildings bunched together across the road from them.

During the feudal ages, Takayama was known as a source of high quality timber and skilled carpenters, whose work was still evident in the buildings of old town. It was a very picturesque area, with shops of local food, arts and crafts and any number of other items. The merchants were so generous in wanting us to taste everything, which is why by nine-thirty in the morning I had had substantial quantities of *sake*. And beans. And peanuts. And more *sake*. And green things and pink things. I figured out that most of the pink things are pickled—pickled what I don't yet know, but they are pickled.

Sake is considered to be one of Takayama's specialties; I think *sake* is one of Japan's specialties. Old *sake* breweries sit across from the market, identified by the *sugidama* or balls made of cedar branches that hang over their entrances.

Everywhere we went we saw these funny little red things called *sarubobo*, which means "baby monkey"; they are characteristic of Takayama—like a mascot or something of that sort of the area. *Sarubobo* was made out of every conceivable material for every conceivable purpose: key chains, dolls, decorations, purses, pens, shoes, magnets, jewelry, linen, clothing—even snack foods, all for sale in virtually every booth of the market and every store of the town. *Sarubobo* was this little (although at times she could be large) red, faceless thing that was supposed to be a baby monkey and bring good health and good luck to babies and other people. It was, without question, one of the ugliest little monkeys I've ever seen. And I love monkeys, even ugly ones. I find it fascinating how different cultures vary in their definitions of "cute." To the Japanese, *sarubobo* was adorable. To my Western sensitivities . . . well, let's just say I've been Disneyfied.

It seemed that everywhere we looked we saw fortunes written on paper—hanging from trees, tied onto fences, dangling from wooden strips. They were for sale for one or two hundred *yen*, with at least one fortune stand on every block, and when the people get their fortunes, they hang them up somewhere outside. It looked to me as if they were hanging out to dry. The fortune contained their wish that will come true. We bought fortunes too, but they were written in Japanese, so I had no idea what they said. Miwako said she might translate them for us, but that was a big job. She was already doing so much for us, putting up with the two crazy sisters, so I didn't encourage her to do so. I didn't want to overstep our welcome.

After lunching at a local noodle house (this time managing to keep most of the noodles on the plate or in my stomach as opposed to on the table), we visited some great museums. One was the *Takayama Yatai Kaikan*—Takayama Festival Float Exhibition Hall. There are two main festivals a year, and each has twelve floats. Four were on exhibit and were rotated every three months, but all the floats came out at festival time. The ones not on exhibit live in little float houses scattered throughout old town. If they were to be rebuilt today, each one would be worth many, many millions of dollars because they were constructed with gold, with exceptionally fine wood carvings; they were really unbelievable to look at. Some floats have mechanical dolls, *karakuri ningyo*, that actually move and dance. It was obvious how much work and craftsmanship had gone into each tiny little piece—the intricacies of all the pieces were staggering to comprehend. All the floats were amazing and all were incredibly decorated. I could just imagine what the festival would be like, with hundreds of thousands of people in attendance, surrounding these magnificent treasures from years so long ago.

One of the best things about the float museum was the bathroom. There were several Eastern-style cubicles (squatters), and then one Western cubicle, but what a Western one it was—it had a heated seat and the toilet did wonderful things to you if you pressed all the buttons. It was pretty amazing! Of course I participated in the pressing of the buttons, limited only by the knowledge that Miwako and Judi were anxiously awaiting my exit from the bathroom so we could continue with our day.

After playing with the toilet (I really do love these Japanese toilets), we went to an old Japanese-style merchant house and checked out what life was like a very long time ago. Two heritage houses sat side by side: Kusakabe Heritage House and Yoshijima Heritage House. They were two of the oldest homes in Takayama, open to the public as museums. We wandered through the wooden homes, looking at many different implements from ages past. Life then was certainly much sparser back then.

Wandering through the old town, we just enjoyed the ambience as we strolled down the narrow cobblestoned roads with wooden houses on both sides. Everything was quaint and little (except the prices). We liked Takayama.

FROM OUR LITTLE *ryokan*, we were able to buy time on the Internet. It seemed a bit odd—being online at a place where I couldn't even sit in my room, but there you go, it's the twenty-first century. It seemed to me that even when people want to go back in time, or experience things the "old" way, we still are not able to completely discard our phones or computers. How sad. I would have been content if there were no Internet connection, but since there was, and there were so many people availing themselves of it, I too, could not resist.

ONE EVENING IN Takayama, we went for dinner to a steak house. We ordered *shabu shabu*, which actually turned out to be a pot of boiling water for our cooking since Judi was allergic to all things from the sea which usually flavours the water. Large platters of raw beef and veggies were brought to the table, and we cooked them in the boiling water. Even without any flavouring, the food was quite tasty. On the menu, they listed "healthy pork," and for the same price, one could also order "healthy pork fatty." We chose the beef. I also ordered frozen *sake*—it looked and tasted like buttermilk, and after the first cup, I got quite pleasantly used to the taste.

But the best thing about the whole restaurant was the toilet. It was a Toto toilet, my favourite kind, with a control panel on the wall. The seat was heated, and the toilet flushed automatically, even if I just fidgeted. The controls allowed me, if I so choose, to wash in many different ways, utilizing a forward spray, backward spray, soft or hard spray, dry with warm air, and many more options. Only time was against me as I knew my dining companions were waiting for me. It did cross my mind that it might not be the height of normalcy to choose to spend my restaurant time alone in a cubicle with a Toto toilet. Just then, a warm, comforting breeze of fresh air covered my nether parts, and I didn't care about normalcy any more for a while.

ONE MORNING, WE were walking down the street to the bus station.
"Oh, fruit!" Judi exclaimed excitedly.
"You want some?" Miwako asked, pointing to the oranges.
"No," Judi said, "I just get so excited when I recognize something."
This got me to thinking. I think there are basically two types of travelers— those who always look for the familiar (I am not implying my sister is of that type) and those who always look for the unusual and different. I have met many of both types. I am of the latter. I am always disappointed when I see something familiar. I could have stayed at home with my dog for that.

WE SET OUT for Hida No Sato—The Hida Folk Village. Not like our Canadian Haidas—this Hida (pronounced Heed-ah) is like a county and also is in the Hida Mountain range. This open air museum was just a short (ten minutes by the "Sarubobo Bus") ride from downtown Takayama. The Japanese had some wonderful old houses that they almost lost in a flood and that were getting very decrepit, so they relocated about thirty of them higher up on a mountain, and made a heritage museum out of them. Most of the houses were built in the 1600s and 1700s and were quite wonderful, with thick thatched or shingled roofs covering attics where silkworms used to make silk. Many of the roofs had sharply steep sides, looking like praying hands and were called *gassho-zukuri*.

The houses had tall gables, and often there were four stories under the sharply angled roof, for the silkworms and the weaving, and all the other things the folks did. Most of the houses had little barns inside them. The people who had lived there felt their horses and cattle were valued members of the family, and they took very good care of them, including bringing them into their warm homes. The whole little village was harmonized with nature. There was a circular rice patty, and other beautiful gardens off in the distance; a waterwheel with swans swimming in the lake gave cause for contemplation, and artisans sewing and carving and dyeing just like in the old days made me feel as though I had stepped back through time. We spent several hours wandering around the village.

But the best thing was the toilet. Even in this old village, there was a public bathroom, where, when I first opened the door, the lights went on. And there, in all her glory, was the Toto toilet, heated seat beckoning. The control panel was on the wall, and allowed me to do any manner of interesting things with water and my body. And then the Toto gently dried me up and sent me on my way.

There were lots of tourist shops at the folk village selling souvenirs—but about ninety percent of the merchandise was food and almost all of the other ten percent was *Sarubobo* souvenirs! Most all of the food items had little sample boxes beside them for tasters.

"Ruth, come here, have a look at this." Judi beckoned me over to a table and held something out to me.

"What are you showing me—that looks like a pair of boobs!"

"It is!" Judi laughed. "Look!" She pointed over to the table behind her. There sat the pornographic food section. I was not interested in buying breast puddings or penis lollipops. There were many other items for sale there as well, but I will leave them to your imagination.

AFTER SPENDING A long morning at the folk village, we had decided to go for *okonomiyaki*—Japanese pizza. It is made with eggs and flour and cabbage and slippery yam, in a kind of paste, and then toppings like pork or beef or cuttlefish or whatever is mixed in, and it is typically cooked on the table which has a small flat griddle in the middle. Judi had a bacon *okonomiyaki*, Miwako had a cuttlefish one, and I had a house special one, which had all the different "toppings" on it. The works! It is also common when eating *okonomiyaki* to put mayo on the top, and all kinds of other condiments like kelp and fish flakes (which always look as though they are alive and moving) and green and black things (no pink things this time). It was really extremely delicious.

And then I had to go to the bathroom.

"It's not Western style," Miwako warned.

"Oh, that's okay." I confidently got up. I had gotten rather good at gathering my clothes just so that I could emerge from an Eastern-style squatter without getting my clothes wet.

I walked to the back of the small restaurant, and I entered the cleanest, most gleaming-est bathroom I have ever seen. The floor literally sparkled clean, and up a large step, was the squatter, shimmering white. So I prepared myself, and began to do my thing. At first, everything was going well, and I smiled thinking how adaptable I could be. But then I lost control, so to speak, and could no longer adequately direct the steam coming from me into the squatter. It went all over the floor, in huge puddles (Of course, this would be one of the times when I really had to go, so there were copious amounts of urine splashing everywhere over the previously-pristine floor (and my shoes and socks). When I was done, I looked around at what I had wrought—how to clean it? There was toilet paper, but it was very thin, transparent almost, and there was a garbage can, but it was truly only about two inches high, in typical Japanese little. I cleaned up as best I could, and flushed and washed, but I know I left it much messier than I found it. And then I sheepishly slunk back to the table.

A few minutes later, I saw the bucket brigade move in. Then they came out of the toilet—three of them—with buckets, mops, rolls of paper, rags, and a veritable storehouse of cleaning supplies. After they finished cleaning, they stood at the back of the restaurant and whispered among each other—I could only imagine what they were saying about the filthy foreigner. I was mortified. I felt like the (North) American devil defiling and desecrating the eastern lavatories. Oh, where was my Toto toilet when I needed it?

LATE AFTERNOON, WE walked through old town. It was very quaint, to be sure. Narrow streets and wooden Japanese houses; it looked just the way I thought a little Japanese town would look. There were sweets stores and *sake* factories, and museums. We took our shoes on and off that day probably one hundred times! Miwako easily slipped in and out of her shoes; she's been doing it her whole life. Judi and I struggled every time, first with taking them off, then putting them on. In each house in the Hida village we took our shoes off; and also in every museum in old town. Some museums even had several buildings so we had to take them off, put them on, take them off, put them on, take them off put them on takethemoffputthemon, ad nauseum. But walking through the streets of old town, we felt as though we were in a different world, a different life, where things were slower and precise and lovely. It was difficult to imagine a twentieth century world somewhere out there while we strolled the narrow streets of old town.

WE WENT BACK to the same restaurant for dinner as the previous night. I immediately went to the bathroom to the Toto toilet. She was so happy to see me, caressing me with her warm seat, as though saying, "What are you doing fooling around with those Eastern squatters? Come sit with me for a while." I pushed all her buttons for a long time. She dried me off gently, waving goodbye. God, I love those toilets! I even visited her twice during the meal.

ONE MORE NIGHT on the floor before leaving Takayama—I would be lying if I said I had been sleeping well. I slept some, but I was so stiff from walking all day that any movement was uncomfortable and I woke up all the time and then lay there worrying about how I was going to stand up. The last night in our *ryokan*, I got up about two in the morning to go to the bathroom. I used my cane, as I was particularly stiff that night. I quietly slid open the door to the tiny toilet room. When I went into the toilet room, I left my cane leaning against the sink.

When I was done with the toilet, I quietly tried to slide open the door, so as not to wake Miwako. The door wouldn't budge.

"What's going on here?" I thought. I tried again. The door that had slid open and closed so easily every time for the past three days was absolutely shut and staying so. I pushed with all my might. Finally, I managed to open the door about six inches, but it was clearly jammed. Then I understood what had happened. My cane had slipped down behind the door while I was in the toilet and was jammed between the door and the wall.

Now that I had the door open a few inches, I tried to call for Miwako. I couldn't call too loudly, because I didn't want to wake everyone else in the *ryokan*. The walls, like the *tatami* mats, were thin.

"Miwako," I whispered. Nothing.

"Miiiiwaaaaakoooo." A little louder this time. I tried the door again. That cane had not moved. I wished that I were a prestidigitator and could levitate the cane, just a few inches, so that I could get out of that tiny toilet room. I was getting stiffer in there. It was so miniscule, my knees were rubbing on opposite walls.

"*Miwako*!" I heard some movement. I went back to a loud whisper. "Miwako, help me."

"Huh, what? Mmmm." I heard her roll over.

"Miwako, wake up. *Wake up*. Help me. Miwako, please. Help."

"What's going on? Where are you?" She was finally awakening. Probably so was the rest of the *ryokan*.

"I'm here, in the bathroom. Get me out."

"Just open the door and come out." Clearly, she was still sleepy.

"Miwako, I can't, I'm stuck. I need you to move my cane. Help me, please." I heard a shuffling, then the cane was lifted and at last, the door moved open. I smiled at Miwako and gave her a big hug.

"Thank you, Miwako. Thank you. If you hadn't been here with me, I would have been in that tiny toilet room forever!"

She shuffled back to her futon and was asleep before I even left the sink room.

That last night in Takayma, after being rescued from the tiny toilet room, I did sleep very well and very long. I guess I was getting used to the floor after all. And probably my mind knew I was not about to be getting up to use the toilet again that night. But I was looking forward to falling into a bed again.

AFTER LEAVING TAKAYAMA the next day, we drove to Shirakowago, high up in the mountains, on our way back to Kuwana City. In 1995, it became a Unesco Heritage Village, when the young folks decided to keep their village looking the way it used to look, even though some of the homes had been modernized inside. These old farms houses were similar to the ones at Hida No Sato—built in the *gassho-zukuri* style, the praying hands style, with high roofs. They still looked as they did hundreds of years ago, and many were open for viewing.

There was a special shrine for *sake*—*dunburoku*—they made the undistilled *sake*, gave it to the gods, and whatever was left over went to the people. I had the privilege of drinking a cup of what was left over from the gods. Like the *sake* from the other night, it resembled buttermilk, thick, opalescent, and very, very good! It was called *dunburoku sake*.

We drove back to Kuwana City, through mountains of multitudinous shades of green, through mountain camping spots where wooden alpine cabins were interspersed with thatched roofed huts. We drove by rivers and waterfalls, and through seemingly hundreds more tunnels, some very long, some not. The neat thing was on all these mountains there was not one patch of clear-cut trees. I realized how much I was used to seeing such an ugly and blasphemous sight at home that its absence becomes noticeable!

JUDI AND I went back to the Udon Noodle House to see our favourite waitress, Mica. Now Mica could not speak a word of English—okay, maybe one or two words, but not much more than that—and our Japanese was not much better, yet we certainly seemed able to communicate. I ordered, in Japanese if you please, dumplings, fried chicken, pork cutlets, beer, and then we pointed to a picture of what looked like French fries.

"Aah," Mica said, "poh-tay-toh."

"*Hai,*" we answered, "poh-tay-toh."

They weren't French fries, but they were indeed potatoes, and we had a good dinner. No fish flakes tonight. Those ubiquitous fish flakes that look as though they are alive were on absolutely everything.

We watched Mica and the other waitresses slip in and out of their shoes. They would come to a set of four stairs, bearing full trays of food, and slip out of their shoes, walk up the stairs and serve the food. They then came down the stairs, put their shoes on (which were facing away from the direction they were now moving) without missing a beat, and didn't stop walking or moving. I have to sit down every time I take my shoes off or put them on. I was fascinated and could have watched them slip out of and into their shoes all evening.

After dinner, we told Mica we were sisters and were traveling around the world, and she asked us to wait a moment. Seconds later she reappeared with her cell phone and wanted to take a photo of us—we happily obliged. We really liked her a lot and felt a sisterhood kinship with her, even though we knew nothing about her. We all hugged each other good-bye, sad that we would likely not ever see each other again.

We were getting ready to leave Kuwana City again, our base in Japan, and go to Ise-Shima, by the ocean. We were very excited about this and were glad that our time in Japan included mountains and ocean.

Chapter Eleven
Ise-Shima: To the Sea Shore

LEGEND HAS IT that once upon a time, Yamatohimeno Mikota, who served the Sun Goddess, Amatherasu o Mikami, made a trip to Futami, an inlet on the Pacific Ocean. So impressed was she with the beautiful scene, she turned to look once more at the beach. The word *futami* means "to look once more." And this is where we had come—to a hotel right on the beach in the town of Futami, in the region of Ise-Shima. This pristine beach was used for purifying body and soul before going to the Ise shrine to pray. The sunrise was supposed to dye the sky and sea such a fantastic color that it was like the dawn of a new age. It was "a sight that lets us make a start for a life worth living!"

We had come to the seaside after staying at our *ryokan* in the mountains. Our first night in the hotel, in a Western bed, I slept ten hours! It was the first bed after many futon-on-the-floor sleeps. Just when I thought I was getting used to the floor. Or was I?

THE FIRST MORNING, we ordered breakfast at our hotel on the seashore. Only Japanese breakfasts were available and Judi didn't want to, actually couldn't, partake, because of allergies. For Japanese breakfast, they served what was termed "half-boiled egg."

We summoned over the manager.

"Good morning, sir." I bowed slightly. "Can we get an egg for her breakfast tomorrow?" I asked, indicating my sister.

"No, sorry, only Japanese breakfasts are available."

"Okay, I understand. But you have a half-boiled egg as part of the Japanese breakfast, so perhaps you could just half-boil it twice?"

I was met with a blank gaze.

"How about taking that egg and scrambling it, or hard-boiling it or cooking it in any other way?" I inclined my head quizzically.

Thereafter followed a discussion lasting a full fifteen minutes, while we were told about kitchen travails and substitutions, or rather no substitutions, and problems of waiters and managers and walruses and kings. But he did agree to try something for the next morning. Exactly what that would be, we just had to wait to find out.

It seemed to me that every discussion or question one would think required only a simple yes or no answer took fifteen or twenty minutes of animated talking with no definite resolution forthcoming. It was a bit frustrating.

Everything was so formal and precise—when I got change, it was given to me on a tray. Our hotel key was presented to us on a tray. Even my take-out coffee, in a paper cup, had the top taped shut, the cup wrapped up, it was put in a bag, and handed to me on a tray! At first, all this painstaking solicitude was delightful to watch, but with time, it began to get a bit tedious.

FINALLY, IT WAS nice to be somewhere *Sarubobo* wasn't. When we were in Takayama and Shirakowago, *Sarubobo* was universal. Little *Sarubobo* dolls and souvenirs were in restaurants and bathrooms, and on the highway at gas stations. We were getting sick of them. And now, we had come to Ise Shima National Park, and there were no more *Sarubobos* and with a shock, I realized that I actually missed them in some bizarre kind of way.

In Ise-Shima, however, were the kitties. The "beckoning kitty," *Maneki-neko*, summoned people into merchants' stores. If her left paw was raised (beckoning), it called in customers and good business; if the right paw was raised, that indicated prosperity. This waving kitty was as ubiquitous as *Sarubobo*, except she was all over Japan, in virtually every store, on signs, in tourist shops, everywhere one looked. I even remembered seeing her in Canada in Japanese stores. There were many different *engimono*, or good luck talismen, but the beckoning kitty seemed to be the most popular.

The froggies were pretty widespread as well. We saw many frogs—in fact, one of the souvenirs I brought home was a wooden frog with a stick in its mouth which served as a percussive instrument. The Japanese cutesy cartoonish characters were very different from ours—I would not call them as cute as ours, but that's because my taste was that of a North American. Most likely the Japanese think our cartoons were pretty ugly and *Sarubobo* and *Maneki-neko*, the beckoning kitty, were adorable! Who knows?

ONE EVENING, AT the seashore, we went for sushi. Miwako wanted to eat it, and I felt as though it would be criminal for me to be in Japan and not eat sushi at least once. Judi was a very good sport and urged us to go, telling us she would manage. And manage she did. The sushi chefs were all very concerned about her and wanted to make sure that she had some food. She didn't want sushi rice, so they went off and made regular rice for her. Then they made eggs over easy and gave her a salad. She probably ate more than Miwako and I together, who both had really good sushi! It was a wonderful evening, full of laughter.

One of the waiters came over to pour my tea. He was a striking-looking young man, perhaps in his early twenties.

"I am sorry for keeping you waiting." He bowed.

"Oh," I replied, "I really wasn't waiting, but thank you." He smiled and filled my cup.

A little while later, he came up to me and once again said, "I am sorry for keeping you waiting." And poured tea.

After the third time, I finally said, "You are not keeping me waiting for anything."

He smiled. I have doubts that he knew of what he spoke.

Our sushi chef was such a good-looking young man! I couldn't take my eyes off his face. He was absolutely angelic, with a smile that could melt icebergs. The whole evening, he smiled and spoke Japanese, and as we were leaving, he said, in excellent English, "Thank you for coming. Good evening."

WELL, JUDI GOT scrambled eggs for breakfast. And we started a new day! And a great day it was. We drove to the seaside town of Toba which had a very good aquarium. My two favourite things were the dugongs and the leafy seadragons.

The dugong is a large mammal that looked like its manatee cousin, and it is said that these creatures are the origin of the legend of mermaids. In fact, their name, dugong, originated from the Malay language where *duyung* meant "lady of the sea." I could see the mermaid resemblance from looking at their tails, but absolutely not from looking at their manatee/sea lion like faces. They are somewhat smaller than manatees, growing only to three metres in length. I was fascinated, watching them swim in their large tank and didn't want to tear myself away. I wondered what/if they were thinking—I supposed they were wondering about my origins and what I was doing there. Maybe they wondered if I came from a mermaid. After all, they were locked up in a human-made prison, so they had lots of time for reflection.

"Oh look at that one over there!" dugong number one said. "She's a strange one—I wonder where she came from."

"She looks like a mutation to me," dugong number two answered. "Look at that face, that hair." She swam up to the glass and stared at me.

"Too bad they are so stupid," dugong number one muttered, swimming up to the glass. "It might be fun to talk with her and find out more about her life. She doesn't look like she is from around here."

"True"—dugong number two flicked her tail—"she clearly is a foreigner. I wonder why the sea goddess made those humans so unable to communicate?"

"Ruth, come oooooon," my sister hollered. "We're waiting for you over here!" I had to leave my little dugong playlet, reluctantly, I might add.

The leafy seadragon was a beautiful creature that looked like a cross between a sea horse and a hairy fern. It was considerably larger than a seahorse, growing to about forty-six centimetres (eighteen inches), and looked exactly like a miniature dragon with fronds all over it. It was a gorgeous orangey-red with gold colour, and its long snout waved about in the water, a speckled darker colour. It was an amazingly delicate and fascinating creature. Like its seahorse cousins, the male carries the eggs on his tail where they are fertilized. He swims around with the babies-to-be for several months until the eggs hatch. I did not want to leave the aquarium where the leafy seadragon swam. I had never even known of the existence of these magnificent creatures before that day. They were stunningly beautiful and exquisite.

Now I love animals and consider myself fairly educated about them. Although I have been lucky enough to see many species in the wild, I'm also aware of the presence of many more creatures whom I have not yet had the privilege of meeting in real life. Yet seeing both the dugong and the seadragon made me wonder how many more critters there were in the world about whose existence I knew absolutely nothing. It was a humbling experience.

I managed to tear myself away from the seadragons to take a little boat ride to Dolphin Island were we saw a dolphin show. Sea World in San Diego it wasn't, but just as well, because usually I am opposed to "animal shows." I would much rather see the animals swimming free in the ocean, than performing for tourists.

WE SAILED AROUND the harbour, ending the day by spending several wonderful hours at Mikimoto Pearl Island, which was my favourite part of the day (could that be because it was the first, the *only* place, that had a significant amount of English translation?).

Kokichi Mikimoto, who died at the age of ninety-six years not that long ago, was the first person to ever culture pearls. The Mikimoto Pearl Island was, in fact, a whole island, with many different buildings. There was a huge museum that explained everything you ever wanted to know about pearls—cultured and natural pearls, growing, harvesting, selecting. There was a second museum relating the life of Mr. Mikimoto. What an incredible life he had! I spent a long time there getting to know about and admiring his life. Mr. Mikimoto, against all odds, and after losing everything in a red tide, finally developed a way to culture pearls and single-handedly revived the pearl industry. His whole life story was truly inspiring; he was a most engaging and wonderful person.

He came from a family who owned a noodle restaurant, in the Ise-Shima region. Recognizing that pearls, which were found in that area, at least the oysters were, had great business potential, he developed the means to culture them. He wanted to decorate all the women of the world with pearls. Many interesting and inspiring things were attributed to him, and some not so inspiring:

"They will get better by just putting a string of pearls around their necks. It can be especially effective in cases of hysterics."

Oh, Mr. Mikimoto, would that that were so!

He met Thomas Edison and many important political figures of the day, and died in 1954 at the age of ninety-six.

On Mikimoto Pearl Island, we saw a demonstration by the *ama*, or women divers. The *ama* have been around forever—the oldest record in a story is from the year 3 C.E. We were told that the success of pearl cultivation would not have been possible without the *ama*. They are no longer needed today with the current modern techniques of pearl cultivation usurping them, at least, not in the way they were needed in the past. But they do educate the tourists at Mikimoto Pearl Island by doing demonstrations.

They harvested abalone, shells, urchins, seaweed, agar-agar, sea cucumbers. Adorned in little white bonnets and flowing white gowns, they look like nuns of the sea. I thought it must be incredibly difficult to wear those flowing gowns when diving, but that's in fact what they wear. The white colour scares away the dolphins and sharks. They don't use scuba gear or anything remotely like that, mostly because when they started doing their work, SCUBA or snorkels were not even flecks in the minds of their inventors.

We sat on concrete benches behind railings over the ocean and waited. Soon a little boat came chugging out in front of us. Six white-gowned women sat in the boat, all wearing white cloth bonnets tied under their chins. I watched eagerly as each one tied herself to a wooden bucket, tossed it into the ocean, and then followed it overboard. The bucket popped up to the surface and floated. The *ama* was close behind.

The *ama* have a particular way of breathing, called *isobue*, which is a whistle-like sound they make upon resurfacing to equilibrate their lungs. We watched as the women dove, resurfaced, whistled, dove again.

These days there were about thirteen hundred a*ma* still living and working in this region, but the average age was seventy-two years old! The ones we saw dive today seemed considerably younger than that, but it was hard to tell. *Ama*, or divers, were all women, because we have an extra layer of fat which makes the cold water easier to bear, and also women can hold their breath longer than men.

THERE ARE MANY positives and negatives to traveling with a local. Some of our best experiences happened when we have had to fend for ourselves in a foreign setting; on the other hand, having a local Japanese with us did simplify matters immensely, especially since we were in small towns where there was virtually no English. The Japanese were all very anxious to please. However because of the language barrier we were totally dependent upon Miwako (or so she thought), which was not necessarily a good thing as we were rarely involved in any determinations. I think we were all getting a bit frustrated. Miwako is a dear person, and she so wanted us to have a good time and to please us, but she made a lot of incorrect assumptions about what we might want and didn't check all that often with us about them. Judi and I also made a lot of probably incorrect assumptions about her. Miwako's English was very good, but it was not excellent and she would get so frustrated. She was not content with just having us understand her, but rather, her English needed to be impeccable, so each sentence was spoken at least four, maybe five or six times, until she got it just right.

For example, she might say, "The emperor, no the government, errr, umm, the emperor called, no, umm, mmmmm, wanted the people to push, no, to talk, umm, mmmm, err, to call, the emperor wanted the people to call the gods not the priests, ummm err, mmmmm to say to the god."

At this point, I might say something like, "The emperor wanted the people to call him god?"

"Yes!" was the grateful reply.

Or

"The taxi driver talk, no, umm errr, said, the taxi driver said that Geku shrine don't, ummm errr, doesn't, Geku shrine mmmmmmm doesn't have attractive, umm err, mmmmmmm, things, so we must go, errrrr mmm, no, should go to Niku first, yes the taxi driver said that Geku shrine doesn't have attractive things, so we should go to Niku first. Yes."

It did become a bit tedious for all of us when every sentence was like that. She was trying so hard to be perfect, rather than just to be understood. And it was easy to understand her—it just took forever for her to finish a sentence! She got frustrated and then we got frustrated. And because she wanted to please us so much, every time we so much as glanced at something, she bought it for us.

I would look at something in the store and mutter to myself, "Oh, that's looks good." And the next thing I knew, she bought it for me, even if I didn't particularly want it. So I walked around trying very hard not to talk too much or appreciate things verbally, something which was very difficult for me, because off she would run to get it.

When we were in Takayama, I had mentioned a coke would be nice, just in passing, and off she ran to buy cokes (which I truly could have done without). While out on this mission, Miwako was hurrying back and fell on the street. She returned to the *ryokan,* bleeding from her face, hands, and knees. I had to do a little first aid and she was fine—well, fine with a bunch of scrapes and bruises all covered with Band-Aids. We all felt terrible. Ah well, we all must adjust as best we can.

SOMETHING I LEARNED, which was continually being reinforced because it seemed like a very difficult lesson for me to learn, was that it was next to impossible to use one's sense of humour with someone who speaks English as a second or third language. I first noticed this in China—if I made a sardonic or ironic remark, it was totally misinterpreted. Many times I had to keep reminding Miwako that I was making a joke. I was actually surprised to discover that a large part of my normal conversation was irony, satire, and humour (or attempted humour). The first time I became aware of using irony and having it misinterpreted in a big way was many years ago with a deaf friend. Of course, my signing capabilities were not fluent, but I could communicate with her using ASL (American Sign Langauge). And when I said something sarcastic, and thought that I had signed it so, she got extremely offended. I realized then the subtleties inherent in all our communications, not only of the language, but of the sound and inflection. And now with Miwako, no matter how much I would try to smile and use body language and any other means I had to get my sarcasm across, it was almost always misunderstood, and for a time, I believed she thought me to be a very not nice person. It made me reassess my normal speech and how I communicate, and in fact, I believe has changed my normal pattern for life. I began talking less and less, which for me was difficult. And so I turned to writing!

OUR HOTEL AT Ise-Shima was very nice, but once more I was amazed that although it was a tourist inn, there was virtually no English here at all, and none of the staff at the front desk spoke English. Of course, I had to keep reminding myself that it was my arrogance that assumed a tourist place would involve English; there were hundreds of thousands of Japanese and other tourists who never spoke English at all, who were very comfortable and very understood at Ise-Shima.

In my room, the bathroom was located about a two foot step up from the floor, and the bathtub was about half my height, and one had to step in and out of it for a shower. But other than that, and the fact that it was Japanese little, it was very comfortable.

But not the prices—wow! It was unbelievably expensive. One day we paid the equivalent of about $12.50 to park for a few hours; a cup of coffee (half a paper cup of bad coffee) cost the equivalent of $3.60; dinner for three cost well over $200.00 (okay, I had two little tiny cups of sake, but it's Japan, for heaven's sake!) Admission to the aquarium was close to $70.00 for the three of us (and I got a senior's discount). It was not a place I could afford to stay for long—not compared to China, which was much, much less expensive on every level.

I found the public bathrooms interesting. There might be six squatters and one Western cubicle. But at least most bathrooms (not all, mind you) had one Western toilet. It always surprised me to see women enter the bathroom and choose the squatters over the Western cubicle. I imagine they wondered why on earth I would want a cubicle with a toilet in it when a normal squatter was there, available for me to use.

Most of the restaurants were eating-on-the-floor type. We always had to check that there were tables, although I kept telling Miwako that I was okay with sitting on the floor for dinner. I didn't think she believed me, but I really meant it. Getting up off the floor was a whole other problem though.

One night, we decided to indulge ourselves in the specialty of the region— spiny lobster. Miwako and I had a special meal for two which consisted of about eight different courses: sashimi, tempura, miso soup, of course, the lobster, and pickles, and green things and brown things, all topped off with brown-sugar-taste-ice cream. And Judi ordered a steak—just a steak with no sauce, no nothing. It came cut in strips, easy to eat with chopsticks. On the plate, artistically arranged, were one tiny round of carrot, one tiny cube of squash, three French fries, and the steak strips. It looked very beautiful. And little.

People here didn't really say good-bye. Everyone said, as we would leave a store or the hotel, *Arigato gozaimaste* (polite form of thank you)—but with a considerable uplift at the end with an increase in volume as well—almost like a sing-song; or else they would say *do itashimashite* (you're welcome) with the same uplilt. No simple *sayonara* for these folks. It was almost like a song of thanks, and it was very similar from place to place.

ONE DAY, WE visited Ise Jingu, not just any Shinto Shrine, but *the* Shinto shrine. The Japanese believe in *kami*, or powerful beings, that reside in nature, like rocks, water, etc. Shinto is the indigenous religion of Japan, and in Shintoism, *kami* are worshiped in *matsuri* or solemn ceremonies. There are more than a hundred thousand Shinto shrines in Japan, but Jingu is the most honored of all Shinto sanctuaries. It is considered to be the spiritual home of all Japanese, most of whom make a pilgrimage there at least once in their lives. Over six million pilgrims and worshippers come to Jingu every year. And so off we went. There were, of course, many *toriis*. A *torii* is a gateway which separates the division between the everyday world and the divine world. They are tall, rectangular structures that one walks under usually, and they look like a Pi sign. They were everywhere in Japan. The main shrines and the bridges are replaced every twenty years—that's quite a feat. The wood from the old shrine is considered holy and is used in other shrines around Japan for restoration, etc.

Jingu was a very pastoral place—aside from the shrines and the priests, etc, there were wonderful woods in which we saw deer and pristine streams full of large *koi*. We walked around for quite a while, and then walked in the streets around the shrine, which was like one big market. We actually did a fair bit of shopping. But even though there were many souvenir shops, again, a huge proportion of what was displayed was food. This always surprised me. I found it fascinating nevertheless, as I was unfamiliar with about ninety-nine percent of it. I was grateful that most places had taster dishes beside many products. I did find something I loved called *mameta*—kind of a Japanese peanut brittle. That was my favourite in Japan, although I liked the goo balls as well.

ONE MORNING WE had breakfast at Komeda's Coffee Shop. Judi and I shared mac and cheese and an egg salad sandwich, and I had a couple of cups of coffee. It was the best meal I've had so far in Japan! No pink or green or black things! It did however, cost over thirty dollars. The negative thing about eating out here was the smoking—everyone smoked and the stink was everywhere. The best thing about the coffee shop was again, the toilet. This one had wall controls with a clock and had thirteen different control dials in both Japanese and Braille. The only English was in one corner where it announced "shower toilet."

I noticed, walking around, that a huge number of older Japanese women were very hunched over, much more so than one would see in North America, presumably from osteoporosis. I imagine it is because they are tiny people, their bones are tiny and so osteoporosis is most likely endemic in this population.

We drove down the coast past many little fishing villages and went to a Sea-folk museum. Again, we were fascinated by the *ama*, the women divers. We saw a video about one, who had to be in her seventies, diving every day with her husband operating the boat. She wore so many clothes, including a wet suit, over which she wore white long underwear and a white bonnet. It was amazing to comprehend. I am a certified SCUBA diver, and I don't even like wearing wet suits because they seem too cumbersome. Yet the *ama* look as though they are garbed in enough apparel to outfit a clothing store. The *ama* continue diving right into their eighties, apparently. And they don't use any SCUBA equipment, just a face mask. Not even a snorkel. They are down for fifty seconds at a time and then shoot right up—why they don't get pulmonary emboli is beyond me, but they seem to do just fine.

WE HAD THE best dinner at a grill house in Ise-Shima. We dined on sukiyaki, but not like any sukiyaki I've ever had before. It was amazing—cooked with lard and brown sugar and a bit of soy sauce. I know, it doesn't sound so appetizing, but really, it was fabulous. So tasty, I even ordered an extra helping of meat. I think it was the best meal I had in Japan—even better than the coffee house! The waitress was so efficient, even with her sleeping infant slung over her back, and the older mother and other daughter were also very attentive to us. They were all so nice and it was soooo good. The only negative was that the meal for the three of us cost about $300.00! And that was just a normal cost here, nothing special! I found myself missing China a lot these days, especially when it came to the wallet.

EARLY ONE MORNING, I couldn't sleep and so got up to go for a walk along the ocean, and then came back through the little town of Futami. As I walked along in the early morning, I would pass folks and we would greet each other, "*Ohayou gozaimaste*" (good morning), and nod to each other. Hmmm, I felt I was really in Japan.

For lunch that day, we hit the vending machines again. The best one was the french fries for Judi—the machine played a little jig while the fries were being prepared and after a few minutes, out came a steaming box, sealed and wrapped, full of hot french fries, with a little package of salt on top. Amazing!

ONE AFTERNOON, JUDI had to see an eye doctor. I knew she had conjunctivitis and needed antibiotic eye drops, but one needed a prescription for them here, so off we went. We entered the doctor's office, after taking our shoes off, of course, and saw other people being examined.

"*Ko, tah, eu, kay,*" the man read from the eye chart. No E FP TOZ LPED for him. There, on the eye chart were little squiggles that I guess meant something to the Japanese, as the man continued to read, "*ay, to, te, kah.*" Judi and I stared in fascination. In no time at all, she got her antibiotic eye drops and will live happily ever after.

THE FOLLOWING MORNING, we headed back to Kuwana City for one more day before Judi and I would leave Miwako. Time was passing quickly. Even so, I would be happy to travel in other countries. I loved China. I found Japan interesting, but it didn't move me the way China did. Everyone in Japan was so polite and so little! I felt I was being petty but really, I did feel like Gulliver in the land of the Lilliputians. It was time to move on.

Chapter Twelve
Kyoto, Hakone, and More

JUDI AND I were getting friendly with the staff who worked at our hotel in Kuwana City. Even though we didn't share a common language, we still managed to communicate to one another. One young woman in her early twenties had a fairly good command of English. She had told us that she was going to be traveling in the US the following month.

"Oh," Judi said, "come visit me. I live in Palm Springs."

"What prefecture is that in?" she asked. Here in Japan everything is in prefectures as opposed to provinces or states or counties. Miwako lived in Mie prefecture. There are forty-seven prefectures in Japan.

BEFORE WE LEFT Kuwana City, we had a goodbye dinner with Miwako and her daughter Aya. Judi and I took them to our favourite noodle restaurant where we also said goodbye to Mica, the wonderful waitress. The following morning we had a goodbye breakfast with Miwako. I think she was sad to see us go, but it was difficult to read her true feelings. Miwako seemed somewhat emotional on bidding us goodbye. Judi and I were glad we came to Japan; we had a most interesting time, and now were very happy to depart, as both of us were extremely excited about our upcoming trip to Russia. We still had a few days left in Japan, but we had arranged to meet friends and tour in other areas of the country and we were quite content to be moving on. Miwako did not seem to share our elation of hitting the road. But I have to admit that it was fairly difficult for us to know exactly how she was feeling. So we just kept indulging her in a significant number of gustatory and other farewell events.

Judi and I hired a car to drive us from Kuwana City to Kyoto. Another emptying of the wallet, but money well spent, really, because we had *so* much luggage, even though we kept sending boxes home. Judi sent some home from Kuwana City, as I did, sending two large cartons, yet still we travel like some sort of luggage store. Every time I travel, I take less luggage with me than the previous trip, and every time it is always too much. One would think I would have learned better after all these trips. I just don't understand how people are able to be away for a significant amount of time with just a backpack. What if they need a hammer, or a toilet plunger or an extra book? Although I must admit that in the 1980s, I did go off alone for two weeks to Isla Mujeres in Mexico with just a backpack. Okay, it was a very large backpack, but it was still one piece, and in my strong days of youth, I actually could cart it around on my back, even though it wasn't very comfortable. I lived in a bathing suit or jeans for two weeks, and still felt very underpacked.

After we had been on the road for an hour, the cab driver pointed off into the distance and said, "toidy."

"Okay," I answered.

He pulled over to a rest stop and parked in front of the toilets. Judi and I obliged him by dutifully performing our toiletries.

Another hour went by and he started talking to me again in Japanese (he spoke no English at all). "Okay," I answered. And again. "Yeah, uh huh, okay," I said. "Mmh hum, I see." I vigorously nodded my head.

"You have no idea what he's saying, do you?" Judi asked.

"Nope, not a clue."

Driving into Kyoto, it was as though we had arrived in America-land. We drove by McDonalds, Starbucks, 7-11, Circle-K, Kinko's, Baskin & Robbins, KFC, Wendy's. Signs urged us to drink Coca Cola in English (all the coke signs previously had been in Japanese).

Our driver stopped for directions and the person whom he had asked was pointing in literally all directions. It reminded me of a line from a play, "He said thanks and went off in all directions." The hotel is this way, no that way, no that way. After stopping four separate times to ask directions, we finally got to the Kyoto Westin, where we were meeting friends and attending a two day conference on health. The Kyoto Westin felt like home: elevators big enough for my body, people at the desk who spoke English, a concierge, people accepting tips, and all the other things that we were used to in a hotel. Up to now, even though we tried to tip people, they would not accept any money at all. None of those lovely, helpful people in the Kuwana City hotels would accept a penny. Or a *yen*. But Kyoto was the jaded big city, after all, and open palms were constantly visible.

Traveling in a foreign country, one can really tell the difference between the big cities and the smaller cities. For almost two weeks now we have been in places with virtually no English, neither spoken nor in signs nor books nor anywhere. And now, all of a sudden, it is everywhere. If people just came here from elsewhere in the world, they would get a totally different impression of Japan than by going to Takayama, for example.

Our first night in Kyoto we were just beat and decided to go to the coffee shop in the hotel for a light dinner and retire early. I told Judi to take advantage of the situation because it was the only time I was prepared to go to a non-Japanese restaurant while we remained in Japan. Between the two of us, we had two small glasses of white wine, two bowls of onion soup, one caesar salad, one burger, and one vanilla milkshake and the bill came to the equivalent of $118.07 Canadian dollars!

The following day we joined a tour. We had a good guide whose English was impeccable! I loved Kyoto! It was a real city of 1.5 million souls, with big city things, yet it also had numerous little roads wandering off the main roads, full of lively shops and people. I remembered all the Geisha books I read in the past and I could just picture them, many years ago, tottering along on their special socks and shoes, *tabi* and *okobo*, dressed in long kimonos, *obis* bobbing behind them, walking towards the teahouse, *ochaya*. It felt positively historic and exciting, especially knowing we were so close to the Gion area (where the geishas live).

Geishas are not prostitutes. One way to tell the difference between geishas and prostitutes, or *oiran*, is that the *oiran* tie their *obi* in the front, while the geishas tie theirs in the back. True geishas are usually beautiful children from poor families, who get sold to provide money for their families. They start their training at six years of age. They continue their education until the age of fifteen and then they become an apprentice geisha, or *maiko*. At age twenty, the woman becomes an adult and a real geisha. A geisha cannot be married, but if she is lucky, she will find a patron, or *danna*. If she wishes to marry, she must retire from the profession. As a geisha, she certainly needs some financial assistance, because one costume usually costs over $1,000.00. I learned that if I wanted to hire two geishas to serve me at a table for two hours, it would cost me over $1,000.00. Considering other Japanese prices, I found that awfully inexpensive!

First we went to a Shinto shrine, Daigo-ji. This five story pagoda, which is a Shingon Buddhist temple, is considered a great national treasure of Japan. Unfortunately, we weren't there very long and so could only appreciate the beauty of the tiered pagoda on the mountain before we were shepherded back onto the bus.

Then we visited Sanjusangendo Buddhist temple, famous for the one thousand and one statues of the Buddhist deity, Kannon, the goddess of mercy (the real name is Juichimensenju-sengen Kanzeion, so it was obvious why Kannon is preferable). This Buddhist temple is officially known as *Rengeo-in*, but its popular name literally means "hall with thirty-three spaces between columns" which describes the architecture of the main temple hall.

There actually were one thousand standing life-sized statues, and one *gi*normous seated statue. As well, there were twenty-eight other wild-looking deities, thunder gods and wind gods and other angry and fierce folks standing guard for the erect Kannons. There is an "aaah" God at the beginning and an "Umm" God at the end—like alpha and omega, which I thought was kind of neat. It was impressive, all right. This temple was classified as a National Treasure by the Japanese government.

We had a nice lunch on the tour but interestingly enough, it was very North American Japanese food—no pink things and green things and black things—it was good food and it was all recognizable—tempura and sashimi, but not at all like the food we had been eating the past few weeks in the country or smaller cities; it was much more like what a North American would consider Japanese food.

Off we went to a kimono factory where we painted our own handkerchiefs in the style used to paint kimonos. It was fun, even if it was like painting by numbers. We all sat at long tables, with all the accoutrements: paints, brushes, etc neatly set up at each seat. We were given a handkerchief and some hints and away we went, painting our own little square of a kimono, which we all were allowed to keep. It was a lovely souvenir, and gave us all great appreciation for those who really do paint the gorgeous kimonos.

We learned that it takes a person over thirty minutes to put on a kimono properly—assuming that everything is made ready the night before. The kids go to kimono school for three months to learn how to appropriately dress in a kimono.

Although the tour continued on to a large store for shopping, a bunch of us grabbed cabs and came back to the hotel. I was shopped out anyway, and I just couldn't afford to keep sending more boxes of stuff home.

During our tour we had visited the Gekkekan sake factory. This factory was much larger than the ones of Takayama or Ise Shima. We all received a little bottle of sake as a gift, and I bought a good bottle of *ichi ban*—number one. I had wanted to get a superior bottle of sake after a good friend prepared a Japanese dinner for me back home years ago. She dressed in a kimono, cooked gyoza and other delicacies, and served the best sake I had ever tasted, telling me she had brought it back from Japan. It was a wonderful evening and for years, I had been waiting to go back to Japan to get a superior bottle of sake. I cradled my new purchase in my arms, thinking about how I would safely bring it home. These thoughts did not last for long as I then got persuaded into donating my *ichi ban* sake to our group dinner that evening. I was happy to oblige.

The sake that evening was indeed delicious, but over the years I have learned that events seldom live up to their expectations if we are wanting to recreate exactly a particularly wonderful enjoyment of the past. I guess it is best to enjoy each moment for what it is, and not try to make it be something else when clearly times and people are always going to be different. A lesson I have almost learned, I mused, as I sipped my *ichi ban* sake.

That evening in Kyoto with our friends was just wonderful, replete with much laughter. Judi and I felt like old pros as some of them only just arrived from Canada the day before and we had been traveling for well over a month. How strange that felt—to see my friends and say I've been away over five weeks now. We were all excited about our impending trip the following day for Hakone, a beautiful place by the lake at the base of Mount Fuji. I had been there more than twenty years ago, remembered loving it, and was anxious to see how much it had changed from my memories.

THE NEXT MORNING, we boarded the *shinkansen* (bullet train) for Hakone. In the *shinkansen*, when the conductor enters or leaves a train car, he bows to the passengers. Similarly, the woman pushing the food cart bowed to all as she entered our car.

The *shinkansens* run precisely on schedule. A rider has two minutes to get on or off. We were hundreds of people on our tour and the two minute thing was a bit harried but we managed.

Most people who work in Japan run. They run and run and run. We were told that sometimes they just run anywhere with no known destination if their bosses are around, so they won't get fired. Clerks in the stores run, front desk folk in hotels run. But when we were in Hakone, it did seem a bit more laid back, and we did not witness too much running.

I loved Hakone—it is on Lake Ashi at the foot of Mount Fuji. I was disappointed that it was too cloudy to really see Mount Fuji clearly, but hoped for cloudless views the next day. There were so many wonderful things here to do or see, but I was plum tuckered out. After the *shinkansen*, we hiked up a very steep hill to get to the bus and drove for almost two hours to get to the hotel. I do not do well in a crowded bus and so I chose to spend most of the afternoon just lying on my bed in our room resting. The room was Japanese small. The knock on the door indicated the presence of the bellboy. I opened the door, and there he stood, in front of a cart with our belongings on it. He picked up a suitcase and walked into the room, with me backing up until I hit the far wall; there simply wasn't room for the two of us to pass. He put down the suitcase. I stepped over it and followed him to the door. He picked up another suitcase, and I slipped into the bathroom, so he could get by. Every time he came in the room, I either had to back up all the way to the end of the room against the wall or stand in the bathroom. Why I continued to follow him to the door each time I will never know, but this little dance went on until all of our prodigious luggage was safely placed on the floor of our room. I had to step over seven bags, one at a time, which almost reached the hallway, in order to finally get close enough to tip him. Later, I realized that some of the toilet cubicles in the hotel were *so* small, that the door cleared the toilet by less than an eighth of an inch. I measured.

Hakone is known for its hot baths. There are many public baths and many of our tour group went to the baths. The main baths are free if one is naked, but if you want to go to alternate baths where bathing suits are worn, then it cost $15.00!

I delighted in sampling the public baths, the free kind. When in Rome . . . er Hakone. First of all, every room has a *yukata*, or cotton kimono. We called to exchange ours for two extra-large ones, as we are extra-large women. However, somehow confusion reigned, because all the extra-largeness went into the length, and very little into the girth. So, as I was taught to do by our guide earlier that day, I stripped down to my underwear and put the *yukata* on, first right side, then left, then tied the belt thing twice around—well, okay, it did gape a bit, but I could kind of hold it shut. I grabbed a towel from my room, put on the Japanese slippers and tottered out the room toward the baths, the long *yukata* trailing behind me. I have to admit, it felt a bit weird riding half naked in the elevator with others.

It reminded me of the first time I was in Japan, in the 1970s. Our women's group stayed at Ginza Dai Itchi Hotel, where kimonos were left on each pillow. Anxious to sample the Japanese baths after a long flight from North America, about ten of the women put on their kimonos and rode down in the elevator to the baths. They could not understand why the Japanese in the elevator were all laughing at them; politely, with their hands over their mouths, but nevertheless, definitely laughing. We later found out that it was a definite no-no to ride the elevators wearing kimonos, or even to be seen outside the rooms wearing them. The next time I stayed in the same hotel, some five years later, there were little signs everywhere asking guests not to leave the room in their kimonos. I smiled, remembering the lovely toothbrushes in the hotel bathroom with "Happy Morning" inscribed on them.

Back in Hakone, I arrived at the baths and a male attendant pointed for me to take off my slippers. I did and looked around to see a shelf of slippers just like mine, so I picked them up and put them on the shelf, only to discover I have put my dirty slippers on a shelf of slippers marked "sterilized slippers." That was my first of many booboos. Then the attendant gave me a little green cloth that I was supposed to take with me into the baths. He pointed the way down a long hall. I walked and turned and walked and went down stairs and walked some more—it was a very beautiful stroll—big pane glass windows through which I saw lovely trees and little Japanese bridges over water, and lots of greenery artfully situated. It was all very natural looking. By the time I got to the women's public bath, I no longer had my little green cloth. I have no idea where it went! So then I took off all my clothes and went into the baths, where first one showers in these sit-down showers. I entered the shower as I had been instructed by the guide previously and I washed my hair too, using the little red pail for rinsing. Then I went into the first hot bath. It was splendid—like being in a quiet, hot tub. I loved it. But I was all alone in it, it was huge, and I felt lonely. I kept seeing women go through another door. I asked a woman who came out what was there, but she answered me in Japanese so I wasn't much farther ahead. I decided to see for myself and went through the door to discover an outdoor pool set in rocks, with water flowing into it, surrounded by trees, all under the blue sky. So in I went. Then I realized that I still had some shampoo in my hair from my shower. It was very bad to have any soap in the public baths. So I didn't stay there very long, but got out and went into the outdoor shower to get rid of all the soap. By then I felt good—the hot mineral water was wonderful. So I put my *yukata* back on, sort of, and got some new sterilized slippers and tottered back to my room, dragging the rest of the extra-large *yukata* behind me like a long, floppy, cloth tail. I liked the hot baths.

The next morning, I went again. Those hot baths sure beat a common shower. I only made one mistake that day—the baskets used for placing *yukata* and personal belongings in are turned upside down. I was supposed to pick one and place my articles in it. The ones right side up are used and dirty. I was so excited to see a friend of mine and as I was talking away I inadvertently used a dirty basket instead of a clean one. Oops. But I switched over quickly and unobtrusively and didn't make any more faux pas that I knew of. That's not saying much.

In the hotel in Hakone, we noticed many stuffed *ook-piks*, or snowy owls, like large cuddly toys. These were huge—some were bigger than I was, and they were everywhere in the hotel. Apparently, the owl is a messenger of good luck, especially in the mountains, and our particular hotel had adopted that as sort of a logo. They were neat to see, but it seemed strange seeing *ook-piks*, which I have always associated with the far north, in Japan.

We checked out of the hotel in Hakone and boarded a bus. As we drove, we were told that four hundred thousand years ago, there was a big volcano in the area, and then afterwards, a volcano erupted in the crater of a volcano. And Hakone was inside the crater, or caldera, of the volcano. The diameter of this crater was six to eight miles, with a circumference of twenty-four miles. The crater, standing at about three thousand feet, was surrounded by mountain ranges. We stopped at Owakudani Hot Springs, which is an active volcano within the volcano (they called it a double volcano). At Owakudani, we hiked up a mountain with Mount Fuji in the distance, finally fully visible. All around us, steam was escaping from vents and there were pockets of steam everywhere. It was a beautiful day, hot, only minimally overcast, so we could see the good mount in all her glory. At the very top of the mountain, we all bought and ate eggs that were cooked in the steamy waters of the volcano. They had black, black shells, but inside, were tasty hard-boiled eggs. We were told if you eat one, you live seven years longer; if you eat two, you live fourteen years longer; and if you eat three, you live until you die. I ate enough eggs so that I will live until I die.

In the 1980s, I also ate these black eggs, but for breakfast one day in the city; they obviously worked, as here I was, standing on the mountainside, definitely still very much alive.

Mount Fuji is 12,388 feet high. The name has many meanings: wealthy warrior, eternity, something to be respected, and my favourite, the Goddess of Fire, which comes from the Ainu words. The Ainu are the indigenous people of Japan.

Japan consists of four major islands and three thousand small islands. I had no idea. The state of California is bigger than all of Japan, which contains one hundred twenty-six million people. Seventy percent of Japan is mountainous so the population density is very high, being concentrated in the other thirty percent. In Tokyo alone there are twelve million people. Yokohama, the port city and second largest in Japan, has three and a half million people, and Osaka has two point six million.

After we left Owakudani Hot Springs, we drove along the Tokaido Highway towards Yokohama. The road was lined with cedars that were planted in the seventeenth century. It was a very beautiful vista, with Mount Fuji now visible behind the cedars wafting away in the wind. We went on a boat ride—Mount Fuji loomed above us. When we stopped for lunch, she kept us company as we ate. She is such a grand mountain, with the top always covered in that little halo of cloud.

We stopped at an incredible hotel for lunch. It was reminiscent of Banff Springs Hotel (in Alberta) meets Japan. Many different buildings sat on a hillside, overlooking a lake, with Mount Fuji visible in the distance. The architecture was stunning as it was creative and interesting and yet looked so organic sitting in its natural home. We followed our leaders into a wonderful banquet room, where an incredible feast was laid out on long banquet tables. Many little round tables were set up around the room. It didn't take us long to realize that there were absolutely no chairs in the room at all!

I looked about the room: unbelievable gourmet food, a blend between American-Japanese, all of it looking inviting and delectable, sat on elegantly set banquet tables along one long wall of the room, while many dozens of people were kneeling around the little tables in order to consume these delicacies. We stood in the food line-up, helped ourselves, found an empty table for our laden plates, and then, like camels at an oasis, slowly lowered ourselves down to feed. It was a very humorous picture—the gourmet American-Japanese lunch, truly excellent, which literally brought us all to our knees. Most of us found the situation very funny, and we couldn't figure out if it was on purpose or not. They served delicious ice cream for dessert, but there were no spoons, so we ate the ice cream with forks, while standing or kneeling around the small tables. It was more than a slightly bizarre experience.

SEVERAL HUNDRED YEARS ago, Japan had no relationship with the western world. In 1854, the Friendship Treaty was signed and the door to the West was open. Shortly after, in 1859, the port of Yokahama opened. Yokahama has the second largest Chinatown in the world, second only to San Francisco. Go figure.

We checked into the Royal Park Hotel in Yokahama, the highest building in Japan. The rooms didn't even start until the 49th floor. We were on the 62nd floor, with a spectacular view of the harbour, truly unbelievable. The room was very large, with a Western style bathroom—although the Toto toilet rules supreme and was still there. There was a real glass shower, and the room was large enough to turn around without bumping into walls and still accommodate all our luggage. The taps still worked in the Japanese way, which was backwards to ours—what we think of as on is off and vice versa.

We spent two days there with friends, attending a convention and drinking lots of sake, then bid *sayonara* to Japan and took to the skies.

I WAS VERY happy to leave Japan. I think if I had to nod my head and bow one more time, my head would fall off. Early that last morning, we drove to the airport at Narita. As usual, we had a driver who did not speak English and a car that was too small for our luggage (even though we had ordered a large one). Now I suppose that if my sister and I were both slight women, and packed much more conservatively, our experiences in Japan would have been radically different. But we are not and we did not and our experiences were what they were.

On the way to the airport, we drove past the many Ferris wheels around the area—I hadn't mentioned before that there are *so* many in Japan—large ones everywhere. I am not sure what the attraction is to so many Ferris wheels in the country.

We arrived at the airport, and the driver took us to Terminal 1. He had a sheet of paper with Simkin on it, and the rest was in Japanese, but when we booked the car, we specified we were flying Lufthansa, and so I assumed he knew where we were going. What a silly assumption. He dropped us off at Terminal one. We loaded our luggage into two luggage carts and in we went, only to discover that Lufthansa was in Terminal 2, the driver had driven off, and Terminal 2 was quite literally miles away (more than a five minute car ride). So we thought we'd grab a cab to go to Terminal 2.

"No taxis!" the security officer shouted, as his hand swept over literally dozens of cabs lolling around.

"What are those?" I yelled.

"Long distance taxis." He snorted and walked off. "Take shuttle."

Not so easy with six pieces of luggage and a purse and two decrepit old ladies. So I went into the begging and whining mode, and finally, just to get rid of me, he got us a taxi.

"Terminal 2?" I asked the driver. He nodded, loaded our luggage in, and then absolutely flipped out when he realized he was going to Terminal 2. But he did deliver us there and got a big tip for it. It took us well over an hour to do the normal check-in stuff and go from here to there, but we arrived at the gate, sopping wet in the heat and humidity, in time to catch the most wondrous of airplanes.

As soon as we got on the plane and looked around, I realized that it was more of a theme park than a flying machine. There were so many choices of what to do and how to sit and where to go that I felt like the proverbial kid in a candy store. I didn't quite believe this at the time, but shortly after take-off, I was online, on the Internet, receiving and writing email, from an airplane, high up in the wild blue yonder. Isn't technology grand! Here we were, flying from Tokyo to Frankfurt and then on to Moscow. The flight was eleven hours long, but I wished it were two weeks. I felt as though I've gone to Disneyland! I had a nice little cubicle, with a seat that would lie flat as a bed if I wanted it to—I didn't—I was having way too much fun. The seat would also go into many other positions, and had a memory button, and as I sat there comfortably, it began massaging my back. Would it marry me? I had an entertainment centre, with movies (I watched *House of Flying Daggers*), documentaries (I watched one on wolves), sit-coms, news, and so much more and they all started exactly when I wanted, just for me. The flight crew could not have been any more attentive, I thought, as I sipped my hot cup of tea. I already had a big meal, and I knew there were two more before the flight would be over. Even the lavatories were large. I was very contented high in the sky. I could have stay up there for months.

Part III

Russia

Chapter Thirteen
Moscow: I Am Really Here!

DOBRYJ DEN, TVARITCH (good day, friend). Here we are, in Moskva. Moscow is of course an English invention and this place is really called Moskva. I love being here the most of anywhere since I've left home! I do feel so at home here.

The first morning, we went to the bank. Somehow, I seem to be able to read Cyrillic—I don't know how that is, but I just seem to know it. So I could read "*Bahnc*." Up we went, two floors, into a little room with three telephone booth cubicles off it. We went to *Kacca* 1—"*Kacca*" in Cyrillic reads "cassa" which we correctly assumed was cashier. It took us over an hour to cash some American traveler's cheques. They said *nyet* to *Canadienskaya* dollars (I'm ready to wring my bank manager's neck; she promised me I would have no problem with Canadian TCs. This is the second country (after Japan) where I could not cash them. So Judi and I are both squeezed into this tiny cubicle, with Elena, the *kacca*, on the other side, in an equally small cubicle. The walls were concrete. She checked every single traveler's cheque under blue light, under natural light, under yellow light, not once, but several times. She counted everything many times. She called in three different *kaccas* to verify. People kept coming to our door (there wasn't room for them to come right in). It took forever, but Elena was very friendly so we said *spasiba* (thanks), took her photo, and went on our way.

We took a cab from the bank. In the car, I was practicing reading Cyrillic. The taxi driver must have thought I was insane. Cyrillic has thirty-three letters, compared to our twenty-six. There are sounds that are fairly different from English, but not so different from Yiddish or Hebrew. It is sometimes confusing as the Cyrillic letters look like the English alphabet. For example, in Cyrillic, the word *PETCTOPAH* reads "restoran" and means restaurant; *KNOCK* reads kiosk.

"Jen-ee-rull ee-lek-treee-k, ah General Electric!" I said excitedly.

"Kom-pyu-torrr. Oh, computer!"

"Koh-fee ch-a-o-s, mmmm, ah, coffee house!"

Oh, I was so excited doing this!

"Tel-ee-fo-n- oh look, telephone."

"Mes-terr bah-nk. Yes, master bank."

I was definitely having fun. And it was good to amuse myself because traffic was unbelievable. The taxi would move two inches, stop, then crawl forward another four inches, then stop. Each time he stopped, the driver yanked up his parking brake. He'd release the brake, we'd move forward another foot, we'd stop, he'd yank it up again. And so we crawled on to the ratchety sound of the brake coming on and going off. There were about eight or ten lanes of traffic across the big boulevards—hard to tell, because no one followed lanes. It was like a very slow Shanghai. Cars were double and triple parked in the streets, like in New York City. There were few traffic signals, which didn't matter much as traffic moved at a snail's pace. Then some roads were tiny because they were built in the sixteenth or seventeenth century, so they were very narrow, not having anticipated being driven on by big machines. Off goes the brake, lurch, stop, squritch, the brake comes on, then off, move forward, then stop, like that for about forty minutes. But we did get to where we were going.

Judi and I were walking in a mall and I saw some neat bejeweled sneakers. In I went.

"Do you speak English?"

"*Nyet.*"

"Okay." I shrugged. I pointed to the shoes, pointed to my feet, and smiled. Ten minutes later they were mine. I do not know how much they cost (well, I knew in *rubles*, but we had just arrived here and I didn't know the conversion yet, especially since *Canadianskaya* money was no good here.

It was unusually hot—over 33 degrees and the humidity must have been higher than rain. At one point in the day, there was a little rain shower, but I thought someone was peeing off the roof because everywhere around that place seemed to smell of urine and body odour (likely because it was so unbelievably hot). That smell was true for that place at that time, but the overwhelming smell in Moscow was lilac. The lilac trees were in bloom everywhere, and it was scrumptious. Just wonderful.

The dress style was pretty modern, but the Russians were larger than the Asians and the women seemed to wear their clothes tight to bulging. There was lots of cleavage and lots of skin.

Russian words kept popping out of my mouth. Judi asked me how to say water.

"*Voda,*" I replied immediately. How did I know that? *Ya nyeh znahyu* (I don't know—and I don't know how I knew that, either). Must have something to do with genes, as all four grandparents were from the Ukraine and spoke

Russian. It's as though it is my forgotten mother tongue instead of that of my grandparents.

In the evening, we went out with some friends of a friend of Judi's. She had been corresponding with them, and I just agreed to go with them. And was I not the lucky person. First Ivan, or Vanya, as he asked us to call him, picked us up at the hotel. What a wonderful man. He and his wife, Elena, or Lena, are in their late forties, and both had lived in the US for some time and are completely fluent in English. They have two kids, nineteen and twenty-one, and two dogs ten and eleven. And they were both absolutely delightful and interesting people, multi-talented, and fun. First we had to walk to Vanya's car, which was about ten minutes away. We walked past the Bolshoi Theatre, and my heart went pitter pat. How exciting.

"Mah-damm Boo-te-rr-fli, *Madame Butterfly*!" I read the Russian.

"Yes." Vanya nodded, as though I were a clever five year old and not just acting like one, "*Madame Butterfly*."

And after we got to the car, we drove past the Kremlin and St. Basil's Cathedral. It is one of the most popular landmarks in Russia with all the multi-coloured onion domes. I even did a 3-D puzzle of it once. It truly was spectacularly beautiful. And driving by the Kremlin—we had passed it in the afternoon in the cab and I recognized it at once—my heart again went pitter pat as I thought of all the history in the red bricks, and what those bricks could tell us if they could talk—all about the pain and joy and living and dying that had happened there. It truly was emotional for me seeing these places I'd heard of so often for the past sixty years.

Moskva is a city of ten million people, but Vanya told us about that many again are there during the day as tourists, shoppers, etc. So twenty million souls are usually wandering around. We drove to Gorky Park, where we met Elena. We walked around the park, and Vanya, Lena, and I went up on a big Ferris wheel to see all around the city. We walked and talked and then drove to Lenin Hill so that Judi could also look around the city. It stays light here until about ten o'clock at night, like Winnipeg, and that night there was a full moon, which was just gorgeous. And then we finally went for dinner. Like true Moskva-ites, we didn't get our food until eleven pm.

"It's a late city," Vanya explained. "People eat late and stay out sometimes until four or five in the morning. There is lots of night life."

In fact, Elena explained that she started work at ten am, although she works until seven or eight in the evening. It's very typical to go for dinner after ten pm as we did. We ate at a Georgian restaurant. Georgian food in Russia is like

French food in Europe—considered to be the best gourmet quality, tasty and inventive. And it was delicious.

I was given a glass of *cha-cha* to drink.

"Hmm, it tastes like grappa," I said, as soon as I could speak again after the first sip.

"It is grappa," Vanya explained. "*Cha-cha* is the Georgian word for grape vodka and it's just like grappa." It was very, very strong, but good. I had two. And we tasted all kinds of Georgian delicacies, and none of us could finish all the food—there was so much and we all took stuff home. They insisted we take home a dessert called "*church-hella*" (more or less) which was walnuts or hazelnuts tied on a string and dipped in grape juice syrup over and over until the syrup was thick on the nuts. We had two boxes of this dessert which we would take with us on the ship to share with others.

We rolled back to our hotel after one am. What a day! We were both exhausted but full and feeling groovy. Actually, I had a splendid time and especially enjoyed meeting two new friends. Vanya and Lena were just great, and I certainly hope they visit in Victoria one day. We shared many, many things in common.

In a few hours, we were to board a ship for the next two weeks to sail up the Volga. I knew there would be no Internet connection there, so used the last few hours in our hotel to send off many communications. And indeed, I got them off just in the nick of time, as all the power went off in about half of Moscow. Apparently this happens often—thought to be due to the excessive heat and too many Internet users.

Checking out of the hotel was a challenge:

"Did you use the mini bar?"

"Not since the woman came in to check the minibar."

"No, she did not go into your room."

"Yes, she did. I spoke to her. She checked the minibar."

"No. She did not go into your room. She did not want to disturb you."

"Yes, she did come in." And round and round went the discussion.

Finally, the front desk reached the minibar woman who confirmed that yes, she had checked our room and then we had to start all over again with, "Are you sure you didn't use anything after she checked your minibar?"

It was hot, and the hotel clerk was bothered. But soon we were on our way.

On the way to the ship, I noticed that all the buildings in Moscow looked old—even the new buildings. It's not like Shanghai, where there are sleek, gleaming monster skyscrapers straining haughtily into space; here, everything looked and felt aged, even the quasi-modern new structures. There were sculptures and art everywhere, and we haven't even been in the metro yet!

As we prepared to board our ship, I bid *da svidanya!* (good-bye) to the hotels of Moskva from me, *P CNMKNH* (R Simkin).

Chapter 14
The Viking Surkov: Our Tour Begins

WE WERE ABOARD the Viking Surkov, a twenty year old ship, on the Moscow Canal leading to the mother Volga. But we were docked as we stayed in Moskva (in Cyrillic it looks like this: MOCKBA) for several days touring the city and environs. Our cabin here was absolutely wonderful! You could fit five, maybe more of the Yangtze cruise cabins into this one—we had two beds pushed together, a sofa and table, a long desk with drawers, a huge closet, and more storage space than even the two of us need! I had totally unpacked, put my suitcase away, and settled in. This might even have been better than the Lufthansa plane!

To get to the ship at the dock, we had to pass security. The weather was extremely hot and humid but we were still not prepared for the sight that lumbered out to lift the barricade: a tall uniformed officer, whose pants were rolled up past the knees, socks dragging down around his shoes, shirt unbuttoned and tied at the bottom just above his belly button which was bulging out over his pants. It was hard to be serious and we both burst out laughing at the sight of this saviour of security.

The day we boarded the ship was "last ring" or "last bell." Vanya had told me that it was the last day of school, and for most kids, it just meant summer holiday. But for the graduating class, it was the end of school, and so they all carried little bells which they rang for the party that was to last twenty-four hours in the streets.

Our first day on board was a very easy day because we were both totally wiped out from the long, hot and humid day before, so mostly we slept. Jane, my travel agent extraordinaire, had most kindly arranged for a bottle of champagne to be put in our room, which I thoroughly enjoyed.

ALL THE GUIDES on the ship spoke impeccable English. Their talk was very idiomatic and they had no trouble understanding questions and comments. What a treat! They all addressed us as "my dear friends" or "dearest ladies and gentlemen." Our guide for our group throughout the entire river cruise was Natasha, whom I handpicked because of her smile; our Moscow guide was Nina, a redhead who was brilliant, spoke six or more languages, and was incredibly knowledgeable. Vladimir was the driver of coach 44, our home away from ship.

We spent the day touring Moscow, the cultural and scientific capital of the Russian Federation, as well as, of course, the political head. St. Petersburg is often called the second capital, and is 700 kilometres away from Moscow. Before 1992, there were much fewer cars, foreigners, and less money available. Now there were lots of all of these, but it was a double-edged sword as streets were so much more crowded with cars and pickpockets and all the other things that came with too many people in one place. The Russian word *tsentr* means city centre, except throughout the country, it is also used to refer to Moscow.

Moscow was founded in 1147, by Yuri Dolgoruki. The ratio in the city of men to women used to be 1:5 in the post-war years of 1945-55, but then equalized until the age of thirty and then started to change again after the age of sixty when women were thirty percent more prevalent than men. So at times, men have been pretty much in demand here! Even though there were more women, of the one hundred richest people in the country, only one was a woman: Yelena Baturnia, wife of the mayor of Moscow. She and her husband subsequently moved to Switzerland after a scandal and charges of corruption.

Driving through the city, we passed a swap meet, but one that was so humongous, it made the gigantic one in Palm Desert, California look teeny. It just went on and on and on and on. It was here that the black market shopping is done, Nina explained. Before Gorbachev, nothing was available here—there were no clothes or much of anything. People were delighted to be able to buy everything, even though the prices were higher.

"We Russians love fur coats," Nina informed us. "We know about Greenpeace, we are aware, but in the winter, it's vodka and fur coats!"

Our first stop of the day was Novodevichy Convent on the Moscow River. *Novodevichy* means "new maidens" and it probably got its name from the market where the Tatars brought Russian girls to sell to Muslim harems. In this convent lived Sophia, the half-sister to Peter the Great. She had rebuilt this convent and used it as a residence. She was older than Peter, and when he was a young boy and sat on the throne, he did not know many answers and so she sat behind him and whispered the correct responses to him. However, he sent her off to this convent, and she tried to wrest control from him twice. She failed both times, and Peter had her supporters hung outside her windows of Novodevichy convent. Sophia lived in the convent with Peter's first wife, Yevdokia, whom he considered a nag and he was happy that both the women were away from him.

Then we went to Sparrow Hill, where we had been two nights earlier with Vanya and Lena, except they called it Lenin Hill. But now, during the day, tourist tables were set up with tourist goodies on them. Everyone was very polite and laid back—no feeding frenzy of the Chinese or huge amounts of stuff like in Japan—just nice tables, with a reasonable amount of *matrushkas* (nesting dolls) and other tacky but often cute souvenirs. The *matrushka* originated in China, and then it came to Russia. Originally they were idols of pagan gods, one inside the other, like the universe, which is why they all have an egg shape. Now in Russia they are the symbol of a mother with a large family. A *matrushka* is a typical tourist souvenir. They are round of figure, which is considered beautiful. Maybe that's why I like Russia so much! According to the Russians, a *matrushka* should be fat, as should be a bride. They are made from larch, aspen, or linden and then the wood is dried for three years. Then they are primed with starch, carved, and painted.

Moscow had wide boulevards lined with linden trees. Linden trees do not have circles showing their age as do most other species of trees, which of course, is very rare. That's why violins such as the Stradivarius are made with wood from linden trees.

We drove by Moscow's "Hollywood" which was a huge complex where movies were made. The city seems to have a big sense of humour, and as I was to later learn, so does the whole country. There are "Moscow jokes" and lots of in-city sayings. People absolutely adore the mayor, Yuri Luzhkov, whom I believe had been elected for his third term. He had been mayor since 1992! He was always constructing things; they say he doesn't eat or sleep—only works to develop Moscow, starting new projects and rebuilding others.

The apartments in Moscow were hugely expensive—a flat could cost $900—$2500 for one square meter.

The tallest buildings were only –forty to fifty stories and they were all apartment buildings. There were not that many of the higher ones, and most buildings seemed to be between ten and twenty stories. Most residents of Moscow owned their own apartments. Single houses belonged to villages where low income folks lived and were associated with poverty mostly. But most people had *dachas* or summer homes as well, which were single family dwellings.

We passed by the largest hotel in Moscow, Hotel Rossiya, built by Khrushchev, which had some four thousand rooms. It was the biggest hotel in the world, in fact, and was right next to the Kremlin.

Also near the Kremlin was the Hotel Moskva, which had two different designs to it. Apparently Stalin was shown two possible designs for the building and because he didn't realize that they were alternatives, he approved both of them. The builders were too scared to tell him he made an error, so they just built it half in each style. Hotel Metropol, near the Bolshoi Theatre, was another famous hotel.

We saw a mother and son on the street selling Lily of the Valley flowers. These flowers were very popular. Lily of the Valley is an endangered species and was not supposed to be sold (and especially not supposed to be picked).

OUR GROUP WENT for a ride on the metro—an exciting outing. Lenin first conceived of this underground project, and Stalin implemented it. They wanted to build an underground that would be more than transportation. It also served as a bomb shelter during the war (in 1941, when Moscow was bombed, the underground saved many lives), and as an artistic expression of the socialist movement, an expression of love for the motherland. All the stations were different from one another; some had bronze sculptures, some had frescos, most all had marble walls, but they differed in color and style from station to station. The walls were marble because they were so easy to keep clean. The benches were original and different in each station, as were the ceilings where mosaics depicted historical events. Because each station was so unique, it was easy to know where one was.

Our leaders, Nina and Natasha, bought us tickets and then we all went down the longest escalator on which I have ever been. And then we ooh'd and aah'd over the art work and boarded the train. We got off at the next station and ooh'd and aah'd again, and once more, boarded the train. This time, we rode for three stops, and then got off. And we had arrived at Red Square!

I was so excited! I kept looking at the red bricks of the Kremlin and feeling the history there, the bloodshed, the tears and the victories. I guess it's because of my genes and heritage, but the history here seems so much more vivid to me than history elsewhere. I remember going to see the film *Dr. Zhivago*, with my mother and her mother. My grandmother, who was deaf and did not attend movies often, was so excited. She watched eagerly the parts about Rasputin—that was her life she was seeing and she recognized it well. I got excited watching her—she just couldn't get enough. Even though the movie was not filmed in Russia (in fact, the book was banned in the Soviet Union for a time), there were parts that resonated with my grandmother's life.

Red Square was surrounded by the Kremlin, St. Basil's Cathedral, and many other impressive buildings and churches, as well as the famous GUM (pronounced goom) department store. Red Square used to be a market place, and it was somewhat reminiscent of Tienamin Square in Beijing. It was where military parades and other formal presentations took place. Lenin's mausoleum was there. Natasha told me there was a two hour line up to see Lenin's embalmed body—but the people waiting were foreigners. She said the Russians were no longer interested!

I ran around in GUM's trying to get some traveler's cheques cashed, but once more, *nyet, nyet, nyet* to *Canadienskaya* money. So I found an ATM and got some *rubles* that way.

ST. BASIL'S CATHEDRAL—it's amazing that it was even real. All the multi-coloured onion domes rising up to the sky were quite glorious. And when Ivan the Terrible saw it for the first time, he was completely struck by its beauty. He called to him the architects who built it.

"Can you build an edifice even more beautiful than this?" he asked.

"Oh yes," they both exclaimed, eagerly anticipating another commission.

But Ivan the Terrible was not misnamed—he promptly blinded both of them so that nothing more beautiful could ever exist.

St. Basil's is named after Vasily (Basil) the Blessed, who was a barefoot holy fool, whatever that is. Vasily predicted Ivan the Terrible's damnation and also predicted (correctly) that Ivan would kill his son. Vasily is buried there somewhere. Ivan the Terrible was the first Tzar. It's interesting how this name came about—when he was ruler, people said, "You are our Caesar," and from the word "Caesar," came tzar.

Another interesting fact: the word "parliament" derives from the French word *parler* which means "to speak." The Russian parliament, *duma*, comes from the Russian word *duma* which means "to think."

In 1990, McDonalds opened in Moscow. five thousand people stood in line waiting and thirty-five thousand were served the first day. It was the first fast food place of foreign origin open in Russia. Natasha and Nina were both fonts of information, some of it being extremely esoteric.

When Khrushchev was in power, there was a music competition. He declared that a Russian had to be the winner, to prove the excellence of Russian music. However, that was the year Van Cliburn rolled into town. The judges all risked their careers, or so they felt, but they could not chose anyone other than Van Cliburn to be the winner of the competition. He became an idol and almost every apartment had a portrait of him. This was a signal that it was the beginning of *perestroika*, rebuilding, and that the people would make their own decisions.

One time Gorbachev spoke about leaders having to be clear and that they should make short, concise speeches. This particular speech about the necessity to be short and clear took him over two hours to make!

IN THE AFTERNOON, I went to the Tretyakov Gallery, where the largest collection of Russian art from medieval times to the twentieth century is housed. Before the sixteenth century, there was no "art" as such; all art was only a religious expression. So there were no "artists," only icon painters. After the sixteenth century, artistic expression came into being. I'm not sure if art historians agree with this explanation or not; however, it is food for thought. I enjoyed hearing some of the stories about the Russian rulers that were depicted in the art works.

After the gallery tour, I met the rest of the cruise people at the Moscow Circus. To be honest, I found it disappointing. I fear that Cirque de Soleil has spoiled me for life. There was lots of posturing and dramatic music and pseudo-dance, and a little bit of acrobatics. The circus performers were good enough, I guess, but the presentation just seemed so tacky. There were three animal acts, parrots, dogs, and chimps. By the time the chimps came on, and this large sad looking animal, dressed in a can-can dress, was urged to kick out its legs, I just felt tears rolling down my cheeks. It was cruel beyond words, and those chimps looked so unhappy going through their paces, it was positively painful to watch. I had seen the Moscow Circus many years ago, and remembered it as being much better than that evening's performance. Still, it was exciting to be there. I was so tired at the end of the day I fell into bed without going for dinner. Good thing too because the next day, we started touring at 7:45 am.

I HAD A long talk with Nina, our Moscow guide. She was such an intelligent woman, and as I mentioned, spoke five or six languages, plus Russian of course, and had three jobs, one of which was a professor at the university. She has been a guide since 1971 for InTourist. At that time, the guides were all very controlled and could not speak with their charges unless they were actually guiding. They could not go for coffee with visitors, or receive tips. Now things are somewhat better, in terms of guiding, but life is still difficult for her. With three jobs, she still has inadequate health care and housing and has many financial concerns as well.

WE WERE TAKEN to the Kremlin on our last day in Moscow. *Kremlin* means "fortress" and that's what it is—surrounded by twenty towers and red brick walls. The Kremlin was first built in the twelfth century and was made of wood. Now of course, it is red brick, and serves as the official residence of the president, although Stalin was the last person to actually live there. The

Kremlin consists of churches, museums, palaces, and barracks, and government buildings, but obviously, only some are open to the public.

A word about Russian toilets: they are not squatters, but some are not overly pleasant. Most public washrooms seem to have western toilets, all right, but no seats. I wonder what they could have done with them? So there are these gaping toilet rims in cubicles. They usually do provide toilet paper, but not in the toilet stall. There is often a toilet paper dispenser hanging on the wall somewhere and one has to remember to take toilet paper with her to the cubicle. One usually forgets. But the toilets of the Kremlin—ah, now those were good bathrooms. Certainly, the best toilets we have come across so far in Russia. They had both toilet seats and toilet paper in each cubicle, and were clean and plentiful. So the Kremlin already was endeared to me before I went very far.

At the Armory Museum inside the Kremlin, we saw all kinds of paraphernalia. Inside the Kremlin in the old days, things were made in factories: clothes to wear, wheels, armour, most things, in fact. Peter the Great decided to close the factories, but he wanted to take the very best of everything and show it as a museum, so in the Armory there are the best carriages, the best clothing, armour, jewels, and so on, all on display. Peter the Great was a tall fellow—about six-and-a-half feet tall. He did not allow people to have beards—he wanted to emulate Europe.

Elizabeth had fifteen thousand dresses in her wardrobe when she died! The dresses were made in the Kremlin, but from material that was purchased from Iran, Turkey, and other countries. The merchants traded kilogram for kilogram—a kilogram of material was worth a kilogram of gold. So the fabrics were incredibly heavy so that the merchants would get paid more gold. I can't imagine wearing some of those clothes, much less walking down a flight of steps with them on. We saw silver tack that the horses used to wear, so that they could produce silver music. And we saw Faberge eggs, clocks, diamond dandelions, and other niceties.

During the Russo-Turkish war, which took place around 1780, the Turks lost, but then gifted the Russians with incredible presents of gold and wealth. It was a political move by the Turks, who wanted to recognize a stronger country and protect themselves; so when Russia defeated Turkey, Turkey lavished gifts upon the Russians. That gifting apparently has led to excellent relationships between the Russians and the Turks. There are almost no borders between the two countries claiming friendship forever.

When the Russian soldiers, the Cossacks, got to Montmartre just after the war of 1812, they were tired and hungry and kept asking for things quickly, like more water quickly, more food quickly, (and presumably, more women quickly too). The French set up these little shops and hence the origin of "bistro" which is the Russian word for "quickly."

All the items on display in the Armory are in cases that have gas piped in so that the silver does not oxidize and also so that the exhibits don't have to be cleaned. I thought that was pretty incredible.

AFTER THE MUSEUM at the Kremlin Armory, we walked around a bit and saw the largest bell in the world—it weighed two hundred tons. But just as it was completed, a fire broke out and burnt the stand it was on. People poured cold water on the bell in an attempt to quell the fire, but that just drastically changed the temperature, and the bell cracked, dislodging a small eleven ton piece from its side. And so the poor bell has never been rung!

After walking around the Kremlin some more, we returned to the ship, as we were to set sail that afternoon down the Moscow Canal. By the next day, we expect to be cruising *Volga Matushka* (little mother Volga).

Chapter 15
Along the Volga With Vodka and Caviar

THE CRUISE FOLLOWED the Volga-Baltic Waterway, which is a very complex system of lakes, rivers, artificial reservoirs, and canals that link the Volga River with the Baltic Sea. We passed through numerous locks along the way as we went from the Sheksna River to the Kovzha River, then Lake Beloye to Vytegra Canal, then traveled in a canal along Lake Onega, then the Svir River to Lake Ladoga and lastly, the Neva River into St. Petersburg.

I WENT TO a lecture on the ship and learned a few more things. Russia was huge—well, we knew that already, but it actually had ten different time zones. Now, that was huge! Ten! Then it went to eleven time zones, and then back to nine. They were changed for some economic reasons. But nine time zones is still very huge, is it not?

The population of Russia was almost 150 million—147.5 million, to be exact. Three-fourths of the population lived in the cities. Russia was one-eighth of the entire world's land mass, and of course, it was the largest country in the world. 49 percent of the country was forest, and only 13 percent was agricultural land.

"VODKA, PLEASE."

"On ice?" she asked.

"No. Straight. Cold. A shooter."

She smiled, nodded, and went to the fridge. She poured the drink, put it in front of me, and waited. Around her stood four bar men and women, looking upon me with interest.

I raised the glass toward them. "*Na zdorovye* (to your health)." I knocked back half, then the other half, and set the glass on the table. The bar men and women stood, mouths agape, not moving.

"Would you like another one?" she asked.

I nodded.

She walked to the fridge, brought out the bottle, and poured.

As I drank that, the mouths on the bar men and women opened more and more.

"Aaaaaah," I said, as I set the glass down. "*kharasho* (good)."

She smiled at me. "Would you like more?"

"No thank you. I think I've done my ancestors proud. Maybe another day." And I smiled.

The bar men and women still stood, waiting for me to fall over, I suppose, but that was not going to happen. When I sat upright for a few minutes longer, they all got bored and moved on.

I looked around me. There were flags from every country. But none from Canada.

"Hey," I asked. "How come there are no flags from my country?"

She looked at me inquisitively, eyebrows raised.

"I'm from Canada," I explained, "and there is no flag from Canada."

"No flag from Canada?" She came around to the front of the bar to look. She then returned behind the bar and rummaged through a drawer.

"Ah," she said. "It must have been stolen."

"Stolen?"

She came around, new Canadian flag in hand along with scotch tape, and hung the flag over my head. We smiled at each other.

"Are you a student?" I asked.

"No." She smiled sadly. "I graduated last year. I work on the ship now, but I think it will be my last year."

"Did you learn English at school?"

"No." She laughed. "I lived in England for six months."

"What did you study?"

"Psychology."

"Can't work here as a psychologist?"

She sadly shook her head. The salaries for scientists and medical personnel are incredibly low. Then we smiled and talked about how the last people we can usually help are ourselves.

"Ah, there's a book title for you, or a research project."

We, Oksana and I, for her name was Oksana, talked about my dog and her cat. And how scientists don't get paid any money in this country. We talked for a long while about work, life, and people who are remarkably the same while being remarkably different. Does that even make sense? It certainly seemed to make sense that evening at the bar on the ship.

WE WERE NOW on the fourth day of our cruise on the Viking Surkov, although for the first few days, we hadn't moved from Moscow. Some things I learned on day four:

In the old days, and at times currently, before a Russian woman could get married, she had to grow linen, make cloth, and then make twelve shirts for her husband-to-be, and thirty shirts for her mother-in-law! So now many Russian girls sing the song, "Mother, don't give me a red dress" which means I don't want to get married. The red dress, of course, is what they traditionally wore to get married. Because Russian women who got married had to cover their hair, when a man presented a woman with a scarf or shawl, that meant he wanted to get engaged, and that she should cover her head from that time on. Usually it was a red scarf.

There was a lot of amber in this region. It came from the petrified sap of fir trees and was considered real amber after fifty thousand years or more.

We continued sailing down the Volga River. We went to a lecture on Russian souvenirs and folk traditions, and another lecture on Gorbachev.

Interesting thought: Did you ever think that the word "*borscht*" has seven letters of which six are consonants and only one is a vowel? It's still an excellent tasting soup though.

ONE AFTERNOON, WE sailed around a bend of the Volga and there before us was Uglich (pronounced oog-litch). Uglich was founded in 1148, and had forty thousand inhabitants. Three hundred years ago, it had forty thousand people, but then it was one of the largest towns on the Volga. But every summer, it has been receiving over five hundred thousand visitors from the sailing boats! Uglich was famous for its clock factory—ten thousand of its residents worked there, a full 25 percent of the population. Needless to say, I managed to buy a bunch of watches in Uglich. The watch factory is called Chaika which means seagull, named after the first woman astronaut's nickname. There were also two cheese factories there which made cheese for the cosmonauts.

There was a Kremlin in Uglich. Kremlin means fortress, as previously mentioned, and it used to have big wooden walls. One day Catherine the Great decided she didn't like the walls, and so now the Kremlin is surrounded by a dirt path instead of oaken walls. When we arrived, along with a whole slew of other tourist boats, there was a large celebration in the town square, with dancing and music. Apparently there was a three day festivity celebrating either the death or canonization (I just couldn't be clear which one it was) of Tzarevich Dimitri who was either killed by one of Boris Godunov's gang, or who accidentally stabbed himself during an epileptic fit. At any rate, the little tyke was just eight years old when he died. Both are considered accurate versions of what happened. Dimitri was one of the sons of Ivan the Terrible and he and his mother Maria, the seventh wife of Ivan, were exiled to Uglich. There was a large church in the town, similar in look to St. Basil's in Moscow with multitudinous domes but much, much smaller, called Church of St. Demetrius on the Blood. The floor of this church was cast iron, beautiful looking really, and in the winter, when the outside temperature could be twenty below zero, they turned on the ovens underneath the floor, and the floor would warm right up. In the church was a huge bell, which was exiled to Siberia for three hundred years. Today, the bell was back in the Church of St. Demetrius on the Blood. The bell tolled to mourn young Dimitri's death and was also used to call for an insurrection for the murder of the young *tzarevich* (son of the tzar). So Godunov ordered the bell to be flogged and its tongue ripped out and then banished to Siberia. The bell has its "tongue" back and has a lovely tone.

Several hundred years ago, there were a hundred and fifty churches and forty thousand people in Uglich and then the Polish invasion took place, leaving the town with fifty churches and only forty families. Five thousand craftsmen came from Moscow to rebuild the city.

Then we went to another church called the Cathedral of the Transfiguration. Around 1928, the Bolsheviks renamed it the Museum of Aetheism, where the main exhibit was an American tractor. But then Stalin decided to open the churches again. Eleanor Roosevelt gave a lot of money to help restore the churches during World War II. Then they renamed it the Museum of History. The museum had hundreds of icons and was now called the Cathedral of the Transfiguration of our Saviour.

Then we had free time. And boy, did we use it. We walked through the market, lingering in front of the hundreds of stalls selling every possible Russian handicraft. But before we went through all the stalls, Judi and I visited the Museum of Russian Vodka. Did we have fun! It actually was pretty amazing—two floors of displays of bottles, and vodka paraphernalia. And Smirnoff came from Uglich! Imagine that! There were still Smirnoffs living in Uglich at the time of our visit. We got all kinds of information from this wonderful gentleman who greeted us there, except he spoke no English and we spoke no Russian; it truly was amazing how easy it is for people to understand each other. And we (er, I) tasted vodka in the tasting room. And bought several bottles. But then I had to go to the market to buy Russian vodka bottle holders that looked like *matrushka* dolls, just so the bottles wouldn't clink together in the shopping bag! Well, that's not the only reason. And we shopped and shopped in the market.

At one point, Judi looked at me.

"You are out of control," she said.

I smiled as I tried to lift my packages and move forward.

WHEN WE HAD to leave Uglich, I really wasn't ready and didn't want to board the ship. On the way to the boat, just before the steps leading down to the gangplank, there were two old ladies, one selling a wilted tulip and the other selling a drooping bunch of lilacs. I gave them each ten *rubles*, declined their flowers and moved on. But when I got to the entrance of the ship, I didn't feel right. I dropped all my packages, and ran back up the steps. I took the hand of the first old lady, looked into her eyes, and said in English which she did not understand, "This is for my grandmother." And gave her a 100 *ruble* note. I repeated that with the second old lady. It wasn't much, really, but their smiles were everything. I wished that I could have followed them home and done more for them. They could have been my grandmothers. But instead I just loved them, got on the boat, and sailed away.

EARLY MORNING, TOO early, of day five on the ship, we arrived at Yaroslavl. Once more the ships were berthed three deep and three long. In order to disembark, we had to walk through the lobby of the Peterhof, our sister ship. But a few days ago, we were moored first, and they had to walk through our lobby to get off and onto their ship.

One day of yore, Prince Yaroslav the Wise sailed down the Volga and came upon a spot where two rivers converged. He liked that spot, called Bear Corner. It was thusly named because the pagans who lived there had a sacred bear whom they worshipped and kept in a cage. Yaroslav wanted to secure the area for use as a waterway to the market and went up to the pagans who lived there to tell them he wanted to stay. The pagans were not impressed and chased him away. He returned with his army. Then the pagans were a bit more impressed. And as was the tradition then, the strongest from each side fought to see who won. Prince Yaroslav was pitted against . . . the sacred bear. And the Prince won with a well-placed hatchet in the shoulder of the poor bear.

Prince Yaroslav went on to become the Grand Prince of Kiev. And the bear— well, he is immortalized in a floral pattern beside the Volga.

We learned about an old Russian saying: "All streets lead to a church." And Yaroslavl definitely illustrated that nicely as literally hundreds of churches sat at the end of hundreds of small streets. The population was about 300,000 so it was a relatively urban place. And the churches—well, most of them are museums now, and only a small percentage of the people actually attend.

When Catherine the Great came to Yaroslavl, she said the street planning was ugly. However, the reality was that there was no street planning. So they started building big squares and streets that all ended in churches.

We visited the Church of Elijah the Prophet, which was a UNESCO protected site. It was pretty amazing with the paintings on all the walls and ceilings, but how many domes and frescoes can a person see in a week? Apparently not enough, because we saw at least one, usually more, at each place we went to.

During the soviet regime, the KGB monitored religious belief very carefully. If a parent gave a bible to a child, he/she could lose parental rights. People who were found to be believers were exiled to Siberia or worse.

Our excellent guide for Yaroslavl was Konstantin, a teacher. He told a lot of Russian jokes, which were really not that funny—more self-deprecating than humorous, I thought. There were lots of buildings in the Stalin fashion that we saw in Moscow, and Konstantin told us that the locals had nicknamed that style "Stalin neo-pseudo-classicism."

Yaroslavl was also one of the greenest towns on the Volga, and has won "green competitions" often. Yaroslavl also had the distinction of housing the very first theatre to ever exist in Russia.

We went to an art gallery where we saw an excellent display of lacquer boxes and other art. After touring the other sights of the city, we had a little bit of free time. Judi and I decided to go to the Internet café. We had wanted to send some email, but once there, they would not let us use our own computers, so obviously, we could not send any of our already written mail off. So I quickly walked around the centre of the town, poking my head into a butcher shop, looking at a local farmer's market, in fact, looking into as many buildings as I could. It looked like an interesting town, much bigger than Uglich.

LATER THAT AFTERNOON, while cruising down the Volga, we attended a Russian tea ceremony on the ship. It seems most countries have tea ceremonies—we went to one in China, and one in Japan. Do we have one in Canada? Probably—called the Pseudo-British Empress Style Tiered Goodies Ceremony. Anyway, the Russian tea ceremony involved a samovar, of course, and they tried to convince us that tea was as popular a drink as vodka, but I don't think anyone believed that! The *blinis* here were very different than North American *blinis*. At home, the *blinis* are more crepe-like. Here, they were thick little pancakelettes. We'd had them several times already. Natasha confirmed for us that the fat little *blinis* were indeed true Russian style.

Although we sailed through the next day, there were lots of activities on board—more than anyone could want to do—political lectures, Russian language lessons, vodka tasting, entertainment in the evening, and much, much more.

THE VODKA TASTING the following evening almost cost me the whole next day! But it was fun! First of all, we learned that there were 2,362 kinds of vodka in Russia. And most of them were very, very strong, 40 percent or more.

We were all seated around long tables in the dining room, with six shot glasses nicely arranged in an arc by each setting. But before any vodka appeared, we were urged to fill our plate with Russian snacks of pickled mushrooms, pickled cabbage, pickled carrots, pickled pickles, and lots of bread. And then they poured each of us a glass of orange juice or water. We started off with Smirnoff. We tasted six types, altogether, going from the good to the sublime. Of course, one was expected to shoot it down in one gulp; there was no sipping for the Russians. Second in line to taste was Mozmya which was 55 percent. When Peter the Great founded St. Petersburg in 1894 and decided to make it the capital, he also decided to make a new vodka. Hence Mozmya.

Of course, after each tasting, we were encouraged to eat snacks. I concentrated on the bread. The third vodka was Russian Standard, which is very good vodka; it is the ship's vodka, so I had already tasted it before. And it was just as good again. Four and five—we were really getting into the good stuff, Diplomat and Tchaikovsky—so smooth, it was like caressing one's insides with a silken warmth. Number six was a little different—it was golden in color. Nemeroff by name, it was made with honey, red pepper, and treated water. The overwhelming opinion of the many tasters was that Tchaikovsky was the best of the bunch. So we all (rather, those who wanted and/or were still standing) received a victor's shot. And then we were shown how to do Russian drinking tricks, like putting the glass on the back of your hand and drinking it (without holding it with your other hand) without spilling. Or putting the glass on one's elbow and drinking from there. At any rate, every time we tried another trick, and there were several, we had a fresh shot. Some eighteen or twenty shots later, Judi, who was my designated walker, pushed me out the door toward our room. By now it was quite late, and I apparently had begun singing the Russian alphabet which I had learned earlier that day. Now Judi claimed that I sang the Russian alphabet all night, but frankly, I had no memory of that. Be that as it may, I did not emerge from my room the following day until four-thirty pm.

I had slept through breakfast and slept through our stop in Goritzy at the Kirillo-Belozerksy Monastery. I had no idea what Judi told people throughout the day, but when I appeared in public for a lecture on Putin, many people came up to me, grave concern upon their faces, asking how I was doing. Actually, I was great. Sana, the assistant manager of the dining room, who was from Uzbekistan, had brought my lunch to the cabin. I still couldn't eat much, but I had some. I had a very relaxing day. But after a night like vodka tasting night, I truly came to realize I was not as young as I used to be.

There was a young woman on the ship, Elena, working on her PhD in Political Science, who gave lectures almost daily. During one lecture, she spoke about President Putin and the Russian people. He is extremely popular, she told us, because he has made such definitive changes in this country. For example, in 2000, right when he first came into power, 31.5 percent of the population lived below the poverty level. And by 2004, that number had dropped to 21.9 percent. Inflation, which had been 20.2 percent in 2000 was 10 percent in 2004. I thought that was pretty impressive.

Russia, although it has the largest land mass, was only seventh in population in the world, behind China, India, USA, and so on. With just under 150 million folks, the population growth was now negative.

Crude oil accounted for 24.8 percent of Russian's exports. And, as I learned later in the day, Russia was not the main exporter of caviar—Iran was.

The poverty level in Russia was set at about $50.00 a month. A typical good salary in the city might be $600 a month; a young specialist might earn a whopping $1000 a month. However, teachers only earned $100 a month.

There was some concern among the political scientists because Putin was such a charismatic, popular, and powerful leader that true democracy might suffer because of this. His support just increased every year. People wanted to extend his term of presidency because he was already in his second term and that's the maximum for anyone. Anyway, it was a very interesting lecture, and Elena was a very bright young woman.

JUST BEFORE DINNER, I attended a caviar tasting. We sat around tables of four, elegantly set with glasses for vodka and champagne (my stomach did a flip-flop but not for too long) and on each dish were four *blinis,* each covered with a different type of caviar. Also on the dish were all the sides, like egg white, egg yolk, onions, sour cream, dill, a lemon topped with a cherry tomato. It looked beautiful.

The ship's hotel manager, Marco, gave us a small lecture about caviar while the drinks were being poured. The largest sturgeon ever caught was 1,400 kilograms—that's well over a ton! There were twenty-four different kinds of sturgeon but I think only a few from which good caviar came. Sturgeons are fresh and cold water fish, but pollution was causing problems. When catching the sturgeon, one has to kill the fish very quickly, so that it does not "suffer" (which is silly—it was being killed, for heaven's sake, so of course it would suffer!). If the fish does suffer, it will release a poison and then the caviar will not be any good. With the big Beluga sturgeons, they have to shoot them quickly with a high caliber weapon. So we tasted four different types of caviar—one red, which was salmon roe, and three black. Even though Beluga caviar is supposed to be the best, and is the most expensive, my personal favourite was Sevruga, which was considered next in line to the Beluga in quality and slightly better than Ossetra.

AFTER A FUN dinner, we went back up to the bar for an evening of name that tune, name it's country of origin, and answer a question relating to that country. It was fun. I only got ten out of eleven correct though, so I didn't win the bottle of champagne (thankfully). I didn't know the symbol for a Ferrari (it's a stallion).

When the game of name that tune was over, it was after eleven pm. It was still light outside. As tempted as I was to stay up and continue playing and visiting I took myself off to bed for some sleep. I was mistaken in thinking that the ship would be relaxing—it was a lot of fun, but there was *so* much to do, with many different programs on board, so that even when we were sailing all day, we kept busy every minute. I figured I could always have down time once I got home.

THE FOLLOWING DAY we started off with a lecture on the Romanovs. The best part of the lecture was at the end. Galina explained that the archives were just opening to the public, and so new bits of historical information were coming to the fore. There was a joke among the Russians that nothing was more unpredictable than the past history of Russia!

I learned more interesting information: Anna Ioannovna, nicknamed the "Tsarina of Terrible Look" married a foreigner who so wanted to be like the Russians that at his wedding, he drank vodka after vodka until he passed out dead on his wedding night.

Pavel I abolished the word "snub-nosed" from the dictionary—he was snub-nosed. All nobility who met him had to bow so low that the sound of the knee touching the floor could be heard down the hall and the sound of their kiss on some part of his anatomy could also be heard down the hall.

It's strange how these are the types of things that stick in my mind as compared to "real history."

As we were sailing down the lake, we kept coming across logging projects—huge areas of logs neatly piled, some being loaded into large barges, others just sitting there with nothing else in sight. It was clearly a logging area, although still, no patches of clear-cut land like we are used to seeing at home in BC.

That afternoon, we attended a great lecture given by Natasha, our guide, on Russian cuisine. What made it so good was that she talked about the food in an historical context. And how and why Russians ate/eat what they did/do. Catherine the Great loved this fish soup called *uha*, which called for a thousand herrings, but only their cheeks.

Peter the Great brought potatoes to Russia, but no one knew how to eat them at first. They ate the leaves, got poisoned, and otherwise did not do justice to the potato. But they were so tired of turnips they were willing to try anything.

We learned about *kvas*, an original Russian drink made from fermented rye bread and yeast. Natasha said the only reason why foreigners would drink it would be to promote international friendship!

AFTER HEARING A bit more about elk lips and bear paws, we docked at Kizhi Island. It was amazing, sailing up to her—Kizhi was famous for this twenty-two domed wooden church, which happened to be the oldest wooden church in Russia, and all of a sudden, there it was, in the middle of the water, really, as it was situated on an island which was only four miles long, and was situated in the middle of Lake Onega. Kizhi Island was one of the most ancient inhabited sites in Russia, and was an early pagan centre. It was now a big open air museum protected by UNESCO. I was pleasantly surprised by the number of ancient places we had been to on this trip, in both Japan and Russia, that were part of UNESCO.

In the tenth century, the pagans lived here. The island was chosen as a sacred place, and it was easy to see why. Surrounded by water on the huge Lake Onega, it was full of trees and flowers and wooden houses and marshes, and radiated such a good feeling! The pagans lived happily ever after until the thirteenth century when the Russians came with their religion. They began to build churches next to the pagan sites. The thing about these churches though, is that they were all made of wood, aspen, and no nails were used. In fact, when nails were first discovered and came to Kizhi Island, the carpenters there said it was not progress, because nails in fact damaged the wood. All the houses in Kizhi were built very elaborately without any nails at all.

We had a great guide, Marguerita, who told us that she lived there for six months of the year (tourist season) and for two weeks over Xmas and the rest of the time lived in a town fifty miles away. She can earn a good living by being a guide for those months. Her English was excellent and she had learned it at the local university.

Marguerita pointed out the Church of the Intercession, the Bell Tower, and the Church of the Transfiguration, all of which form a triangle so they can never overshadow each other. These three buildings used to unite a hundred and thirty villages. One was a winter church and one was a summer church.

WE WALKED THROUGH the little village into the home of a wealthy farmer who lived hundreds of years ago, and also peeked into their *banyo* or steam bath on the water. The houses were huge because the horses, cows, chickens, and other animals all lived inside as well. Chickens can't lay eggs when it is cold. In the winter, the house functioned as a fortress, where humans and animals awaited spring. The centre of the home was the oven, and children and old people had the privilege of sleeping on it. The stove was all important, for cooking, sleeping, bathing, etc. Although they were farmers, the local women never made jam, because there was no sugar. There was a cradle hanging from a rope attached to a long, long wooden staff, so the mother could move the cradle over the beams to be anywhere in the house.

In the sauna, old women cured people, sorcerers worked, young girls told fortunes. Every week the families bathed together, sitting in the hot sauna, and then jumping into the icy lake. The lake was very frozen in the winter; in fact, trucks crossed it in the winter, as it was over a meter thick with ice.

Everything was made of wood. The trees were logged only in the winter, as the resin was three times the amount then and it acted as a preservative for the wood. Trees were dormant in winter. The houses were built with very ornate features, but they all served a purpose. The homes were surrounded by a gallery, or balcony, as I would call it. Every house had this balcony surrounding its outside, because there was yet another Russian saying that a "house without a gallery is like a man without a beard," that is, unattractive, although I might not entirely agree with that saying.

The Church of the Transfiguration was 292 years old. It was amazing that it was built with no nails, and everything was geared to snow and rain water washing right off and leaving it clean. The aspen caused the domes to change colors often. It was truly an architectural marvel. It was built by local folks who couldn't read. There were no plans for it. Yet it turned out to be this most amazing edifice. When the carpenter who built this church finished, he threw his axe into the lake, so there would not be anything like it again. But a few years ago, they had to close it for safety reasons because it was, well, old and no longer safe. But they weren't sure how to fix it. They figured it out though. Starting the following year, they were going to raise the entire church up a few meters. Then they were going to take log by log down, and build it up again. Any log that needed to be restored, repaired, whatever, would be fixed and strengthened. And within ten years, in time for the structure's three hundredth birthday, it will be completely renovated. Hopefully.

WALKING AROUND KIZHI Island, one could really get a feel of farming life there and what it would be like to live there. I didn't want to leave, but leave we must. When we first arrived, we had to walk through three ships to get to land. Returning to our ship some hours later, we had to walk through *four* different ships to get to ours. In a way, I was glad to see so many ships there, because tourism had really become the livelihood for these people. Before all the tourists, they were starving peasants, and now they could at least make enough money in six months of guiding to support their families for a whole year. And of course there were all the obligatory gift/souvenir shops by the dock and by the village museum. And because we loved it so much, we had to leave a few *rubles* behind.

Back on the ship, I took myself up to the bar to Oksana, my favourite bartender. We had gotten into the habit of having at least one good chat a day. That night was to be the staff/crew show—sketches and singing and dancing, most of it silly and funny, and some of it remarkably good. The following day would be the passenger talent show. I thought out loud to Oksana, "I might be in it—I might not be. I'll see how I feel when I wake up in the morning." I had signed up to be in the talent show when we were in the Arctic, and had really been looking forward to that, but it ended up happening *so* late, that I simply could not stay up for it, so went to bed and missed it. I explained all this to Oksana and said that maybe I could try again. We would see. She was very encouraging.

The passenger talent show occurred after the captain's dinner and I did perform in it. My magic tricks (so to speak) were extremely well received.

At eleven-thirty pm, we all went out on deck to watch the amazing sunset. It would rise again before five am—not sure how much before. I have only heard people talk about it as I had always been sleeping. Which I needed to do imminently. *Dohbry vyecher* (good evening).

ELENA, THE YOUNG political scientist who had been giving lectures almost daily, presented the last one on Russia and Democracy. She gave us the results of a survey from 2004, where 54 percent of the people said Russia was not a democracy. She ended her lecture by saying, "Russians are engaged to democracy; we are not yet married to democracy." Very astute.

All the tour guides also gave a presentation—of the type "ask us anything you want about us and Russia." There were six guides for the 212 passengers. They were all incredibly well educated, multi-lingual, with multiple graduate degrees. I certainly have been very much impressed with Natasha, whose knowledge of history, geography, languages, customs, and social science, and much, much more has been absolutely amazing. She has an encyclopedic knowledge. Plus she has a great sense of humour!

We sailed down Lake Ladoga, Europe's largest freshwater lake. It was ice-free only six months of the year. Then we took the River Svir from Lake Ladoga to Lake Onega, which goes to the White Sea, and sailed into St. Petersburg after eleven pm.

Chapter 16
St. Petersburg: City of My Heart and Soul

WE SPENT AN entire day touring St. Petersburg. What a wonderful city! What to me was intriguing was watching the excitement of Natasha and the other guides as they came home and were telling us about their home city. Their love and excitement for the city and its positive changes over the last decade and a half were palpable. Towards the end of the day, as Natasha pointed out a statue of Pushkin, she sighed and said, "Ladies and Gentlemen, you can't know how nice it is to show you statues of Pushkin instead of Lenin!"

Natasha told us that St. Petersburg weather leads to nine months of great expectations and three months of disappointment. But that day it was quite beautiful and pleasant outside. The city had 4.2 million people, and more than four hundred bridges. It was founded in 1703 by Peter the Great, who among very many other things, defeated the Swedish King and got access to the Baltic Sea, thus ending Russia's life as a landlocked country. In 1712, St. Petersburg became the capitol of Russia, but in 1918, that was changed over to Moscow. And of course, St. Petersburg has had several names. Natasha said that you can always tell someone's politics by how they answer the question "Where do you live?" depending upon whether or not they answered "St. Petersburg" or "Lenningrad."

St. Petersburg was the eighth most expensive city in the world in which to live. There were over two thousand UNESCO sites there; in fact, the entire city was one unit under the protection of UNESCO. The concentration of culture there was enormous. Forty-two percent of the adult population had higher education. However, the divorce rate was 65 percent. There were eighty theatres, two hundred and fifty museums and more than five hundred palaces. There were also twenty-five McDonalds and seven KFCs. All buildings there stood on pilings because of floods and the riverbeds, and so there were no real skyscrapers. The city lay in the delta of the Neva River. *Neva* means swamps, marshes. The Neva River had the strongest flow in Europe. It was a young river, only ten thousand years old. All that information certainly gave me cause to think about things.

The metros are incredibly deep; as deep as a thirty-three story building is high. That's because they have to go below the riverbed because of the marshes.

The soil is frozen about eight months of the year. The temperature in February can be minus 8 degrees. April is warm, about 20 degrees. Frost can come back in May. The city is only five hundred miles below the Polar Circle. All the lakes are frozen from the end of November to the end of March. Natasha told us that there are sixty cloudless days a year, a hundred days a year where it rains heavily, and a hundred and forty-five days with heavy frost. That only leaves sixty days unaccounted for. Like today, which started off cloudy and ended up with blue skies. Yet the climate is milder than Moscow.

There are a hundred thousand Jews in St. Petersburg and several synagogues. 91 percent of the population of the city are Russians, with the next group being Ukrainians, then the Tatars and Belarusians.

Peter the Great wanted to emulate everything Western and he particularly liked Amsterdam so there were many canals in the city. It was sometimes called the Northern Venice. Why it was not called the Northern Amsterdam was beyond me. The city was built by the very best of Western European architects. And it shows. The architecture was stunning. And because the weather was often gloomy, the buildings were in colours, not necessarily bright, but nevertheless, blue, gold, rose, terra cotta, green, even red and purple. They were just lovely.

St. Petersburg was unique in that it was almost perfectly planned, with its islands, canals, bridges, streets, and squares, all done on such a grand scale. In 1867, Lewis Carroll wrote about the city: "It is as though one walked through a city built for giants." And aside from all this grandeur, St. Petersburg was known for its "artistic soul." Many of the great Russian authors and composers called St. Petersburg home.

Unlike other Russian cities, St. Petersburg had no kremlin. Peter the Great based the city layout on Amsterdam, where he studied shipbuilding when he was young. The canals, squares, everything, were built from scratch. Peter forbade the use of stone in building anywhere else in Russia. Everyone coming into St. Petersburg had to bring rocks and stones with them, no matter what else they were carrying, or else they were subject to large taxes. Masons could only work in St. Petersburg. But because of all this planning, and all the bright minds that Peter brought into the area, St. Petersburg was incredibly sophisticated, surpassing even the European cities it was meant to emulate.

OUR FIRST STOP was Pushkin Palace, Catherine's Palace. Catherine, the second wife of Peter the Great, was the Russian Cinderella. Catherine I, originally Marta, a peasant from Lithuania, at the age of sixteen was married and at the age of seventeen, was widowed. She was a prisoner of war, a whore, a mistress of many powerful men, and lastly mistress and then wife of Peter the Great, who renamed her Catherine. They had six illegitimate children and married twice. After they were married, they had five more children, one of whom was Elizabeth. Then Peter the Great crowned Catherine, the first time that had happened to a woman. When Peter died, Catherine seized the throne and ruled for a few more years until her death.

After she died, Catherine's daughter, Elizabeth, built the palace and named it after her mother. Elizabeth wanted to turn her palace into another Versailles when it was being built; but when it was done, she said, "I don't like it." It was rebuilt six times until she liked it, but then she loved it. And it was easy to see why. It truly was magnificent, and like nothing we have seen so far. It was finished in 1756. After the Russian Revolution, it became a museum, and then in 1941, the Nazis moved in and destroyed pretty much everything of beauty. It had since been restored, of course, and they were still working on the restorations. The Nazis cut down all the surrounding trees for fuel, and when they were leaving, they blew up parts of the palace and left another eleven bombs in the basement. 92 percent of the original palace was ruined, but the restoration had been very effective. The décor was carved from linden wood. One hundred percent pure gold was used for the regilding.

The castle had three hundred rooms. During Elizabeth's time, there were over six hundred people staffing the castle. We walked through only twenty-two of the rooms, but how grand they were! Natasha pointed out the wonderfully ornate and gilded décor and said, "Everything that glitters in Russia *is* gold." This palace was just one of many summer residences.

We walked through a dining room where the table was in a unique shape— it represented the Cyrillic letter that started the name of Elizabeth. We saw another room, with portraits of dead game hanging on the walls; they would only eat hunted game there. When Elizabeth wanted to hunt, her staff would release game that had been kept in cages into the Alexander Gardens, and off they would go to hunt down dinner.

The kitchen was always kept in another building, because it was considered lower class to have an odour from the kitchen in the palace.

The trees were planted in such a sophisticated manner, that when they were in bloom, they would change colours in stripes, red, gold, and so forth, but after the Nazis chopped them down, they were replanted in a haphazard manner.

One of the rooms we visited was the famous amber room. Wow! It was splendid! Two years previously, it was re-opened by Putin and the head of Germany. The original amber room was an ambassadorial gift from Germany to Peter the Great. It was stolen by the Nazis and disappeared. They totally wrecked the room. So Germany donated 3.5 million dollars towards the fourteen million it took to restore the room. Had the original amber room survived, its current value would be sixty million US dollars. The German masters kept the secret of the amber work and had to help reconstruct it. Amber was everywhere; mosaics were made of amber, the walls were solid amber. But instead of just flat amber, the walls were multi-coloured, alive, glistening, and ornately carved and displayed. The paintings and mirrors in the room were wonderful; indeed, the entire room was just amazing!

Catherine the Great had said that too much gold depressed her. Elizabeth couldn't get enough of it and had it everywhere. I have always found Catherine the Great to be a fascinating woman. I remembered from my history class in 1960 that she was the first in Russia to be vaccinated for small pox. Catherine the Great had many lovers. When she died, she was sixty-six and her current lover was twenty-seven years old. Poor Catherine the Great—she died of a stroke at the age of sixty-six when the Swedish King refused the hand of her grand-daughter two days before the wedding, because Catherine would not allow her grand-daughter to change religions.

WE WENT TO Peter and Paul Fortress, which was the first building constructed in St. Petersburg. It served as a jail, and the first inmate was Peter the Great's own son, Alexei, who was imprisoned and ultimately executed. Dostoevsky was also imprisoned there. Peter the Great was buried there, and so were the last of the Romanovs. When Natasha was taking us there, she promised we would not see more icons. She told us about a tourist who had a notebook on which was written "ABC" in columns, page after page. When the guide asked the tourist what "ABC" was, she got the answer, "Another bloody cathedral." So Natasha promised us it would not be another bloody cathedral. And true to form, she was right.

Peter the Great died from bladder and kidney disease. He couldn't pee for two weeks before he died and his doctor had to puncture his bladder to relieve his pain. He was very stressed out, and he called to his aide, "I want to write something. I want to leave my will." He began, "Leave everything to . . ." lost consciousness and died.

The true Anastasia is buried there as well. There were three hundred laurel wreathes made of solid gold and silver. Two hundred and ninety-nine disappeared during the revolution.

There are so many stories of life and death and plotting and executions, and the names were so similar or identical even, so at times, I found it difficult to keep track of who was whom. But I loved all the stories.

WE CONTINUED DRIVING around St. Petersburg. Every time we would pass something, Natasha would say, "On your right is the Marine Museum, founded by whom?" and we would all echo dutifully, "Peter the Great."

Natasha: "On your left is the Museum of Natural History, founded by whom?"

"Peter the Great."

"Straight ahead is the University of St. Petersburg, founded by whom?"

"Peter the Great!"

And on and on it went, our history lesson.

NEVSKY PROSPECT, THE main street, was the most famous street in St. Petersburg. It was four miles long, and every single building was protected by UNESCO. It was an open air museum. It was built in 1704, and was very straight and wide. It was a beautiful street, full of shops, galleries, boutiques, with every building being architecturally different, every building a different colour. It was quite wonderful. At the end of the street was a cemetery with the remains of renowned citizens such as Tchaikovsky, Rimsky-Korsakov, and Dostoevsky.

The day ended with a trip to the ballet, where we saw the St. Petersburg Ballet Theatre perform *Giselle*. It was absolutely stunning. I think I sat with my mouth open for the entire performance. It truly was magical, and I was so delighted to have the opportunity to attend. The dancers were as good as I've ever seen, probably better. And after the ballet, we drove around a bit, and returned to the ship after eleven pm. The sun was still shinning. The sun set these days around midnight, and it rose again by four am. By solstice in three weeks' time, there would be less than two hours of semi-darkness per twenty-four hours.

THE FOLLOWING MORNING, Judi and I used some free time to—you guessed it—mail more packages home! So far, I have mailed packages home at least once from every country! I'd like to say I've learned my lesson about over-packing. I'd like to say that, but if I did, I suspect I would be lying.

Elena, one of the women who worked in reception on our ship, and Vladimir, the second mate, had very graciously volunteered to take us and all of our goodies to the shipping place. We were told most emphatically not to mail anything from Russia, as the postal system was horrendous. So we had been looking for a shipping company like Fed Ex. Elena had made some phone calls the previous day, and assured us she had found a place that would ship our boxes to the US and Canada.

So off we went on a beautiful St. Petersburg day and drove for an hour. We found the office, where the first thing we had to do was to fill out forms. Of course. We filled out multiple copies of forms in great detail. Then Elena translated everything into Russian, even though the forms were bilingual. There were many consultations with the *kacca* (cashier), then the manager. Then we had to fill out more forms. Then we had to go back to the desk to sign more forms, each one requiring five original signatures (carbon copies wouldn't do). Both Elena and Vladimir were helping us with the forms, the signing, the *kacca*. Finally, they were ready to look at the items. They took Judi's boxes, which were sitting open on a scale, and started removing each item to say what was allowed and what wasn't. In the meantime, the line-up for the *kacca* was growing and growing. The stares were not quite so friendly any more. The *kacca* held up a small bottle of hotel shampoo which Judi took from Japan because she wanted the Japanese writing on it.

"Not allowed," the *kacca* said.

"Not allowed?" Judi asked.

"*Nyet*. Cosmetics. *Nyet* cosmetics."

Then she found little wooden magnets, worth about one dollar each. These took some examination before she decided, "Allowed."

She came across a few small paintings that we had bought on the street the other day from a young artist.

"*Nyet*," *kacca* said.

"Why not?"

"Antique paintings."

"Antiques? The man who painted them is only twenty-five years old!"

"*Nyet*. Not allowed."

The line behind us continued to grow and we were now aware of some fidgeting in the ranks.

Finally, she finished with Judi's boxes and called up the bank to validate the credit card. And then it was my turn. But I think because the line behind us was still swelling, she just took my boxes to the back room and spared me the indignity of going through all my personal belongings in front of an ever-increasing audience. After placing my signature on five more forms and filling out several other forms, it was time to pay. I handed her my VISA and she dialed the bank.

And we waited. And waited. And waited. Suddenly, after talking in Russian with Madame *kacca*, Elena announced, "You will go to toilet now. He will show you." She pointed at a stubby looking gentleman. *Kacca* handed me back my VISA.

"Uh, okay," I muttered. What could I do but go to the bathroom then.

Off we went, through the back room, to the toilets, with symbols that made distinguishing our sex very difficult. One was a triangle one way, and the other was an inverted triangle. We opted for the first.

When we returned with the gentleman who had been waiting for us, I handed the *kacca* my VISA card and we started all over again. It seemed to take forever, but she finally did get through. When she found someone on the other end of the telephone, she began to talk and type in the computer and fill out more forms for over fifteen minutes! Just to validate the VISA. And finally we were done. We gave the *kacca* a Canadian pin, smiled *spasibo* (thank you) to her, and left. Vladimir must have had ants in his pants or had been late for work. He transformed himself from a regular driver on the way there to a maniacal speedster, zigging and zagging, bouncing over the innumerable pot holes and train tracks, honking, swerving, and quite terrifying us. It was actually unpleasant, but nevertheless, an experience, and we did return back to the ship quite safely. So to mail a few parcels took us an hour and a half in the office, and close to an hour each way in the car for a total of three and a half hours! And now it was afternoon, and time for the Hermitage.

ON THE WAY to the Hermitage, we were caught in a traffic jam. We passed many cars jammed in, all facing each other and unable to move. All the cars were at different angles and traffic was backed up for miles. Natasha used the time to tell us all about the Hermitage as well as stories of Russian lore.

The Hermitage is visited by thirty thousand people daily and three million people a year. If a person spent one minute in front of each exhibit, and did that eight full hours a day, seven days a week, with no breaks, it would take eleven years to see the more than three million pieces in the collection at the Hermitage.

"Hermitage" is a French word and means a place for a hermit. It was an original idea of Marie Antoinette and developed by Catherine the Great. Everywhere Catherine lived, she built a small, quiet house where she could live with her best friends, and she called it a hermitage. In the winter palace there was such a room, a hermitage. That name passed on to the whole palace. It is a place of retreat.

Today, the Hermitage consists of the Winter Palace plus four more buildings. The winter palace was built in 1756 for Elisabeth I. She died three months before it was finished, but Catherine the Great did enjoy it. She had amassed

222 masterpieces in her private collection. In 1764, she wrote to Voltaire saying "only mice and me admire all these treasures." She said she was like a glutton for the artwork. She loved it! Purchases of art work stopped with WWI.

The Hermitage displays only 10 percent of the collection at any time; there is no room to display the other 90 percent. The Hermitage is the biggest and most important art gallery second only to the Louvre. (I've been to both, and I really liked the Hermitage.)

During WWII, three bombs hit the Hermitage. 60 percent of all the artifacts were taken to Siberia and were all returned back after the war. There is a staff of fifteen hundred—art historians, restorers, attendants, and many others hired to protect the art work.

Natasha gave us all this information on the bus from the ship and then told us she was going to show us the Hermitage in three hours. We were going to walk three miles (which we most certainly did) and see all the highlights. It was actually funny, as I don't believe I've ever moved so quickly through a museum or art gallery as I did at the Hermitage.

"Look, there is a de Vinci. Sneak in, look at it, and then meet me over here." (There are twelve authenticated undisputed de Vinci paintings in the world; the Hermitage has two of them.) A Madonna was found in an open air market, with mold, all wrecked, somewhere in Russia. The guy who bought it knew what he was looking at, and took it to France to the Louvre, where it was authenticated as a real de Vinci.

"Quickly now, go look at the Rembrandt and return to this corner." (The first Rembrandt was bought by Peter the Great.) And so progressed our tour.

What I really loved was walking though the buildings. How grand that place is! The ceilings and walls and floors were just incredible. And everywhere one looked there was the most amazing art. I was just trying to absorb all that into my being.

In 1986, a man walked through the control check with a bottle of "water." He asked to see the best painting by Rembrandt and was told to see "Danae." He then stabbed the painting twice and poured sulfuric acid (which was in the water bottle) all over her. In moments, 30 percent of the painting was gone, even though he was stopped immediately. The maniac was arrested and is still in an institution. He wanted to protest some political demands. He said that he originally wanted to blow up Lenin's tomb but when he saw how heavily guarded it was, he changed his mind and went to the Hermitage instead. Russians joked that they wish he never would have changed his mind. (Lenin's Tomb was very expensive to maintain, and there was lots of talk about finally burying him). At any rate, the Rembrandt was restored, more or less. The foreground is new, the background is new, but the middle is still the original. And that is why no water is allowed in the Hermitage.

Two families in Russia bought up most of the French Impressionists before they were even famous, and brought the paintings to Russia. So there is quite a good exhibit of Monet, Manet, van Gogh, Gauguin, Degas, Cezanne, etc.

In 1837, there was a fire in the Hermitage. Nicholas I was listening to opera at the Mariinsky Theatre. For three days he worked side by side with others to help to put out the fire and save the building. He heard some people were trying to save this Venetian Silver mirror. He told them to go out because he was worried for their lives. They said no, that it was a great piece of art. He then took a chair, threw it at the mirror, and as it cracked into pieces, he said, "Now it is no longer an art piece. Leave." He saved their lives.

After the fire, the Hermitage was rebuilt in another style, and so half of it was in the classical form and half in baroque.

We saw a piece of decorative carved jasper that was so big that when it was brought down from the Ural Mountains by twenty-four horses, it would not fit in the doors. They had to remove the roof and then rebuilt the building around the piece.

Then we found ourselves in a room with exceptionally high ceilings, held up by magnificent marble torsos. The chandeliers were glittering, sculptures abounded, it was *so* grand!

We looked at a painting by Carravaggio, "The Lute Player." Natasha asked, "Is it a he or a she?" Hard to tell. It was a young person, but it could be of either sex. "No one knew for a very long time, but then a music expert found the answer, right here in the painting." And she explained how the piece of music in the painting sitting in front of the lute player is a famous piece of the times for a man's voice, and so it was a he.

We went to the world famous malachite room. Malachite is mined in the Ural mountains. The room had huge columns of malachite, malachite fireplaces and tables and a huge malachite urn. It was beautiful.

Probably my favourite display in the Hermitage was the Gilded Peacock Clock by James Cox. The clock was built in England and arrived in Russia in 1797. However, it arrived in pieces, and re-assembly took more than ten years. I think it was incredible that it was rendered fully functional at all when one considers all the levers and cogs and moving parts as well as the actual clock. It was an extremely impressive piece, with the peacock, owl, squirrels, mushrooms, and much, much more.

It was originally owned by Prince Grigory Potemkin, who was the secret husband of Catherine the Great. Of course it was now a main display in the Hermitage. It was the only large example of robotics from the eighteenth century which still survived unaltered now in the twenty-first century. It only did its robotic thing at certain times on certain days and we did not see the clock "perform." However, I did see the clock, this magnificent peacock, with the time and works in a little mushroom with a dragonfly dial, and learned that every Wednesday at five pm, the clock was set to go off, and the peacock opened up its tail and the owl did something with his eyes, and the dragonfly told the time, and so on. It was enough for me to come back to St. Petersburg and the Hermitage to see it in action. And I will. (And so I did).

THINGS NATASHA TOLD us during our bus rides:

A typical Russian church has five domes—one for Christ, and four for the four evangelists (Matthew, Mark, Luke, and John who were attributed with creating the four gospels of their names).

After the Russian Revolution, things did not go exactly as anticipated. All the great reforms were not happening. Someone had to be blamed for this. An enemy, most likely from the west, was in our midst, the politicians said, and all these things wrong are the enemy's fault. And thusly came into being the KGB.

In Russia, when a woman has a baby, she gets paid from the seventh month of pregnancy to the second month post-partum while she is off work. She then takes three years off to raise her child, but her job is held for her, along with its seniority. There is no salary, but a small monthly child payment.

And so Natasha told us how the Communist Party was responsible for the births of her children. She was a young married woman just finishing university. Twenty young women were singled out to come work in the KGB headquarters. These were women who were extremely bright, whose families were "clean," who had all the right characteristics to work there, most likely as interpreters. So Natasha was asked if she would take the job. If she said yes, well, then she was in trouble, because she didn't want to do it, and her husband had told her he would never lie in the same bed as a KGB agent. If she said no, well, then she could end up in Siberia. So she said she was pregnant and then had Paulina. Then ten years later, she had a job and was very quickly being promoted. She was higher up than most people twenty years her senior. (Once you meet Natasha, you can understand why; she is very brilliant.) Anyway, one day, her superior came up to her and said, "Natasha, we would like you to join the Communist Party, because we want to make you head of the department (or something akin to that)." Well, Natasha thought, what to do, what to do.

"Ladies and gentlemen," she explained, "to join the Communist Party, well, this I could not do. But to refuse, this could be very bad for me and for my family."

"I am pregnant," Natasha said, and that is how Pavel (Paul or Pasha) came into being. And how the Communist Party was responsible for her children.

AFTER THE HERMITAGE, the bus, which was to return us to the ship encountered the traffic jam that we had skirted on the way there. But now it had escalated to the point of incredulity.

"Ladies and Gentlemen," Natasha announced, "never in my life have I seen a traffic jam like this. I promise you. Never."

And so we spent hours in the bus, trying to get around the traffic jam, but it was a truly unbelievable and incredible experience. Cars would all go into an intersection, at all angles, and other cars would come up right behind them and more cars right behind them and then nobody could back up or turn around and the traffic just backed up more and more for miles and miles and miles. Alexii, our wonderful bus driver, kept trying to go around it, but couldn't get out of the jam. We literally could not get back to the ship. One of the guide buses sat without moving at all for over twenty minutes. But our bus, group 44, with the wonderful Natasha, had decided to pull over at a kiosk (that's *KNOCK* in Cyrillic). Natasha and her son Pasha (who rode with us as it was his birthday and Natasha was going out with him after she safely delivered us) interpreted for all thirty-five of us as we purchased beer and vodka and chips. We then had a bus party, telling jokes, and Natasha continued to regale us with Russian folklore and stories. It was the best time. Everyone laughed and laughed, and when our bus finally returned to the ship some three hours late, we were all very happy, not even wanting to get off to board the ship, while all the other buses dislodged grumpy, unhappy travelers. The only problem with our bus party was no bathroom, which was starting to be a problem just about the time we managed to return. Apparently, a traffic jam of this magnitude was a first for St. Petersburg, but some felt it was a presentiment of times to come.

"Natasha, tell me really, does this happen often?" I asked.

"Look me in the face," she said, removing her sun glasses. "Look into my eyes when I tell you I have *never* seen traffic like this before."

DRIVING THROUGH ST. Petersburg, we had seen so many brides—they were everywhere, taking photos in front of the Hermitage, or in the park in front of the statue of Peter the Great—many, many brides. Well, it was June, after all.

I found it very interesting to see the foreign food restaurants in Russian—like Russian Chinese restaurants, and Russian Japanese or Mexican restaurants. When I come back to St. Petersburg, and I will (and did), go to a Russian Chinese restaurant.

The bridges of St. Petersburg open from two to five every morning to let the big ships through. Every hour, they shut again to let traffic through for ten minutes, and then they open again.

Do you know why the domes of Russian churches are onion shaped? Natasha told us. In the old days, buildings were one story high, belfries were two or three stories high. When the belfry was topped by a dome, from off in the distance, it looked like a welcoming candle with a flame. That's one of the reasons for the onion shapes.

ABOUT FIVE MINUTES after we returned from the Hermitage and the Traffic Jam, we got onto another bus to take a canal cruise. I am so glad I decided to go because it afforded a totally different view of the beauty of this city. And it didn't hurt that we were served vodka, champagne, and caviar on the small boat.

I loved watching the Russians do their thing. Some were fishing, some drinking and partying beside the water. Lots of folks were flirting. I saw an area of town that looked to be a gay area, and when I later asked Natasha about it, she told me that yes, there are areas like that, with lots of gay clubs and restaurants. After so much repression, with the new freedom now comes acceptance and liberation, and she said lesbians and gay men are totally accepted now.

Many of the buildings in the residential sections had huge facades with large archways that led into courtyards around which the apartment complexes were situated. Inside these courtyards lay a whole other world, with gardens, animals, and people living their lives.

Architecturally, St. Petersburg is the most beautiful city I have ever seen. I have totally fallen in love with this city, something I haven't done for a very long time. I was blown away by the beauty of this city, her complexity and variability. I could hardly wait to return to explore her further.

Chapter 17
The Yussopovs and Rasputin

WE USED OUR time that last morning on the ship to pack and get organized as we were to leave the ship in the early evening, but we still had one more tour. We went to Yussopov Palace, along with the two million visitors a year who go there.

The palace is famous and beloved not only because of its beauty but because it was where Rasputin was murdered. The Yussopovs were one of the richest families in Russia. They were the fifth most wealthiest and owned many estates, fifty-five estates, actually. They owned over two hundred factories and many other enterprises. They also owned several palaces. The Yussopovs were of Moorish descent, and came to Moscow centuries ago. A sultan's son married into Russia and had a grandson. His name was Yussof, a good Muslim name, and it was Russianized by adding the "pov."

One reason for the popularity of the palace is that in 1916, Rasputin was assassinated there. Rasputin was born in Siberia. His father was a peasant, but he was a "rich peasant," whatever that might be. Rasputin was married with three children. People referred to him both as a holy man or an evil spirit. He had the ability to predict the future and to hypnotize people as well as heal them. He was only half literate, but knew the Bible by heart. When he came to St. Petersburg at the beginning of the twentieth century, no one knew of him. Somehow, Rasputin got himself introduced into the royal houses. He never disguised who or what he was; he looked very different. People felt Rasputin could see right through them. When Felix Yussopov started planning to murder Rasputin, he planned for two years, and he always avoided a direct glance so that Rasputin couldn't figure out what he was plotting.

In 1904, Nicholas and Alexandra had a son, Alexei, born with hemophilia. No one could stop the bleeding. The empress had heard about Rasputin from the ladies in her court. She was a desperate mother who loved her son. She invited Rasputin to the court as the child was suffering terribly. Rasputin put his hands on the child's forehead and healed him. By morning, he was better. The royal family didn't want people to know he had hemophilia. Rasputin was often seen coming out of the Empress' bedrooms (where the child was). At the time, children rarely were raised in their parents' bedroom.

Rumours started. They abounded. They hinted that the Empress and Rasputin were having an affair. The gossip spread saying Rasputin was having affairs with many women in the royal family. At that time, Russia was losing in WWI and the country was on the edge of revolution. Felix Yussopov, feeling patriotic, decided to get rid of Rasputin, a person whom people would ask for benefits at the court, insuring he became a very powerful person. Yussopov wanted to restore the ruined honour of the empress and to get rid of Rasputin, who had such political authority and negatively influenced the royal family.

Yussopov palace was just splendid—so elegant and lush. Those Yussopovs were rich! The princess used to send her laundry to Paris. They never knew how much money they had—they just knew they had a lot. Alexei Yussopov saw a marble staircase in Italy, fell in love with it, and brought it to St. Petersburg—a huge double-sided, winding marble staircase. The Yussopovs were charming and enchanting as well. The mother of Felix was thought to be the most beautiful woman in all of Russia. Felix himself was a bisexual, and everyone of both sexes fell in love with him, as they did with his mother. The Yussopovs were very hospitable and often had hundreds of guests; they were very generous. They had a huge collection of art, which was confiscated.

Natasha: "The family's art collection is where?"

Us: "The Hermitage."

DURING WWII, THE palace was used as a military hospital. Could you possibly imagine regaining consciousness after being shot, opening your eyes and looking at gilded cherubs blowing kisses at you from the ceiling? Three bombs hit the palace during the war. It was restored. I kept thinking St. Petersburg should be renamed Restoration City.

There was a curse on the Yussopovs because in the 1600s they had converted to Christianity. The curse had something to do with children (sons) not reaching the age of twenty-seven and inheriting the family's fortune. Nicholas was Felix's older brother. Felix and Nicholas knew that one of them was going to die because of the curse. Their mother never stopped praying that they both would live. Nicholas fell in love with a married woman. When he was twenty-seven, he was challenged to a duel because of his lover, a duel which he had to accept to maintain his honour. He was shot and killed. The mother was so shocked she was paralyzed for six months. So then Felix, at the age of twenty-four, inherited this massive fortune and became one of the wealthiest men in the world. He did get the title of "Prince" which was his brother's title after his mother did some negotiating.

Natasha: "And where do we see Felix's fortune now?"
Us: "In the Hermitage."

THE PALACE HAD a "home theatre," which was unlike any home theatre I had ever seen. We walked down a grand staircase, and there was the theatre, a mini La Scala, unbelievably ornate, the only rococo style theatre that survived WWII (which is one of the reasons UNESCO protects it). The theatre had a capacity of a hundred and thirty people. It had perfect acoustics. We sat in front of the stage on chairs (covered, of course) that Nicholas II could have sat in. The theatre was stunningly beautiful. Liszt, Chopin, and Schumann performed there. That place certainly gave new meaning to the expression "home theatre."

The family also had a hundred and twenty-six musical instruments, including of course, Stradivarius and Amati violins and a lot more of that ilk.

"And where do we see these instruments now?" Natasha asked.

"In the Hermitage," we dutifully responded.

We then went into the oak dining room which was one of five dining rooms in the palace. Felix wrote that his father was very strict with the children and hated when they were late for dinner—but how to know in which dining room they were dining?

Felix was as beautiful as his mother. When he was a teenager, and his parents would be at another palace, he used to sneak into his mother's room, put on her clothes and pearls, and go to the bar and flirt with men. One night he used the pearl necklace as a lasso and it burst. The police were called, and Felix was put under home arrest for a month, but every day he would crawl out his window to play some more.

Felix ultimately immigrated to France and had one daughter and there was also one grand-daughter. She was thirty-two at the time of our visit, and the daughter was sixty, but there were no kids and no Yussopov name. Natasha guided the daughter through the palace a few years previously, and she had been praying for an heir, but still there was none.

For two years, Felix plotted to kill Rasputin. He invited Rasputin to the palace under false pretenses. They fed him his favourite food and drink (Madeira) laced with cyanide. He did not die. Two hours passed, still he was living. He wanted to leave, but Felix kept stalling him. Felix got a gun and shot him. The doctor in the group said he would be dead in a few minutes, so they all went upstairs. Eventually, Felix went back to the basement to check on him—he leaned over to see if Rasputin was still breathing, and Rasputin grabbed him by the neck, and started to strangle him, saying, "Felix, Felix." Felix escaped, ran upstairs, got more weapons, ran back downstairs—no Rasputin. He was gone, leaving behind only drops of blood. But it was wintertime, so they tracked the drops of blood outside in the snow. They caught up with Rasputin, wrapped him in a fur coat, and threw him over a bridge. However, the coat got caught in the ice and shortly thereafter, Rasputin's body was found. He did not die of poisoning or bullets, but he finally drowned. The empress wanted the death penalty for all the plotters of Rasputin's death. The five plotters were heroes, but they were exiled to far-away estates and all eventually emigrated.

Five years before his death, Rasputin wrote to the empress that he would die by the hand of one from the royal family, and that he would bring down the family with him. He wrote it would be the end of the family and of the Russian people.

The whole tour through Yussopov Palace was just awesome and I would love to return. I just couldn't seem to get enough of it.

THE ENTIRE CITY of St. Petersburg is so amazing, I will be very sad to leave it. Everywhere I turn I look upon statues, castles, bridges, and unbelievable architecture. The facades, the arches, the artwork are all just incredible—it is truly mind-blowing!

Upon our return from Yussopov Palace, we quickly finished packing and said our good-byes to our new friends on the Viking Surkov. We then bid farewell to St. Petersburg, a city that has now crawled deeply into my heart and soul.

Part IV

The Ukraine

Chapter 18
On the Train to Kyiv

JANE, OUR WONDERFUL travel agent, had arranged for us to be picked up at the ship and taken to the train station, where we had a sleeper cabin booked for the trip to Kiev or Kyiv. So I approached the driver.

"Do you have our train tickets?"

He looked quite askance at me, and it became immediately apparent he did not speak English.

So I did what most tourists do in such situations—I repeated the same question, much, much slower.

"Do

you

have

our

train

tickets?"

And he did exactly what he did before—looked puzzled and shrugged.

I looked around me at the almost empty pier. Ah, there was Julia, the head guide, talking to some people.

"Julia, can you help me please?" I called over.

"Yes, of course," she responded.

"Please ask him if he has our train tickets."

She did.

He didn't.

"Oh no," I cried out. "What are we to do?"

"You do not have them?" Julia asked, indicating a bunch of papers and documents I was holding.

"No. I only have our transit visas here."

After much more talking in two languages, and my getting a little nervous as the clock was ticking and trains leave ultimately, Julia asked to see all the papers I was holding.

"Sure," I said, "but these are the travel visas I picked up the other day before the ballet."

Julia looked at them and burst out laughing. "These are your train tickets." She laughed. "Of this, I am sure."

"Where are our transit visas?"

They actually were stapled into our passports, right where they were supposed to be.

So after profusely thanking Julia, we set off for the train station, leaving the giggling Julia behind us.

THE DRIVER LET us off, and a porter immediately took our bags. We just showed him the tickets/travel visa pieces of paper, and he nodded and away he went. We followed. One porter took us up some stairs, while our luggage disappeared around a corner with a second porter. But somehow I wasn't at all concerned. I know there is so much out there about being careful and about theft, but most people are quite helpful and honest. Sure enough, the porter with the luggage met us on the track. He walked us down to our car, but it was too early to board the train. So he unloaded everything, and we sat on our luggage and wondered how long it would take until we could board. The porter told us something in Russian. I told Judi I thought he was telling us he would return to help with the luggage. And sure enough, just as the train opened, a nice young man appeared to deal with our luggage. He carried it all into our little cabin. Shades of the Yangtze cruise. Well, this cabin was little-er. With a bathroom down the hall. But that was okay, it was after nine pm, and we figured we would sleep soon anyway.

WE WENT INTO the PECTOPAH (*restoran*, or dining car). We wanted some dinner. Judi saw a plate of food on a table in front of a gentleman and pointed to it and to us, and soon we had what the gentleman was having. It wasn't half bad Russian food! Put on the table in front of us was a huge plate of potatoes, and beef, and salads and corn and beets, and the ubiquitous sour cream and dill. It was great, really.

Then I wanted to plug in my computer. Earlier, Zena, the conductor, showed me the plug. So I went to plug it in and wait for a bit with it while it was charging, as it was in a hall beside an outside door. Zena came up to me, and with much gesticulating, told me to follow her. She then showed me that the power was not on—so I was sitting there plugged into a dead plug! By now it was close to midnight—I thought it might be time to turn in.

Zena approached, and kept asking me a question in Russian. I had no idea what it was. She finally got another passenger who interpreted:

"What time do you want dinner?"

"You mean tomorrow?" I asked.

"What time you would like to eat?"

"You mean breakfast?" I asked.

"No, tonight, when will you eat?"

"Oh, no, we already ate. Why?"

"Because you have vouchers here for dinner, your dinner was paid for."

Oops. Because we had already eaten and paid. Well, live and learn.

IN THE MORNING, we went to the dining car.

"I want some eggs," Judi said.

"I don't know how to say eggs," I said, "I only know how to say potatoes."

"That's okay," Judi said. She then called Zayir over, went "cluck, cluck, cluck" and flapped her arms cum wings.

A big smile spread over his face, and soon she was eating a huge plate of eggs, potatoes, salads, and the quotidian sour cream and dill. But for some reason, I only got coffee. They asked Judi if she wanted tea by showing her a used tea bag. After waiting about half an hour, she clucked and flapped again, and soon, I had my breakfast in front of me too.

I THEN ASKED Zayir if I could recharge my computer in the PECTOPAH. Then, as I started to type, he understood, and got an extension cord and set me up at a table, and I literally spent ten hours there, catching up on all my writing. It was a most pleasant, relaxing day. Judi decided to get out all her paraphernalia for printing pictures, and took pictures of all the folks working there, Zena, Zayir, Lena, and more and then printed out little photos for all of them. We were totally surrounded by staff and passengers the entire day. And of course, the staff were all thrilled with their photos. I was trying to write, but the distraction was only minimal, and definitely worth it.

There was always a TV on there—if it was an American movie, there was Russian voice-over; otherwise it was in Russian. I was always very happy to listen to it.

IT WAS AMAZING to me how much we are able to interact with people when there is no common language. For example, we knew that Zena had a thirty-year-old daughter in Austria and a father in Washington. At least, that's what we think we knew. Zena "*shprecht deutch schlecht*" (speak German bad), like me. But with a few German words among the Russian, we could certainly understand each other. And Zayir knew that we passed through the town where our grandmother was born. And that we were sisters.

Indeed, we did pass through the town of Gomel, Belarus, where we believed our maternal grandmother was born. It was a very strange feeling. I stood at the side of the train looking out. It was a very short stop, but it was thrilling, nevertheless. This is where my ancestors were from. I smiled. Zayir got it.

We were not allowed to disembark in Belarussia. We were told this by our conductors in no uncertain terms. When the train stopped at Gomel, I went to the area between train cars, where there were steps down to the station. An armed soldier looked at me and negatively shook his head distinctly meaning "do not come down here" as he walked alongside the train, rifle up in the air against his shoulder. But this was the town where my grandmother had lived, for heaven's sake. I just had to put my feet on the ground there. So I waited for the soldier to walk a bit further down along the train, and then very quickly hopped down, shuffled my feet on the land of my grandmother, and then quickly hopped back up onto the train before any harm could befall me.

Gomel was in Belarussia. We had to pass the border, first from Russia into Belarus, and then from there into the Ukraine. In a way, it was helpful not speaking the language, because all the customs and immigration men just shrugged, stamped our papers, and moved on.

ZENA, THE CONDUCTOR on the train, had truly taken a liking to us. She talked to us all the time. Except she talked very quickly in Russian and I probably understood about 0.1% of it. If that. And I keep saying to her in Russian "I don't understand" and she smiled and carried on, chattering away in Russian. Judi and I would laugh and shake our heads and Zena just shrugged and kept on talking!

WE WERE ABOUT two hours out of Kyiv. We had no idea what would happen there, as we did not think we were being met at the train station, so we would have to make our own way to the hotel. It would be another adventure, but isn't that one of the reasons we were traveling? For the adventures?

Chapter 19
Kyiv and Babi Yar

WE ARRIVED IN Kyiv. Zena immediately found us a nice strong porter who helped with our bags. And much to our surprise, we immediately saw a sign with our names on it. Holding it was a smiling Sergei, who couldn't really speak English. In no time flat we had our luggage off the train and onto the porter's cart, and then we started walking. And walking. And walking and walking and walking. Down the tracks. Across the tracks. Up the tracks. And finally we made it to the car, and eventually to our hotel.

The Hotel President-Kyivsky reminded me of the old Chinese hotels—huge buildings with high ceilings and large rooms. Things didn't necessarily work with Japanese efficiency, but I sure am glad to be in the land of the large and doubled chinned.

We stopped at the cashier to get some local money. Since Independence, of course the Ukrainians have their own money. So we traded in our *rubles* for *hryvnias* and *kopiyok*. The main currency is a *hryvnia*, and the Yiddish-speaking folks out there can understand why I keep mistakenly calling them *gribbenes*.

We were tired and hungry and so after taking care of our basic needs, fell into bed for a very good sleep.

We enjoyed breakfast, which was very like Ukranian dim sum, with little meat ballies, and dumplings, and a few things I didn't recognize but tasted good, and then took our computers to the business centre. But cyberspace was not to be for this computer, as their wireless connection was broken, and they would not let us hook up our computers to their one hook-up. There was a huge line-up waiting to use the one connection.

WE ONLY HAD one day in Kyiv, so I had arranged a tour guide for the afternoon, and thus we met the Ukranian Natasha. She was a good guide, excellent in fact, but I'm afraid no Natasha or any other guide will ever come close to our Russian Natasha.

Before we even got into the car, Natasha started talking about all the churches we would visit. Judi and I both rolled our eyes and groaned.

"Can we go to Babi Yar?" I asked.

"You want to go to Babi Yar?" She turned to me.

"Yes, I very much would like to go there."

The good Natasha picked up on this immediately and said, "Good, first we go to Babi Yar, then we go to the Jewish section, then we go to the synagogue . . ."

Judi and I nodded.

"Great!" we all said, and we were off.

KYIV IS THE Ukrainian word for the city and is pronounced k-y-iv; Kiev is the Russian word and is pronounced key-ev. This is what Kyiv looks like in Cyrillic: KNIB.

Kyiv was founded in the fifth century. There was an old gate to the city which was ruined by. . . I hear my other Natasha asking the question and hear my obedient answer: the Tatar Mongols, of course. The city was occupied during 1941 to 1943. Golda Meier's family came from Kyiv, but they immigrated in 1903. Shalom Aleichem was also from here. Lazer Brodsky, who lived just at the turn of the nineteenth century, was called the Sugar King of the Ukraine. He built a synagogue in a good part of town but he outwitted the authorities. He knew that if he would apply to build a synagogue, it would be refused. So instead he applied for a permit to build a business building, and thus got approval. After the building was already built, he then turned it into a synagogue. Which was still there in the city and we would come to it later on. He also built a hospital and tried to get Jewish students accepted into the University.

During the Nazi occupation, almost everything was destroyed. We drove down a wide street with good-looking shops; it was the only street that survived the occupation. On week-ends, the whole street was shut off to vehicular traffic and pedestrians ruled. It was a big avenue—eight lanes for traffic and many trees.

Under the downtown area, there was a huge shopping mall, sort of like Winnipeg underneath the corners of Portage and Main.

The Ukraine achieved independence in 1991, and at that time, Ukrainian became the official language.

WE ARRIVED AT Babi Yar. This was the site of one of the largest mass murders ever, where thirty-four thousand Jews were massacred by the Nazis in two days in September, 1941. It is estimated that well over a hundred thousand people were killed here. I had heard so much about this when I was a kid, yet I never thought I would arrive at the ravine. We studied it every single year in

Jewish school. Every year for nine years, we heard about the slaughter that took place there.

Baba means old woman and *yar* means a deep ravine. Many centuries ago, an old woman lived at the bottom of the ravine, hence the name. It was a very isolated place, which is why it was used for the massacre.

In 1941, the Nazis were in Kyiv. On September 28, they ordered all the Jews to report the following morning, with their passports, warm clothes, and with all their belongings. The Jews all thought it was part of a resettlement plan.

On the morning of September 29, 1941, the Jews arrived at Babi Yar. First their passports and other documents were thrown into a huge fire. Then they were made to leave their belongings, strip off all their clothes and walk naked toward the ravine. Once they walked that long kilometre, they were lined up at the edge of the ravine and shot. Those that didn't automatically fall into the ravine were pushed. Thirty-four thousand Jews were thusly massacred. It took the Nazis less than five days to do that. The bodies were never buried. Every day, the Nazis got one hundred men, usually Ukrainians, to burn the bodies and to cover them with dirt. The Nazis tried to hide this massacre and keep it a secret, but some of the people who were hired to burn the bodies told the truth about what they were seeing.

Some people actually escaped. There were twenty-nine known survivors. They were wounded, fell into the ravine with the dead, and then at night, crawled out, some of them through piles of dirt that had been tossed over the bodies. Some of the Ukrainians hid Jews but at the risk of their own lives.

One woman, Dina Pronicheva, survived Babi Yar. She jumped into the ravine, falling with dead bodies, just before she was actually shot. She lay on the huge pile of dead and not quite dead bodies, hearing them cry and feeling them move, pretending to be dead. Germans walked over the bodies, occasionally bending down to take a valuable or two. One SS man kicked his foot against her and became suspicious that she was not dead. He picked her up and struck her. She remained limp and showed no sign of life. Her kicked her again and crushed her hand, cracking the bones. Still, she pretended to be dead. He was finally called away and shortly after, she felt earth fall on her as the bodies were covered with dirt and sand. Still, she did not move. Choking as dirt covered her face, she scraped the dirt off and finally dug herself out of the mire of bodies. It was night and very dark. She managed to grab a little bush at the top of the ravine and pulled herself over the top. Dina Pronicheva survived and told the story of Babi Yar. Subsequently, she became an actress in the Kiev Puppet Theatre; books have been written about her experience.

There was a big discussion about what type of monument should be built on the site of Babi Yar. First the Soviets built a monument, but it was to all victims. The Jews wanted to build a monument specific to the lost lives of the Jews, and after Independence, they did exactly that. It is in the shape of a menorah with writing in Ukrainian, Hebrew, and English.

Every year on September 29, Jews and allies come to Babi Yar for a huge memorial service. The Jews are now very well integrated into Ukrainian society.

At the turn of the century, there were ninety synagogues and three hundred thousand Jews. Now there are four synagogues which serve well the Jewish community.

WE WERE THERE, at Babi Yar. We began to walk down that last kilometre. It was covered in cobblestone and surrounded by trees. The whole ravine was now surrounded by trees, which were not there before. The Jews walked down this path, naked, cold, passports already burned, obviously not going to be resettled anywhere except under the dirt in the ditch. My steps got heavier and heavier, slower and slower. I was pulled to progress down the path, and I wanted to go, to bear witness, but it was hard to walk. In 1941, we would have been surrounded by barbed wire and barking, snarling dogs. My heartbeat quickened. "*Yisgadal v'yishkadesh shmei raboh*" (Hebrew prayer for the dead) came out of my heart and my mouth, automatically, like a surprise. We walked up to the ravine. It was a powerful moment.

When I wrote this, I could feel the tears in my eyes; that morning, I did not dare cry. I didn't know if I would be able to hold it together. So many people died, mothers, children, lovers, *babas*, people other people loved.

We walked down the path along the ravine for a while in silence.

The ravine is two kilometres long and fifty meters deep. Over a hundred thousand people were murdered there. Besides the Jews, the Gypsies were wiped out as well. There was no monument specific to the Gypsies; I wondered why.

There was a concentration camp there as well, also called Babi Yar. The Nazis registered it as a construction company.

We walked by a small section of a Jewish cemetery. It used to be a huge cemetery, but it was wiped out when the Soviets wanted to build a stadium. But after the cemetery was destroyed, the stadium was never built. We saw a headstone that looked like a high shoe lying on its side.

"It has that shape," Natasha explained, "so that when the Messiah comes, it will be easier to leave the grave." Something I never knew.

In 1976, the Soviets built a monument to Babi Yar. It was across the street from the ravine and the Jewish Memorial menorah. There was an artistic competition for the monument and a group of Russian artists were hired. These artists were quite brilliant. From the front, the imposing monument looks like a typical Russian monument, strong people, out of stone, standing upright, etc. But as one started to walk around it, you could see the people slipping into the ravine in the back. In the front, the mother who is feeding a child, is now slipping down in the back. The overall effect is devastating—very brilliant and effective as all the strong figures slide down dead into the ravine.

Right beside this monument, the Jewish Cultural and Heritage Centre was going to be built, by Americans. Construction was to start almost immediately.

At Babi Yar, the area was now full of lush vegetation. Before it was just a deep ravine.

Walking around Babi Yar, I realized I had never looked up; always I kept my eyes down, searching, looking for clues and answers in the ground. They were never found.

WITH GREAT DIFFICULTY, we left Babi Yar to continue our tour of Kyiv. Part of me wanted to stay there. It seemed as though a few hours was such a small amount of time to spend at a place I had heard about over and over in school, a place about which I had nightmares, a place that was never too far from my conscious mind. For some reason, after hearing about Babi Yar so often in school, the massacre had affected me greatly. I learned about a young woman who managed to escape, who found safety in a farmer's home. How could her life ever have become normal after her family all fell dead beside her, after she crawled naked out of a mass grave filled with friends and neighbours, after she made her way, naked and frightened, to a place of safety. When I was young, her age, I thought of this young woman often. And now I was there, still thinking of her. I never knew her name. We learned about other places as well, including of course all the big concentration camps and crematoria. But Babi Yar really stayed with me. And it was painful to leave.

THERE ARE A hundred and fifty political parties in the Ukraine! Victor Yuschenko belongs to the party called "Our Ukraine." There are about four hundred deputies in parliament which represent about four or five parties.

According to Natasha, the biggest positive since 1991 was interesting to me. As Natasha explained, "Now we are Ukrainians, not Russians."

We drove by buildings that were built by Khrushchev in the 1960s. They were all five-story apartment buildings.

KYIV SITS ON the Dneiper River. We drove to Podol, the Jewish district. *Podol* means situated on the Dneiper River. Eighty percent of the population here was Jewish. The big synagogue here was built by Brodsky, "The Sugar King," at the turn of the nineteenth century. It was turned into a stable by the Nazis but is now restored.

In Podol, there are very old buildings, interspersed with very new ones. During the Soviet times, Ukrainian people used to love to shop in Podol, the Jewish district, because their shops often had produce and other things while the other shops had nothing. In this area, it is now not allowed to build multi-storied buildings as the government is trying to preserve the atmosphere. During those days, people lived right on top of each other, in apartments. Often seven families shared a kitchen. The shops were on the ground floors and the families lived on the second and third floors. But most of the people in Kyiv had a *dasha*, as they do now, and during the week-ends, the city is practically deserted.

IN 1811, THERE was a terrible fire, and most of the buildings burnt up. There were twenty-six big fires all together, and then after 1811, the people stopped building their houses out of wood and started using brick.

Between the fourteenth and seventeenth centuries, the Ukraine belonged to Poland. Then there was the war of liberation against the Poles, and the Ukraine became part of the Soviet Union.

Kyiv is very proud of her greenery. She became the capital in 1934. Around that time, the Church of Michael was blown up to make way for a government building (which was never built). This church was first built in the twelfth century and was destroyed by the Tatar Mongols. Of course.

IN 1932 TO 1933, there was an "artificial famine," and –six to ten million people starved. During Stalin's time, people were punished who did not join the state farmers or the collective farms. Stalin did not want people to be independent farmers. One million people were sent to Siberia. There is an incredible exhibit of photos and other artifacts in front of St. Michael's church about this. This atrocity is not well known and was of unbelievable magnitude.

The Saint Michael's Church was built in the twelfth century. It had been completely restored to the identical way it was before, and it was very, very beautiful. It was coloured blue and yellow, (Ukrainian colours) on the grounds of a monastery, and was quite something to see. In the Ukrainian church, like in the Orthodox Russian church, every one stands, even the elderly and infirm, for three to four hours during services. I don't think I could do that! Before the church was blown up, they had managed to save some of the frescoes and mosaics and now had identical copies up in the ceilings. The originals were now in Kyiv, Moscow, and . . . Did I hear an echo from the soul of Russian-Natasha's groups yelling in unison, "The Hermitage!"

I asked Natasha about the reason for the standing in church and she said, "I don't know. Maybe it is just a tradition." I subsequently found out that the standing is done to express respect, like one would stand in the presence of a king. Somehow a very elderly person having to stand upright for four hours at a time does not seem like a respectful act on the part of whomever made the rules for the church in the first place. My back hurt just thinking about it.

St. Sophia church was across the way from St. Michael's, and it was the only remaining church in Kyiv from before. And of course, it was a UNESCO site.

In the square was a lovely statue, and one of the figures was St. Olga, who in the tenth century, went to Constantinople, was baptized there, came back and tried to introduce everyone to Christianity. She was ahead of her time, and it wasn't until the time of her grandson Vladmdir, that people listened to them and began to convert.

WE DROVE BY Red Square, the Main Square where the Orange Revolution took place in December, 2004. For three weeks, people were camped out in the streets. Victor Yuschenko was recovering from his poisoning of the past year and people were cautiously waiting to see how he would do.

Then we went to the Synagogue Lazer Brodsky built. It was renovated in 2000, and was quite posh, with crystal chandeliers. The synagogues were orthodox in style, with a separate place for the women upstairs, but there was one reform synagogue where the men and women could sit together. Brodsky died at the age of fifty-six, in 1904, just six years after the synagogue opened. He was known as the sugar king and yet he died of diabetes.

We walked across the street to see a lovely statue of Sholem Aleichem, the pen name of Solomon Naumovich Rabinovich, a leading Yiddish writer. *Fiddler on the Roof*, the musical, was based on Sholem Aleichem's stories about Tevye the Dairyman. He wrote about Jewish life in Eastern Europe. We used to study about him in Jewish school, and it was really very nice to see a monument dedicated to a Jewish author, a first for me.

THEN AS WE were returning back to the car, we were met by two youths, maybe nine or ten, perhaps a bit older, praying, holding their hands out for alms, pious looks upon their faces, quietly mewing for money, with absolutely angelic faces. And I almost bought it until I looked more closely at their clothes—they were very, very contemporary, new, clean, and the boys definitely weren't starving. So I didn't say anything, but just got into the car without giving them money. As we drove away, the young man stuck up his middle finger at me. I stuck mine up right back at him. There really are some unfortunates on the streets, but these two were definitely not them.

Driving back to the hotel, we went by a building that was going to be thirty-three stories high, and would be the tallest building in Kyiv. There was a need for office space there.

When we told Natasha we were talking the train to Dniepropetrovsk, she told us we had to get some food to eat on the train. We were happy to hear that, as it was almost four pm, we had eaten an early breakfast, and had nothing since. So she took us to a supermarket. There we bought some great salads, chicken, cheese, and other wonderful goodies. I so looked forward to our picnic on the train. We bid *da svedanya* (good-bye) to Natasha and prepared for our train trip to Dniepropetrovsk.

Chapter 20
Traveling to Dniepropetrovsk

SERGEI THE DRIVER picked us up at the hotel, delivered us to the train station, and drove off after putting us in the care of a porter. This porter took the long way to the train. We walked down the tracks, farther and farther, then across the tracks, then up the tracks, farther, then farther and farther still. Then we had to wait until the train was available for boarding. Once it was, all hell broke loose. This train, from Kyiv to Dniepropetrovsk was an express. And we each had a ticket for one seat, but no seat for our luggage. After a lot of hassle, we understood that we had to buy another train seat for our luggage. Which was fine. Mr. Sourpuss was already in our little train compartment of six seats. The porter put the luggage, all seven or eight pieces of it, on the seat across from him. The conductor came in, we played charades again, we paid him some money, and thought we were set. But we had only purchased one extra seat, and there were five people and our luggage sitting in this compartment, none of us any too happy about the turn of events. We tried to buy Mr. Sourpuss a beer, but he declined. And so I was wedged into a seat, surrounded by luggage and people, and literally unable to move or stretch for the next five or more hours. *Oy*. Needless to say, we did not have our picnic on the train. There was no room in there to move, much less unpack. I decided I would try to sleep or otherwise lose consciousness until we got to Dniepropetrovsk.

JUDI WAS SITTING beside someone quite unhappy to be squished between her and her luggage, and I was beside someone else between me and Mr. Sourpuss. None of the guys seemed friendly.

Mr. Sourpuss looked at me.

"English?" he asked.

"*Da* (yes)," I answered. "*Kanada*."

"Ah Kanada."

"English?" I asked him.

"*Nyet*," he responded. Then he asked, "*Francais*?"

"*Un petit peu* (a little)," I answered. With my eyebrows I asked if he spoke French.

"*Nyet,*" was the reply.

Then he asked, "*Deutch?*"

"*Ja, ein bißchen* (a little)," I answered. "And you?"

"*Nyet.*"

Why was he asking me if I could speak all these languages if he could not? I went to sleep.

HOWEVER, EVEN THOUGH this train was an express, it made several stops, and after one of the early ones the guy sitting between me and Mr. Sourpuss got off. That relieved the situation in our compartment somewhat, but Mr. Sourpuss still wasn't smiling and the other fellow was fairly grim as well. I started running a high fever quite suddenly for some reason and fell into a deep sleep for a while, so my body could sweat off some of the fever. When I awoke about two hours later, Judi, who could make friends with a stone, and the fellow next to her, were having an intense but very friendly conversation (in English) and Mr. Sourpuss was smiling—well, maybe that's an exaggeration, but nevertheless, the ambience in the compartment was much friendlier.

I looked out the window and saw that it was getting dark. We had grown used to "white nights," and were not used to darkness at night. It was ten pm and although I could make out the houses and trees, it was beginning to darken considerably.

Soon we stopped at a little town called Pyatikhatki (means five houses). I looked out the train window and saw hundreds, maybe thousands, of stuffed animals, some very large, sitting on the train platform.

"Wow, what is this?"

Konstantine, for that was the name of Judi's new friend, explained that it was a toy market, and all these stuffed animals were made in that region. They were really beautiful, individually, and what a sight to see so many of them sitting passively watching the trains go by.

KONSTANTINE WAS A lawyer who was returning from Kyiv after taking his second out of three exams to become a judge. He and Judi talked for hours while I dozed, waking on and off for another cup of Russian tea and lemon. Once I woke and they were talking about Moscow. I heard Konstantin say, "I think Moscow is not a city—it is a country!"

The train traveled down the track between Kyiv and Dniepropetrovsk. I sat there in my febrile state, thinking about my paternal grandmother, who may have ridden on these very rails. When she was a young woman, she went with her mother to marry my grandfather who was in Ekaterinoslav, which used to be Dniepropetrovsk before 1926. I don't believe she had yet met my grandfather. On the train, quite unexpectedly, her mother died. My grandmother got off the train at the next town, sought out the local rabbi and asked for direction. She had no idea what to do. The rabbi told her to bury her mother in that town, and get back on the next train and go marry my grandfather. Which she did. I can't imagine a young girl of eighteen, burying her mother alone in a strange town, and then getting on a train to marry a man she had never met. As it happens, the next part of the story turned out very well, as my grandparents had a great life together and things did work out extremely well for them both. For all my grandmother knew, the man she was going to marry could have been a wife beater, and/or an alcoholic, or who knew what else. However, as she soon discovered, he was a lovely man, intelligent, gentle and loving. But the story of my great-grandmother had been haunting me and I had wanted to come here to tell her that everything turned out okay. So I did. On the train tracks. And wherever she may be, I'm sure she received the message.

As we got closer to Dniepropetrovsk, I kept thinking, my grandmother could have seen this, my grandfather might have sat there; everything I looked at I tried to relate to them.

Then we arrived. No porters in Dniepropetrovsk, this city of 1.2 million people. But luckily for us, our excellent travel agent Jane once again came through for us and there was a sign with our name on it. Yuliya and her driver met us and helped us carry our prodigious baggage to the car. After loading all the luggage and four people into the car, one of whom was still partly comatose (me!), we were off to the tourist hotel.

"WELL," YULIYA EXPLAINED, "we do not have too many tourists here, so our hotels are not really so good." It was a big hotel, with a large lobby, but something about it was, well, imposing in a not very welcoming manner. But I was too tired to care. I let everyone help me, collapsed into bed, and slept it all off, waking up the next morning good as new and ready to start a new day of touring in Dniepropetrovsk. Now that I have learned how to pronounce it, it is kind of fun. No more "D-city" for me, which was what we called it before.

OUR ROOM AT the hotel was much smaller than the one we had in Kyiv. When we got our luggage in, there was virtually no floor space left. There were two beds, but they were like camp cots, really, and there were two tables and a fridge. The bathroom was interesting. There were taps over the sink and a hose which led to the shower so you turned on the sink taps, flicked a switch, and voila, instant shower in the tub. It was funky and would do nicely. It had manual air conditioning (we opened the window) and it had been fairly hot and muggy out, but we managed.

Every floor had its own attendant who was the keeper of the keys and I suppose, all the news and gossip about all the guests. They were very nice to us.

YULIYA HAD ARRANGED to pick us up at ten am as I wanted to sleep a bit. So we went down for breakfast into the breakfast room. The waitresses were all dressed similarly—in silky white blouses with telling vents in the sleeves and other parts, the shortest tight black skirts I have seen in a while, and shoes. No socks and stockings. I guess they thought it looked attractive, I'm not sure. They all looked like very nice people to me, but I didn't get why they dressed like that, especially first thing in the morning. But we did get our breakfast—Judi got her eggs, and away we went, ready to tour Dniepropetrovsk/Ekaterinoslav.

DNIEPROPETROVSK WAS a city of 1.2 million people, and it was situated on the Dnieper River. There were five cities in the Ukraine with over one million people—Kyiv was first and Dniepropetrovsk was fourth in size.

In 1251, the Tatar Mongols destroyed everything. Of course they did. And then everything got restored. Of course it did.

The city had its own circus as most of the larger cities did. There was a metro and "electric" transportation—streetcars or trams. There were fifteen higher education institutes or universities there.

There was a large bridge in the city, which was built in 1873 by Russian engineers. At that time it was the largest bridge in the world. My ancestors most likely crossed that bridge. After the bridge was built, the region started to develop. There were lots of rich mineral resources around there, iron, coal, and manganese, and they all came together in Ekaterinoslav as the city was then called. Large plants came to be built, and the Germans, Poles, and Belgians all contributed to them.

Ekaterinoslav was named after Catherine II, but in 1926, after the Russian Revolution, the city's name was changed to Dniepropetrovsk after Petrovsky, who was the first head of the Soviet Ukraine, and the Dneiper River, on which it is situated. There used to be a huge plant in the middle of the city, a silk cloth mill which made uniforms that were worn by the emperor even. But then it was decided that no plants could be in the middle of the city. The silk plant remained, but it was now a bakery. This "bakery" was amazing—eight huge

Doric columns in front—it looked like such a grand building. I should have asked to sample the bread—I'm sure it would have been delicious coming from such a noble edifice.

AFTER DRIVING AROUND the town a bit, we stopped at the Dniepropetrovsk Historic Museum. Outside the museum, we saw the stony *babas*. Now *baba* does mean grandmother, although usually it is *babushka*, but *baba* also means idol. These grave monuments were –nine to twelve centuries old and were positively prehistoric looking. Very amazing.

The whole museum was quite neat, although we were mostly interested in the parts dealing with Ekaterinoslav at the turn of the century, as that is when our ancestors were there. However, they had amazing exhibits which dated from Paleolithic times. They had unearthed a grave of a person who was in a fetal position and then the archeologists discovered that they were buried in the same way that they were born. It was most fascinating.

Then we went into the section of the museum about the Cossacks. They had wonderful exhibits about them. The Cossacks lived in these fortress things called *siche*s. There were five in this area out of a total of eight. The *sich* was divided into an inner section, with a church, of course, and a courtyard and that's where they had their meetings and gatherings. Then there was an outer section and even a third citadel, all enclosed by a huge fence and high walls. The only women allowed were those who worked in the outer circle. No women were allowed to live in the *siches*, or even visit. Even Catherine II. No wonder she liquidated them!

The women lived on settlements, where they gardened and lived peacefully until their Cossack men came home for the winter.

The Cossacks originated in the fifteenth century or so. A Cossack was a "free person who can carry weapons." The Cossacks didn't care so much about clothes, but they always had to carry a pipe and a sabre. They smoked both regular tobacco and "happy tobacco." They built these *siches* and close to four thousand men lived in each of them. They became very strong. They organized originally because they lived in a very fertile area; lots of fishing and hunting and good growing, and people (particularly the Tatar Mongols) were always trying to move in. So the Cossacks formed to protect their land. Later, the Cossacks were also running from religious persecution.

The *siches* became so strong they were like an independent state. They were starting negotiations with Turkey, and Catherine II was afraid that the Cossacks and the Turks would join together against her. So she eradicated them all. The last *sich* was destroyed in 1775.

Then Catherine II invited different people to come settle in the area. Everyone would be free. In 1778, Catherine did come to the area. A lot of people were given titles, Cossacks too. They had this huge book, with all the titles written into it. There were very many. The last entry was in 1914. They tried to hide it after the revolution because it was forbidden to have titles. The revolutionary brothers would not have approved.

Prince Potyomkin was a favourite of Catherine II. He helped plan Ekaterinoslav, built the church, and erected a huge palace for when Catherine would visit, but she never did. In fact, he never even lived in it. Now it is a place for the students, where they have conferences, meetings, gatherings, etc. It is constructed in the shape of an eagle. From the air, it looks like a well-proportioned eagle with wings out. It was bombed during WWII. The students helped to reconstruct it, so it was given to the students for their use.

In the mid-nineteenth century, the population of the land was one-third Russians, one-third Ukrainians, and one-third Jews. At times, the Jews were even in the majority.

I particularly liked the photos and other depictions of life around the turn of the century, because that's when my grandparents were there.

Pushkin was exiled to Dniepropetrovsk as well, for his "freedom loving poetry."

I LAUGHED MANY times about how we were so misunderstood because of our accents. In the museum, I had said something like, "Oh, we saw something similar in Kizhi."

Yuliya asked, "Oh, is that in Japan?"

"No, it's in Russia. Kizhi."

"Ah," she got it, "Kizhi." I had not pronounced it properly.

And yesterday, when Judi was talking to Konstantin about his life, she asked if he had a *dasha*.

"A what?"

"Dasha."

He looked at her so puzzled.

"You know," she started to explain, "a *dasha*, a house where you go . . ."

"Ah," he exclaimed, "you mean a *dasha*!"

"Yes, exactly."

DNIEPROPETROVSK USED TO be a closed city; tourists were not allowed to visit here. Dniepropetrovsk wasn't even on most maps because of the military installations. They had nuclear rockets. Now the Ukraine is a nuclear free country. During the cold war in the 1950s and 1960s between the USSR and USA, in Dniepropetrovsk they invented a war rocket which had in its warhead ten nuclear charges a thousand times stronger than the ones used in Japan. They also had two hundred false charges. Enemies couldn't distinguish which was true and which was false and these rockets were impossible to defeat (so they said). The rocket was called "The Devil." But it was because of this rocket that the cold war came to an end.

The plant was still there, and was the capital of the rocket industry, but they built modern satellites for space, underwater exploration, forest fires, weather satellites, and much more, all very advanced.

The city opened to tourists in 1985-86, but they didn't really start coming until the 1990s. The city was still not really geared to tourism. There were no air-conditioned buses, no tourist facilities, and as Yuliya says, "Well, as you could tell, the hotel is not the best."

I asked Yuliya what the biggest difference was for the Ukrainians since 1991 and Independence.

"Well," she answered, "we are no longer Soviets, we are Ukrainians." It seemed as though that was the answer from just about everyone here.

AFTER THE MUSEUM, and just one church, we went for lunch. The church was beautiful, and was in the process of being restored. It was on the site where Potyomkin built the church for Catherine. Inside it was very ornate, with lots of paintings and gilded artwork and much blue and yellow. But what impressed me the most were the constant number of old *babas, babushkas* in place, and young people as well, coming in, bowing and crossing themselves and ardently praying and lighting candles. There were no formal services when we were there, but there sure were a lot of folks doing their religious things.

WE LUNCHED AT the *Kosatski Forteytsya* or the Cossacks' Castle or fortress. It was a charming restaurant, with wooden tables ornately carved, and carved wooden decorations on the walls and ceiling. As well, embroidered fabric hung on the walls. The waitresses were in typical Ukrainian dress, and Ukrainian music played in the background.

The waitress first brought some bread and house appetizers, which she insisted I try. She didn't have to do much insisting. First there was this creamy spread called *sala* which was pure garlic. She took my knife, put some on a piece of bread, and practically fed it to me. It was good. Next was this red stuff.

"What do you call this?" Judi asked.

"*Chrain,*" was the answer.

I tasted it and *chrain* (horseradish) it was, a very good *chrain.*

The third stuff was *garchisa*, a mustard that was so hot it made the hottest *wasabi* I've ever had seem like water.

Then I had *borscht*. It was a huge bowl, really huge, and as delicious as it was, I could only eat half of it. Yuliya told me the waitress wanted to bring me the Cossack *borscht*, which was *borscht* in a loaf of bread, which would have been twice as big. They eat big portions here! And after the *borscht*, I had what was turning into my favourite Ukrainian meal (could it be because I can order it in Ukrainian?). I had *cutleta*, and *kartoshiki ukrainski* (meat and potatoes). Mmmm, good.

AFTER LUNCH WE went to the big synagogue in this city. It is called the Golden Rose, no one quite seemed to know why. It was initially built in Ekaterinoslav in 1800, burnt down in 1833, and then rebuilt. After the revolution, the Soviets used it as a cultural club for a sewing factory. In 2000, it was restored to a synagogue. Adjacent to the synagogue is the Jewish Cultural Centre, which functioned as a school, a library with archives, a computer room, a deli which sold kosher foods, and more.

IN 1913, IN Ekaterinoslav, there were seventeen Orthodox churches, four foreign churches and thirty-eight synagogues. The main one was the Golden Rose synagogue, called something else at the time. Actually, in 1907, there were forty-one synagogues in the city, and 134 in the surrounding area. Today, there is just this one synagogue for praying, and another very old one which functions as a *yeshiva*, and where they do social programs for the elderly and infirm. There are about fifty thousand Jews in Dniepropetrovsk now, but only several thousand of them are involved in Jewish life.

We hung out in the library of the cultural centre for a while, chatting with several people there, perusing old historical books telling about the life and times at the turn of the century.

THEN, BECAUSE JUDI wasn't feeling too well (her turn today to be under the weather), she went to lie down while I went to the supermarket with Yuliya to do a bit of shopping. I loved going to the supermarket. Most things were familiar, even if occasionally they were unrecognizable. Not like Japan where I had no idea what I was looking at—here I sort of knew and just enjoyed reading all the labels and seeing the packaging and especially, watching the local people.

FOR DINNER THAT evening, Judi and I walked across the street and strolled along the Dneiper River until we came to the Red Cock Restaurant, thusly named after one of Pushkin's fairy tales. It was a wonderful place, all wood, heavily decorated in *Ukrainski* modern. We were seated outside on a balcony hanging out over the river. It was delightful. A singer strumming on his guitar entertained us intermittently, and the other diners entertained us all of the time. Unfortunately, Judi wasn't feeling too well and wasn't eating much, but I managed just fine with my *kartoshke ukrainski* and *shashlyk* (well, I wasn't going to have exactly the same thing for every meal!).

After dinner, we strolled back along the river, past lovers and friends also strolling, or sitting on the walls, or past diners in other restaurants drinking and singing. Yup, we were in the heart of the Ukraine.

We kept looking up at the bridge and saying, "You know, I bet *bobbe* and *zaide* (grandmother and grandfather) used to walk over this bridge all the time."

Or, "I bet they strolled down this very street, don't you think?"

THE NEXT DAY we were to leave for Poland and the land of the Euros. For my last night in the Ukraine and Russia, I would like to present my version of a very abridged Russian and Ukrainian history, (which probably applies to all the "stans" and other countries around here as well): It goes like this:

1. The Tatar Mongols destroy everything.
2. Everything is restored, especially the churches.
3. There is a revolution.
4. Independence is gained.

Part V

Europe

Chapter 21
On To Poland

YULIYA ASSURED US that people at the airport at Dniepropetrovsk would speak English as she waved goodbye to us. She lied. The driver dropped us off, helped us with our luggage, but had no idea where to go. After running around the airport with my ticket flapping from his hand, he shrugged, pointed to a bench, and said, "Wait." So we did. And did. And did. I asked every uniformed person I saw if he or she spoke English. "*Nyet,*" was the consistent reply. I went to the Information counter at the airport.

"Do you speak English?"

"*Nyet.*"

Finally, a lovely young woman dressed all in white like the savior angel she was told us, "I am going on the same flight to Kyiv as you are. I will tell you when to go. But now, wait." And we did.

Airports there were very different than what we were used to. There was no formal check-in counter as far as we could tell. We were told to be there two hours prior to our flight, which we were, but everything was locked up until less than an hour before flight time. All our luggage was still with us, of course. So tickets in our pockets, we sat down to wait.

Finally, we followed the white angel into a departure lounge after an announcement in Ukrainian was made. We still had all our luggage and had to put it through a security conveyor belt. When we finally found a counter with an attendant, I asked if we could check our luggage through to Warsaw, even using the Ukrainian name for Warsaw. The answer? "*Nyet.* Only Kyiv."

"Okay."

We loaded all our luggage on the scale to be ticketed.

"You have excess baggage," the agent said. All of a sudden, she can speak English. "You will pay 220 *hryvnias.*"

"Okay."

"You will put your luggage there." Her English was rapidly improving. So after she ticketed the luggage, I had to go behind the counter, and lift all our luggage onto the conveyor belt.

"Okay."

Then a bunch of people were getting onto a bus, presumably to get on to the plane, so we stood in line.

"*Nyet*," said the agent at the door. "Wait."

So we sat down again. And waited. And waited.

THE PLANE WAS a cute little prop job. But it really was quite a pleasant flight and soon we were in Kyiv. We picked up our luggage and navigated through one terminal into the international terminal, checked in, and were off to Poland.

WE ARRIVED IN Warsaw, not sure if we were being met or not. The plan was to get ourselves to the train station, and get on a train for the hour ride to Krakow. Neither of us relished the idea of loading our stuff in a cab, unloading it at the train station, loading it onto the train, unloading it at the train station, loading it into a cab, unloading it at the hotel. You get the picture.

And then a voice in my ear said, "Maybe you are looking for a ride?"

Enter Jan (pronounced Yahn). He was a cab driver, and after we ascertained that no one was there to meet us, we thought we would use him to take us to the train station.

"Maybe you would like to ride in my car to Krakow?" he asked.

Now this definitely tweaked our interest.

Here is this strange man, in a strange city, offering to drive us to another strange city. Hmmm. I know it doesn't make sense, but something about him was just fine. Maybe when he said his first, "*Oi yoi yoi.*" Somehow that endeared him to me immediately. We started to walk with him to the car park, because at the very least we needed to get to the train station. He immediately took care of our luggage.

IN THE UKRAINE, the cars had been, well, pretty minimalist. So I didn't relish sitting for several hours in a car like the ones we had been driving in for the past few days.

"Well," asked Jan, "to the train station or to Krakow?"

"Hmm, what kind of car do you have?"

"A Mercedes. Good car." He smiled. Indeed.

"How long will it take us to drive to Krakow?"

"Three hours," he responded.

It was 3:45 pm, the train was not supposed to leave until six pm, arriving at seven, so the time would have been the same, and getting into one car and being delivered directly to our hotel was very tempting.

I looked into his face. Jan was forty-eight years old, a large man, who was wearing a fashionable sports jacket. He had a very friendly look about him and twinkly eyes which brought a smile to my face.

I looked at Judi and we both nodded.

"Okay, Jan, off to Krakow."

And off we went. We had a fabulous time! First of all, we chatted. No, first of all, he really had a Mercedes, which was intensely comfortable. We chatted a bit about his life, his wife, and his two sons. His English was good enough for us to talk simply about things. He was totally adorable.

"Do you like Italian music?" he asked.

"Sure, why not."

He slid a CD into the slot. A nice Italian love song came on. The next song was a bit more upbeat, and I thought I kept hearing strange things. Wasn't that "pepperoni" I heard? And "coca cola"? Sure enough, there was this song called "Zuppa Romana," where for three minutes and nineteen seconds the musicians sang only words of food and drink, and it all rhymed. It was absolutely hysterical, and it pleased me no end. We played it over and over and over again until we could all sing along: *mortadella, mozzarella*, on and on we sang.

JAN LOVED HIS Mercedes and drove it well. And fast. It was sort of fun going fifteen thousand km/hr, or so it felt, kind of like the MagLev in China, while listening to this inane Italian song, "Zabayone, minestrone," as the Polish countryside slid by. *Vino seco, amaretto, ricoletto.* I did, however, wear a seat belt for the first time in weeks (they were not an option in the Ukraine), not only because they were there but because Jan was driving excessively fast. *Langostini, tortollini*, the song continued.

But we laughed and sang and talked and very soon we were in Krakow. After going to our original hotel and being told we had to stay down the street, at another hotel, we were soon settled, more or less, at Hotel Matejko, named after a famous Polish painter.

When we checked in, all our luggage was sitting in the lobby.

"What do we do now?" we asked Blondie behind the desk.

"You go to your room." She pointed. We both burst out laughing and went to our room. Our luggage followed after a while.

WE ASKED BLONDIE where to eat and she recommended a place just down the block. The restaurant was called *Restauracya Jarema—Polska Kuchnia Kresowa* (Eastern Polish Cooking).

The menu was in three languages, Polish, German, and English. Many people here speak German; in fact, when we first came in, the woman who greeted us did not speak English and so I had to speak German with her to arrange for dinner.

I passed over the appetizer of "sparagrus with garlic sauce." I almost went for the "Dumplings with liver and grits" and the "backed (sic) potato pudding," but instead had a specialty of the house, which was very good. For a drink, I ordered *Wesola Dama*, the ingredients of which were *passoa, wodka, sok pomaranczowy*. I had no idea what that was, but I recognized the vodka in it, so how bad could it be? In fact, it was delicious. We had a wonderful dinner, eating well and copiously.

IN THE MORNING, Agnes, our guide for the day, awaited us. One of the reasons I came to Poland was to go to Auschwitz. I felt it was important for me to go at least once in my life, to bear witness, to walk through that horror of the past. But I am ahead of myself. First Agnes. She was a delightful twenty-eight year old; a slight woman, with short cropped red hair and an intelligent demeanor. She turned out to be an extremely clever and well-informed young woman. She came together with a driver and a very fine (ie comfortable) van. And so we set off. As we drove, Agnes told us a little about Poland.

Poland was situated in the middle between east and west, and, as Agnes explained, the "souls and character" of the people were a mixture. Poland shared borders with seven other countries, and Krakow was in the southeast corner. Krakow was on the Wisla River which flowed into the Bay of Gdansk.

Krakow had a population of about 750,000. Warsaw's population was over 1.5 million.

We drove by a huge "meadow" in the city, called Blonya Meadow. Agnes explained that it was a place where people gathered for certain events. When the pope died, there were over one million people in that meadow. When the pope was still alive, he would hold masses there for two million people at a time.

Agnes spoke a bit about the past pope, who was from Krakow. When he was young, he wanted to be an actor, and he wrote poetry and drama as a young man. During WWII, he went into the seminary, and rose through the ranks quickly. He became pope in 1978, and had many friends and family in Krakow.

We heard about the dynasties of the past in Poland. At the end of the eighteenth century, Poland was partitioned between Russia, Prussia, and Austria. For over one hundred years, Poland did not exist on a map. Warsaw belonged to Russia, Krakow to Austria. After WWI, Poland regained independence. The Poles never lost their sense of identity, even though the children were not allowed to learn Polish before the war. People were sent to Siberia for studying Polish.

Just before WWI, the first Polish organizations were set up, and in 1918, Independence was achieved. But then after twenty years, WWII happened. Ninety percent of Warsaw was destroyed. The uprising in Warsaw involved young people, the ones who grew up in an Independent Poland. The uprising lasted two months. The Soviets sat there and watched. The British sat there and watched. The Soviets were happy to see all the young people die as they were the very ones against communism. After Warsaw and most of the young population was destroyed, the Russians moved in and took over.

From WWII until 1989, Poland was ruled by the Soviets. Then there was the big round table talk and the situation changed.

In 2004, Poland joined the European Union. Poland does not use the Euro yet though. The currency is the *zloty* (which means gold), divided into 100 *groszy*. As soon as the economic situation strengthens a bit, they will switch over to Euros. The unemployment rate was about twenty percent. There were virtually no social services. Agnes told us that things overall were starting to get better, there was a slow improvement, but there was still no money. The previous day, Jan had told us almost the exact same things. Apparently the younger generation had embraced capitalism, but some groups had not fared well in the transition; groups like old age pensioners, farmers, the unemployed, still suffered financially.

The question: Is it better to have everything available now and no money to buy any of it *or* have things given to the people, for example, social services, but not have a choice or not have very much variety.

The answer: No one seemed to know.

Many people spoke German in Poland. Kids were all learning English in school at an early age. When Agnes was in primary school, she learned Russian. Now the primary second language has switched to English.

The situation between Poland and Russia was difficult. There was a lot of enmity between the two countries. Putin was seen as a major controller. It was interesting after coming from Russia where Elena, the young, intelligent political scientist, thought Putin was wonderful, and now here in Poland, Agnes, the young, intelligent political scientist, thought Putin was terrible.

We talked a bit about what it meant to be an EU member. Agnes said that now at least Europe listens a bit more to Poland's voice. Poland is the ninth largest country in Europe, but has been ignored for so long. Poles remember when no one helped them during partition, during WWII, after WWII when the Soviets controlled things. It all happened without blood being spilled. Poland was just forgotten. And now, they just want to be heard.

The Poles are upset at being ignored. They are somewhat anti-Russian because of this, as Putin tended to ignore the Poles. The President of Poland, Kwashniewski, then in his second term, went to Russia for a big event, and the Poles felt he was quite ignored on that trip. However, he said he went to pay tribute to the Poles who were buried in Russia, and he did that. We shall see what develops in the future.

Poland has much to offer the European Community. There was lots of coal mining, as well as iron and salt. Agriculture was very strong there. And tourism had started to become a big industry.

A word about tourism: Poland, and especially Krakow, was one of the biggest surprises of the trip. It was absolutely wonderful. The hotel was definitely one of the very best we had stayed in on the whole trip. It was a smallish hotel, but the rooms were large, well-appointed, clean, everything worked well. Cars were big and clean. Most people spoke English or German or French. There were lots of great restaurants with wonderful Polish food. There was a myriad of fascinating things to see, and it was very easy to get around. Krakow was a walking city, with many of the main streets closed to vehicular traffic. I wish I could have spent at least another week there, as I had barely scratched the surface. I felt two days was probably enough time to be in Dniepropetrovsk, but two weeks would be nothing in Krakow. I knew I would be recommending it highly for anyone wanting an interesting and stimulating holiday.

Chapter 22
Auschwitz

WE WERE IN the van driving to Auschwitz. Agnes told us that when she was a teenager in school, it was obligatory for all students to go to Auschwitz. I wished that were the case in North America!

Auschwitz was about an hour by car out of Krakow. First we arrived at the town of Oswiecim. This town was established in the thirteenth century, and was a nice Polish city when we were there, with a big Jewish community. It has/had a very good rail junction, and there were many empty barracks that the Polish army used before the war, so the Germans decided to use that area for their camp. It was easily isolated and camouflaged. Oswiecim was a normal city of 45,000; that was where the Auschwitz museum was situated. Oswiecim was the Polish name; Auschwitz was the German name for the same place.

In pre-war Krakow, there were seventy-thousand Jews, twenty-five percent of the population. After WWII, there were five thousand Jews in Krakow. Agnes said that now there were a hundred and fifty Jews in Krakow. Somehow I found that difficult to believe, but I guess it may be so.

Auschwitz camp was initially started for Polish political prisoners. In 1940-41, only Poles were interned there. Mostly these were the intellectuals and radicals, anyone considered to be an enemy of the Nazi system. Then the Nazis brought Russians, and then . . .

In 1941, Himmler, head of the SS, came to Auschwitz and ordered them to extend the camp. Then in 1942, there was a meeting of fifteen Nazis, mostly lawyers, all educated men, and they developed the "final solution" concept, which was extended throughout Europe. Auschwitz was chosen as a "death camp" in 1942.

I AM NOT inclined to write about the history of Auschwitz and all that happened there; hopefully, this information is already known. And I have to say that spending almost a full day at Auschwitz and Birkenau, there really were not any big surprises for me, nothing astounding or new that I learned. But the feelings we had, well, that was why I went there.

The first thing, of course, was the sign. There it was: *Arbeit Macht Frei* (work sets you free), just the way I'd seen it in countless images. My heart rate increased when I first saw it. It was so familiar in one way, and yet so horrible. Auschwitz was originally supposed to be a show camp. Prisoners had planted trees, and although it was surrounded by an electrified fence, it was supposed to be the show place for the Nazis to send images back through Europe.

When prisoners first got off the train and walked under that sign, they walked past the camp orchestra. Every time work details came and went, they walked past the camp orchestra, playing marches, while the Nazis filmed much of it. But the real reason for the orchestra was that it helped prisoners keep in step and was easier that way to count them as they went to and from work. What a macabre concept.

If a prisoner escaped, their family was rounded up and brought to the camp. There, they had to stand (or sometimes were hung) until the fugitive returned. The Nazis did this to maintain discipline through fear. It worked.

AUSCHWITZ HAD BECOME a museum. There was no entry cost, so as many people as possible could come through it. I saw some amazing things there. I saw an urn containing ashes from the ruins of crematorium #5. It was set up as a memorial, to commemorate all who perished. Those ashes could be anyone, Jewish, Polish, Russian, gypsy, male, female, child, old person. It was a moving memorial.

Our Auschwitz guide was Sebastian, a twenty-eight-year-old economist who started guiding visitors seven years ago when he was in university. He thought it would be for the summer, but he was still there. He was amazing—such a wealth of information. And of course, he had met so many people, survivors, Jewish, Nazi, Polish. His own grandfather died at Auschwitz. Sebastian had a four-year-old son and a ten-month-old daughter. He gave tours at Auschwitz in English, Spanish, and Polish.

Sebastian told us that they could prove that 1.5 million were killed there for sure, but that is a minimum. Most likely it was 2.5 million or more, but he said he was only allowed to say what they could absolutely prove. But they do know that because so many of the people who came to Auschwitz went right from the train to the gas chambers without being registered, that the numbers are actually much higher than those for which they have documentation.

We walked into a large room with photos and other displays. There were groups there touring in Hebrew, Korean, Polish, English, German, French. That was a good feeling.

ACCORDING TO THE Nazis, at the time of the "final solution," there were eleven million Jews living in Europe. We saw the papers that documented all of this, so serious, as though they were doing something of importance for the world, not decimating it. The Nazis wrote about "the nest of European insects." There were three million Jews in Poland, so they wanted a death camp in the middle of the "nest."

The conditions in the ghettos in which the Jews lived were so bad, that they desperately wanted to believe resettlement was an option, a hope for the future. They eagerly embraced what the Nazis told them in the hope of wanting to be resettled. The Nazis even sold Jews non-existent plots of land, or offered them work in fictitious factories. Sebastian told us about talking to one of those people.

"Didn't you hear rumours, weren't you suspicious?" he asked him.

"Of course we heard rumours," the survivor answered. "My father wanted to believe in resettlement and felt that as long as there was a war and the Nazis needed labour, the Jews would be okay (Nazis had said that all the "subhumans" would work for them). My mother felt we would be killed. I felt that even if the rumours were true, they did not apply to me."

This is not unlike the fact that every day millions of people die in car accidents, and yet when we get into our car each day, we do not expect to be one of them.

As the people came into the camps, the selection was made. The Nazis told the prisoners they were protecting the weaker people from harder work. The weaker people were, of course, killed, but they didn't know that until the very, very end, which is why they were all so docile. Seventy to eighty percent of Jews that came to Auschwitz never stopped there; they went from the trains directly to the crematoria. They died before they were even prisoners.

I HAD HEARD an anecdote years ago about an incident at Auschwitz and wanted to ask Sebastian if he knew about it. This was what I had heard: A group of naked women were in line waiting to go into the gas chamber. There were about twenty armed Nazis standing around, making remarks about them and laughing. All of a sudden, one woman started to do a very seductive dance and focused on one of the Nazis. They started to laugh and cheer her on. She got more and more seductive and came right up to the Nazi soldier. The Nazis roared with approval. As she wound her naked body around his, she grabbed his gun and killed him. She was immediately shot.

Sebastian said he was not sure if that was a separate incident or if it was one of the "urban myths" that came from another true incident: There were about twenty Nazis standing in changing room #2. One woman started shouting at them, saying they were human swine, etc. The Nazis laughed at her. She walked up to one and in a struggle, shot him, but only wounded him. He apparently walked with a limp for the rest of his life. She, of course, was immediately shot.

WE WALKED INTO a room where we saw cans and pellets of cyclone B, which turned into hydrogen cyanide and killed everyone. Cyclone B was originally a disinfectant. The Nazis used over twenty tons a year.

When the people were being gassed, they really had no idea of what was happening. In the changing room, there were told to undress, put their clothes on a hook and remember their number. The children were asked to keep their shoelaces together. The prisoners were proud to be Jewish, would be singing *Hatikvah*, and they never showed any fear. *Hatikvah*, which is now the national anthem of the state of Israel, had previously been a popular anthem of the Jews. *Hatikvah* means "the hope." The fact that they sang and showed no fear was basically because they had no idea what lay ahead.

We talked for a long while about Mandelbaum, the last survivor of the *Sondercommandos*, who lived forty kilometres away from Auschwitz. Sebastian had met him on many occasions. The *sondercommandos* were Jewish work units whose main job was to dispose of the bodies in the gas chambers. They were forced into these units by being threatened with death if they did not follow their orders. The *sondercommandos* helped the Jews keep their dignity until the very end. Their job wasn't entirely negative, as the people who were being killed went into the showers with dignity, and with no fear or pain. However, in fifteen to twenty minutes, one thousand people would be dead.

Then the *sondercommandos* had to remove all the gold fillings, and cut all the hair off the women. All of the women had to have gynecological exams in case they had hidden something of value. The *sondercommando units* did all this under the watchful eyes of the Nazis.

The *sondercommandos* lived in the attic above the gas chambers. Their barracks were kept separate and they were fed better than other prisoners because they had to be very physically able to do the work assigned to them, which of course benefited the Nazis. Because they knew the Nazis' "secrets" about the gas chambers, they were regularly executed, sometimes every three months, and new units were formed.

Mandelbaum was an amazing man—I had seen him being interviewed on TV shortly before I left on this trip. He seemed to have hope for the future. He had forgiven the Nazis and harbored no hatred for them.

If a young Nazi at Auschwitz "had enough," they had no choice really—they could ask to leave, but they would get sent to the Eastern front which was a death sentence.

At one point, Mandelbaum was feeling suicidal and angry and went up to a young Nazi, Jurgen Kunstleman. He called him a swine as well as other epithets, fully expecting to be shot. Jurgen looked about, and after ascertaining no other Nazis were around, turned quietly to Mandelbaum, and with tears running down his cheeks said, "The worst thing is that you are right." And he walked away. After the war, Mandelbaum wanted to meet him and apologize for calling him a swine. He felt Jurgen had no more choice in his job as a Nazi than he did in being one of the *sondercommandos.*

"The more I work here, the more confused I get." Sebastian sighed, as we talked about moral right and judgments.

IN PARTS OF Poland, in the 1940s, Canada had become synonymous with being wealthy. Canada was thought to be a place of great riches and resources, and so it was a natural that the Polish prisoners nicknamed the huge warehouses "Canada." The Nazis picked this up from the Polish prisoners, and hence *Kanada* I and *Kanada* II, the two huge warehouses, came into being.

We walked by two tons of human hair, used for mattresses, pillows, robes, cloth, etc. The Nazis did not want to waste a thing. The hair was found in a warehouse at the time of liberation.

We walked by exhibits of eyeglasses, and exhibits of *talleisim* (prayer shawls). We saw more exhibits of artificial limbs and disability paraphernalia. With all these displays, it always took a minute to figure out what we were looking at, what we were seeing, because the piles were so big and so out of context, in a way. Huge piles of dishes and cups, mounds of leather suitcases, with names and addresses written on them, ninety thousand shoes (just a tiny part of those confiscated), piles of brushes (many without handles as they were valuable) were all displayed with information about where they were found.

GONZALES WAS BORN in Auschwitz. His mother was from Italy. He survived the camp and was liberated. Kids under fourteen (except twins) were killed immediately, but Gonzales was born quite late in the war, and apparently, the Nazis were amused that he was there. He lived in the camp for two years before he was freed. I thought it was almost unbelievable that a baby could be born and survive for more than two years under the conditions that existed then.

Mengele, of course, did experiments on twins. Only forty-six twins survived from a total of over six hundred. Sebastian told us about talking to one of the surviving twins. She couldn't believe that "Uncle Josef" had killed their friends. Mengele was known for treating the twins well, giving them chocolate, toys, food, and other goodies—until he killed or tortured them, of course. But the living twins didn't know Mengele was involved in the deaths of the other twins.

THE NAZIS THOUGHT the Slavs were "dirty bloody sub-humans" and that the Jews were "animals."

Every time we came out of a barrack, where we had seen some exhibit, I found myself gulping for fresh air, breathing it in, looking up at the sky. I could not imagine, ever, what it must have been like.

We looked at the "death wall," where the executions took place. The prisoners had trials, but it was a kangaroo court. The Nazis tried to do everything efficiently, and run things "right." So the prisoners had a "trial" and then were shot at the death wall.

We saw the place where Rudolph Hoss, the first commander of Auschwitz, was hung in 1947. First he testified at the Nuremburg trials, then he was hung at a place between his house and crematorium #1.

Walking into the crematorium, I could hear the birds singing. It seemed like such a contradiction, yet the birds seemed very happy. The crematorium took two days to burn six to seven hundred people. It was way too small for the purposes of the Nazis and was not big enough for mass extermination. So we went to Birkenau.

BIRKENAU IS 425 acres. There were three hundred barracks, which were only half of the overall plan, which had been curtailed by liberation. Five to six hundred people lived in one barrack. We saw the barracks and the bunks and they looked just like all the pictures I have seen. But to see them all together, on the land, adds another dimension to the reality of what happened.

We toured the collective toilets. People could not go to the bathroom when they wanted. They went once in the morning before going off to work, and once when they came back from work. There was excrement everywhere, as most people had starvation dysentery. The toilets were disease ridden, and absolutely gross, so they became the safest place to be as the Nazis gave them a wide berth. The black market happened here. If the prisoners needed a *minyan* (ten people) to pray, they did it here. There were three hundred holes cut in long concrete benches, one hundred holes per bench, three benches. The "Shit Patrol" was a good job in a way. Outside, in winter, workers froze or got frostbite. Inside, the heat of the excrement kept the place warmer. Sebastian again told us about a survivor he met who was on the Shit Patrol. He literally had to swim in shit as he cleaned the latrines. "If you were going to survive, you had to make some compromises in your mind," he told Sebastian.

WE WALKED BACK to the main road and said goodbye to Sebastian. There's not a whole lot one could say about Auschwitz-Birkenau that has not already been said. I only hoped we never forget that this happened, and never let it go. The cruelty, the sickness, and the perversity of the death camps were almost incomprehensible to a sentient human being. I read a quote somewhere in Auschwitz—something to the effect that those who don't understand history are doomed to relive it. I hope the world understands it very quickly. We have not done a good job so far as humans. Maybe going to Auschwitz will spur us on to do better. Who knows?

I thought of Sebastian's words: "Maybe it is time to stop talking about the history and start talking about the future." Let's.

I THOUGHT WITH much interest how the Poles and Germans and other European nations have accepted their part in the Holocaust, and through schooling and other governmental means, are attempting to make amends as best they can and to insure that something like that doesn't happen again. But not the North Americans. We do not accept responsibility for our wrong-doings and do not know how to say, "We're truly sorry—we will try not to have this ever happen again." I think Canada is trying a little with the First Nations to reconcile wrong-doings, but the United States—not so much. The Germans have extensive programs in school, and the Poles have maintained Auschwitz for the world and it is clear that they all feel a sense of responsibility and want to prevent anything like the Holocaust from happening again. Why can't the North Americans follow their examples? Instead we have to deal with people proclaiming, indeed, teaching in our schools, that the holocaust was a hoax and never happened, or not dealing appropriately with the slavery system in the US. What will it take for us to grow up and act like responsible adults?

AFTER WE LEFT Auschwitz, we wanted to live and to eat. We stopped at a Polish peasant place, *Zagroda*, and had a huge meal and talked. Agnes was with us of course. We had Polish *smaletz*, which is *schmaltz* with *gribbenes* (skin cracklings with sort of burnt onions). That's served instead of butter with bread.

We returned to Krakow and walked around the main centre. The old city used to be surrounded by walls hundreds of years ago, but now, where the walls used to be, there is greenery and parkland. It's great to look at a map of the centre of Krakow and see all the green where the walls were. There are bits of the original walls left though and they will stay. They are just lovely. Some politician said that the old wall had to stay up for two reasons: one was for the next generation, so that they would be able to appreciate it, and secondly, because to take the wall down would increase the wind, and that would cause ladies dresses and skirts to blow up and that would be inappropriate. Truly! So this beautiful part of the old wall stands for the wrong reason, but still looks lovely.

IN THE THIRTEENTH century, guess who ransacked Krakow. Three times, the Tatar Mongols came. One time, a guard up in the watchtower saw the enemy and blew the trumpet to warn everyone. A tatar mongol shot an arrow and hit the trumpet player in the throat. He only managed to play five notes before the arrow hit him. So now, every hour on the hour, twenty-four hours a day, the watchman of the tower plays the short melody, only five notes. And he plays it four times from four windows, for the castle, for the counselors, for the guests, and for the firemen. But luckily for the Krakovians, there are no Tatar Mongols on the horizon.

We were in the main square of Krakow, which the pigeons share with the people. It was a very laid-back place, a place where artists obviously thrive. Agnes told us that Warsaw was a place for working and Krakow was a place for living. You could really feel the soul of Krakow in this square: pigeons abounding, kids playing, musicians and artists everywhere, people drinking coffee or vodka at small outdoor cafes, small shops selling any number of things, flowers and fruit on display, and everywhere, people laughing, talking, strolling. Everywhere were *obwarzanek* or Polish pretzels. There were new cherries and fresh fruit and many other types of food as well. It felt like a party, but apparently this was a daily happening. We loved it. I wanted to come back, as there was not enough time to not only visit the places we hadn't seen yet, but just to hang out. What a wonderful city is Krakow!

Chapter 23
Getting to Switzerland

I DID NOT know that Switzerland didn't use the Euro. I thought all the European Union countries used the Euro. Firstly, I found out about Polish *zlotys*, and now, we were using Swiss *francs*. I still had not been in a country whose first currency was the Euro. The cab driver accepted Euros, and I paid for dinner with a credit card, so it was not a problem.

But what a day I had getting to Switzerland! I was now on my own again, as I was when I first started out on this sojourn. Judi and I bid each other farewell in Krakow; she went off to meet some of her friends in Italy, and I was booked to take a three day boat trip on my way back home to Canada.

AIRPORTS WERE DEFINITELY not my forte on this trip. I was brought to the airport in Krakow feeling rather smug. I had managed to pack up my stuff so that I had only one bag to check in (true, it was a bit on the heavy side, but I could maneuver it myself), and one carry-on (true, it was a bit on the heavy side, but it had wheels). I thought this would be very easy—one bag to check, one bag to take with me. But I forgot I was in Poland.

The agent looked at me and said, "You cannot check this bag. It is too heavy."

"Yes, I understand. I am prepared to pay excess baggage."

"No. This bag cannot go."

"Well, what do you suggest I do? I am on my way home now, and I need my luggage with me."

"You cannot take it with you."

"I must take it with me."

"No, sorry."

"Okay. What do you suggest I do then?"

"Repack."

"Repack? But it will still weight the same!"

"Yes. I know. But you must repack into smaller bags."

"Where am I supposed to do this?"

He shrugged.

The nasty manager lady came over. She didn't want to let any of the luggage go on the plane, repacking or not.

"Listen," I said, "I have been traveling for many months with exactly this luggage, and I have not had any trouble until today"—this was a bit of an understatement, of course, but she didn't have to know that—"I understand you want me to repack. I will do whatever you want, but my luggage needs to come with me."

There was much more discussion and argument and after a while, I went off into a little corner of the very crowded airport and started to unpack all my personal luggage into smaller bags. They also told me my carry-on was too heavy, so I repacked that as well.

I showed up at the counter now with three bags, two of which I wanted to check and carry on the third.

The nasty manager lady said I couldn't carry on my bag.

I sighed. "Look, it is a legal carry-on size. I have taken it on planes for months now. I must take it with me."

"There is nothing to discuss," she snapped. "It is not going with you."

Back to my corner I went. After more unpacking and repacking, I arrived at the check-in counter with three bags and my computer briefcase and a net bag into which I just stuffed full of things I didn't want out of my sight (like my pills and pictures of my dog!).

So finally my luggage was acceptable to them. I was then carrying on two packages and checking three bags. This seemed fine. The agent was starting to feel sorry for me, I think, and was really trying to help, but the nasty manager lady did not wake up in a good mood that morning.

The agent tagged my luggage through Munich to Basel, and I was just about to walk away when the nasty manager lady said something to him in Polish. I could tell it was not good.

"What?" I asked.

"Your plane is delayed. You will not make your connection."

"Well, what can I do?"

He shrugged. "Be here in five minutes."

"I am here."

He shrugged again. We had a long discussion about how I needed to leave today because I had a ship to catch, etc. They were going to fly me out tomorrow, maybe, and I tried to tell him, as nicely as possible, with tears in my eyes, that I couldn't do that. Please, please help me.

"Wait." And off he went.

After a very long time, he returned with a smile. The airport was a madhouse really, full of people, and planes were late or cancelled and many people were upset and having to rebook. But he managed to rebook me on Swiss Air so he reticketed all my luggage, and sent me off to the lounge to wait for my late plane.

I FLEW INTO Munich and had about an hour to connect with my Swiss Air flight. However, some of these new airports are like cities—they are immense, and I had no idea where to go. I knew I had to check in at the Swiss Air counter first for a boarding pass (why they couldn't do that in Krakow, I don't know), and then find the gate.

I was standing in a deserted hallway looking at a monitor and my watch, aware that time was very short, and not knowing where to go, when an angel appeared driving a golf cart.

"Do you need help?"

"Oh yes, please."

Gaby picked me up in her cart. Since I had shipped my wheels and my backpack, my two packages were quite heavy and I was very grateful for the ride. But had Gaby not picked me up, I later realized, there would be no way that I, or even a sprinter, could have made that connection. We drove to Lufthansa first; they directed us to Swiss Air. Of course it was in another terminal. Of course it was literally miles away, past the beer gardens, past the shopping centre, past most of the huge airport. And Gaby, my little Germanic angel, was so sweet, and so helpful. She was forty-two years old and had been driving wheelchair-bound and other people for twenty-three years at the Munich airport. She looked as though she were twenty-one. She had an angelic smile, a calming voice, and she was truly beautiful.

"Do not worry. I will help you," she reassured me. I almost cried in gratitude.

We got to Swiss Air, and then had about ten minutes to get to the gate. There was a huge line-up at passport control.

"Oh, you will never make it. Come with me," Gaby said as she hopped out of her vehicle and marched right to the front of the line with me in tow. She said something in German to the passport officer, wished me well, and disappeared into the crowd. I made my plane with a minute and a half to spare. God bless Gaby.

I CHECKED INTO my hotel in Basel, took a shower, and felt like a new person. The day's traveling fell off of me, and I decided to go for dinner.

Ruth Simkin

The hotel recommended a small Swiss restaurant not too far away, called *Elsbethenstuebli*. I strolled through a park, passed part of the university, walked down the street and into *Elsbethenstuebli*. I was starting to feel a bit tired again, and when presented with a large menu, was not sure what to order.

"This is very good, it's the specialty of the house," the woman said, presumably Elsbeth.

She pointed at something, I didn't quite see what, but I said, "Okay." I mean, how bad could it be?

"Salad or soup?"

"Uh . . ."

"The potato soup is very nice."

"Okay."

"Wine?"

"Yes, perhaps a glass of white."

"Red would be better."

"Okay."

"A glass or perhaps half a bottle?"

"Uh . . ."

"Half a bottle, yes?"

"Okay."

And so Elsbeth and I ordered dinner. Which was excellent.

And when it was time for dessert, Elsbeth ordered the flan, which was *so* good, that I found myself actually moaning out loud in pleasure as I savoured it.

I noticed under the table beside me a doggie dish of water. Oh great, pets. But where were they? I didn't see any four-leggeds. Much later, I looked over at the table next to me and noticed the gentleman had a rather large and fuzzy shoe. Then I realized that the dog was lying across his and the woman's feet, sound asleep. Oh, how wonderful to be in such a civilized country!

After a while, the dog people turned around and asked me if I minded if they smoked.

"Of course not," I said, putting politeness and appreciation ahead of desire. I was so taken aback by the fact that they asked, that they could have done anything. What nice people! Even if the smoke makes my eyes tear and my nose plug up, who cares? Besides, the half bottle of red wine made the smoke much easier to take.

I FOUND THAT there was a delay of about thirty seconds from the time someone spoke to me in German until the time I actually comprehended what was said. I usually had a dumb look on my face and the people had already either turned away or switched to English by the time I understood what was said and formulated an answer. Maybe in a few days I would respond quicker, I thought, but this delay really made me get a feeling for people who did not speak English as a first language. So many times I have been quick to think other people were not as bright or interested when in fact their brains were just processing the language and they were getting ready to respond. I know that in the future, I will be much more patient with all my friends who speak English fluently but not as a first language. I believe I had become quite arrogant about languages and this trip had really made me realize how little I knew or understood. When I return home, I wanted to study languages, although it was probably too late for me to become truly fluent the way I was with Greek some forty years ago.

I WAS ENJOYING being in Switzerland—it was so neat and clean and orderly. There was something very calming about it. But I decided instead of running off for yet another city tour and seeing the old walls and the old churches, I would just use my time there to write and sleep and explore on my own. My hotel was very modest, but clean and comfortable and I was not inclined to wander too far away. It had a nice little mini bar for which we were supposed to "note consummation" on a sheet.

LATER THAT DAY, I boarded another Viking Ship for a few days as we traveled down the Rhine. I had no idea what to expect or even where we were going. I was just looking at this next week as the start of making my way home. I was ready to go back home now.

Chapter 24
The Viking Deutschland: Traveling down the Rhine

I WAS ON yet another Viking ship, the Viking Deutschland. This ship was built over thirty years ago, and it must have been very beautiful then. My cabin was sweet—a sofa, chair, table, a bed which came down from the wall, lots of closet space, sink area, bathroom. Not luxurious, but certainly comfortable enough. The ship held a hundred and ninety passengers or so, and I think there were about a hundred and seventy on board, most of whom spoke German.

I boarded in Basel, Switzerland. I got to the pier two hours before official registration, and they let me go up to the sun deck to wait where I immediately fell asleep until it was time to check in.

SEATING IN THE dining room was assigned, and the maître d', Jurgen, a stuffy, squat little fellow about as high as my chin, was fairly snippy that I had not come to see him prior to dinner for my assignment. I would have done so had I known I was supposed to do that. However, he sent me over to a table of four, where two women were already sitting. They did *not* look happy to see me. The situation was not improved by the fact that when I was seated, the maître d' said "Bon appetit" and turned to leave, and I responded by saying, "Ginsboig." The two women and the maître d' looked at me as though I were an alien. I couldn't help it. I always say "Ginsboig" when someone says "Bon Appetit." This comes from one of my favourite jokes which goes like this:

Mr. Ginsberg from New York had always wanted to take a transatlantic trip. Finally, he was able to do so, and the first night in the dining room, he was shown to his table where a French gentleman was already seated. As Mr. Ginsberg approached, the French gentleman stood up, inclined his head, and said, "Bon Appetit."

"Ginsboig," Mr. Ginsberg replied, who sat down and began to eat. The meal passed without a word being spoken by either man.

The next night, the same thing happened. Mr. Ginsberg approached the table, the French gentleman greeted him with "Bon Appetit," Mr. Ginsberg responded with "Ginsboig" and they proceeded to eat their meals in silence.

For the entire trip, the maître d' watched this in horror. He couldn't stand it any longer, so two nights before they were to dock, as Mr. Ginsberg was leaving the dining room, the maître d' stopped him and explained, "Mr. Ginsberg, the French gentleman is not telling you his name, he is wishing you an enjoyable meal. That is why he says 'Bon Appetit,' it means 'good appetite,' he wants to wish you a good meal."

Mr. Ginsberg was horrified and not just a little embarrassed, so the last night on the ship, he made sure to be there very, very early, before the French gentleman arrived. He sat in his chair waiting for hours, and then, when the French gentleman approached the table, Mr. Ginsberg stood up and with a smile, said, "Bon Appetit."

"Ginsboig," the Frenchman responded, as he sat down to eat his meal in silence.

Ever since I heard that joke, I respond to "Bon Appetit" with "Ginsboig," even though most people have no idea why I say that. At times if they ask, I would tell them the joke, but most times people just look at me as though I am very weird and ignore it.

And so it was at our table on the ship. It was fairly tense at first, and I didn't know what to say, as both of the women totally ignored me. Finally, the one beside me said something to which I had a chance to respond, and then, one day later, we were all best friends.

Meet Shirley and Marilyn, a mother and daughter team, who traveled together every year around that time. How I missed my own mother with whom I used to travel! They were strongly Jewish, their family escaped from Russia and headed for South Africa, but now they lived in Florida, where they came to via Texas! Their accents were delightful—a mixture of all of the above. Shirley was the mom and had heart problems. As soon as they found out I was a doctor, I was in their good graces. I'm not being fair—they really were nice. I think initially they had just hoped to have that table to themselves and were disappointed when a stranger sat down. But things eventually became more than tolerable for all of us.

Our waitress was the lovely Lucia. She and I hit it off immediately. I always liked talking with the staff more than the other tourists, it seemed. Probably because the staff were local folks, and after all, that's one of the reasons I travel—to learn about local folks. The bartender was Zoltan, from Hungary. We quickly bonded as well. Zoltan and I discovered an interesting connection—the previous year when I went to the Arctic Circle, my ship was the SS Akademic, a Russian ship. A few years earlier, Zoltan was working on a ship going through the Northwest passage, they hit a sand bar and had to be rescued by—none other than the Akademic. And so we had this Russian ship in common.

I felt that being back on a Viking Ship was so familiar, as though I had come home. The food was good, better than the Russian ship. We had a good first dinner, and then had to wait until the "briefing" which happened at ten pm. It was past my bed-time, but I managed, with some difficulty, to stay up for the safety lectures. As soon as it was over, I went to bed.

I HAD NO idea where this ship was going and I really didn't care much, either. As far as I was concerned, I was now on my way home. Six more sleeps, and I could be with my dog, Reenie. So imagine my surprise when the following morning on the tour bus, the guide said, "Ladies and Gentlemen, welcome to France."

France? When did that happen? I had no idea. Come to think of it, the signs were in French, but I guess I thought we were in Canada or it just didn't register. The Rhine here forms the boundary between Germany and France.

We were in Strasbourg. In the morning, I had looked out my window to see swans swimming serenely around the ship. How lovely it was. Later that morning, I was on a tour bus, a big tour bus that held over forty, with only about six tourists, two of whom were Spanish speaking. We picked up the local guides—the male wore a maroon woolen neck scarf, shorts, and sandals, causing him to look a bit off balance. Our guide was Adrienne, welcoming us to "Frahnss."

We drove by a small church where Albert Schweitzer used to be pastor before he studied medicine at the University of Strasbourg. We drove by the Faculty of Medicine. Patients used to be treated with wine there in the middle ages; the faculty had a large wine cellar. Today they sell the wine and use the money to buy new machines for the Faculty of Medicine.

We were driving through Strasbourg and Adrienne pointed out the River Ill, which is the main river of Alsace Lorraine. It was a sweet little river, meandering through the town. Strasbourg was created 300 BC because of this river, as it was easier to ship on the Ill than on the Rhine, which was quite dangerous at the time. Currently it was a town of 260,000, but if one counted all the surrounding area, there were 435,000. 64 percent of the people were Protestant, and it had a large Jewish population as well. We saw the Peace Synagogue— quite an imposing building.

The mayor of Strasbourg was a forty-five-year-old woman, in her fourth year as mayor. I didn't think she was too popular at that time. There were flowers everywhere and the guide said, "The young lady is mayor and she thinks it is very important to have flowers everywhere." Well, I do too. Adrienne told me she liked the old mayor better.

We drove past a palace that was a copy of Versailles, but just a bit smaller, as Adrienne continued with the history. In 1871, France lost the war to the Prussians, lost Alsace Lorraine, and the Germans created the German quarter. To prove that the University was very German, they built a big monument of Goethe outside. Goethe had attended the university in 1771.

We drove by the famous storks of Alsace. There they were, nesting high up in trees along the street and in the park. They were beautiful storks, quite large, with babies in their nests. When the babies got older, they would be captured and tagged and kept in cages in the park for two years. They would lose their migratory sense and then they were let out and they lived the rest of their years free in the trees, but they didn't go anywhere. The reason for this was that otherwise they would migrate to Africa where they were hunted and they would all die. There were about three hundred and fifty storks, and they lived to be about twenty years old.

STRASBOURG WAS FAMOUS for the European Commission of Human Rights, the European Science Foundation, and the Council of Europe. It was the home of the European Parliament. There were twenty-five member states of the European Union and forty-six members of the council of Europe. We saw four large pieces of the Berlin Wall as a symbol of freedom.

I learned that day that there was now a European army, created a few years earlier. It was currently in Afghanistan to "ensure peace."

ADRIENNE KEPT TALKING about the huge differences between the German and the French buildings, squares, people. Later I asked her if there was still animosity between the Germans and the French. At first she said maybe still among the old people, but then admitted as to how old habits are hard to break, and yes, perhaps there still was some antipathy between the two cultures. The town itself seemed to be split in terms of German names and French names.

There were three universities, with forty thousand university students from ninety different countries.

WE LEFT THE bus and started a walking tour. Strasbourg was a delightful town, with quaint and interesting buildings.

We walked through the big square where the Cathedral de Notre Dame was located, and then into Gutenberg Square, where there was a huge monument to the inventor; it was in Strasbourg that Gutenberg's printing press first saw the light.

We walked into the tanners' quarters. This section was full of history. The tanners used to lay their hides out upon the roofs, and all the buildings were surrounded by tannin plants. These were used to make lohkas, a cheap fuel, which smelled absolutely terrible. There was also a huge hospital for syphilis there. Syphilis was called the French disease because so many French soldiers had it. These days, tanning had lost its economic importance of yore, and syphilis could be easily cured, and now the buildings just looked atypical and interesting sitting in the winding, cobblestoned streets.

IT WAS SHORTLY thereafter that I lost my group. I had asked for an ATM (still can't cash Canadian travelers cheques—let this be a warning to all Canadians traveling abroad—don't take Canadian TCs). Adrienne pointed to one across from Gutenburg square, and I thought she meant for me to go use it. So I did. When I came back, my group was gone. That's okay, I thought, I knew I could get back to the meeting place. So I spent a lovely one-and-a-half hours wandering the streets, sitting in a café, drinking a latte, and watching the tourists and a mime. I thought maybe my own tour group would pass by, but they didn't. There was a Charlie Chaplin type mime/clown/robot guy who was very funny and entertaining. At times he had huge crowds around him laughing uproariously.

I went back to the main square, which was really a happening place. There were musicians of all kinds, a calliope, more mime/mechanical-man guys, tons of tourists, and I suppose Strasbourgians as well, walking their babies and doggies or sitting in cafes. It was all very wonderful.

THE TOILETS HERE were underground. The men's was always before the women's, the door was always open and I always saw much more than was necessary. But at least there were lots of them, they worked, they had the necessary supplies, and so I was happy.

BACK ON OUR ship, I sat in my cabin, watching the Rhine go by. The countryside was positively pastoral. We went through a lot of locks, but other than that, there were trees and farms and animals, and it was lovely.

I thought it was very interesting that the Germans called their river "Father Rhine" while the Russians had their "Mother Volga."

We were in a lock, going down. It was amazing that outside my window, probably not more than six inches away, was a black concrete wall. The whole cabin became dark and I had to turn on a light. I heard squeaking and creaking, and just saw darkness outside as we descended. Then we got to the bottom, and slowly inched forward, just millimeters on each side from the wall of the lock, and as we came out of the lock, it got light again in the cabin. And these huge walls towered above us. Pretty amazing.

WINE WAS BROUGHT to the Rhine by the Romans, through France, but Riesling and other wines were drunk by the Egyptians. This area was particularly good for the white wines. All the viticulture was destroyed after the Thirty Years War, but built up again, and continued to present times to be famous, at least in my house, because we drank a lot of Gewurztraminer and Riesling there.

THIS CRUISE WAS so much more relaxing than the Russian one. In Russia, we were always on tours or at lectures, which was truly great, but there was very little down time. This was much more laid back. We had a four hour tour one morning, and then nothing for the rest of the day. So I slept the entire afternoon. I was really starting to feel tired.

By five pm I went up to the bar where Zoltan was giving a demonstration on making cocktails, but by five-thirty, I was back in my cabin fighting sleep again.

I SENT OUT some laundry one morning—lots of it—and it was back by lunch. How different than our Poland experience. We sent out laundry one night and the next night, it still wasn't back. Judi kept phoning them, and going down to the desk to check, especially since she had changed her plans and was leaving that very evening. Finally, there was a knock on the door, and someone dropped a huge pile of damp, very, very wrinkled laundry on our bed. So then we had to round up an iron and ironing board and make some of the clothes wearable. It was pretty funny, really.

IN A TWENTY-FOUR hour period, I had been in three countries (Switzerland, Germany, and France). I remained content to sit and watch the Rhine and time go by and count: Six more sleeps until I leave for home. Five more sleeps until I leave for home. Four more sleep . . . I'm ready.

The Rhine was pretty long—820 miles, and ran through six countries. It was connected to the Danube by a canal which then flowed through another eight countries and into the Black Sea. The Rhine was the most heavily frequented waterway in Europe, although the few days on the ship had seemed very quiet; true, we'd seen barges and cruise ships and pleasure craft, but it hadn't seemed overwhelming at all.

WE HAD A special French dinner on the ship because we were in Alsace. For dessert we had Bavarian cream with fruit sauce or a Banana split—not exactly my idea of French food but there you go; main course was Goulash or roasted salmon. Okay, the cream of sugar pea soup with ham strips could have been French Canadian and I'll allow that "Gratinated Onion Soup" (sic) was French although did not taste so. And we did have Quiche Lorraine for an appetizer, but with sour cream—shades of Russia!

ONE MORNING, WE got off the ship in Mannheim, got on a bus, and drove an hour and a half to Mainz. I am not sure why we did it that way, but we did. To me, Mannheim was known as the home of the leading character from the *Bagdad Café* movie! We passed by fields of wildflowers of brilliant colours, farm lands with people breaking their backs in them, and beautiful scenery all along the autobahn. Then we took the *ausfahrt* (exit) to Mainz and our guide for the morning.

Meet Johanna, a Dutch woman who had lived in Mainz for many decades. She spoke four languages fluently and I didn't know how many more not so fluently. I really felt inferior, that's for sure. I wish we all grew up speaking at least four languages; it would make such a big difference in how we all got along, at least I would like to believe that.

MAINZ GOT ITS name from Celtic origins, from the Celtic word meaning "sun God." The town was founded by the Romans two thousand years ago. Only after 1330 were Christians allowed to erect any buildings for churches though.

I learned that the Holy Roman Empire was the First Reich, from Charlemagne in 800 to Napoleon in 1800; the Second Reich lasted from Napoleon for another thousand years. The Third Reich was also supposed to last one thousand years, but of course, it started in 1933, and thankfully ended in 1945.

AS WE STOOD on the banks of the Rhine in Mainz and looked across the river, I realized we were looking at Weisbaden. Wait a minute—Weisbaden—I was going there in a few days. So then I started to inquire about how far it was to Rothenburg, where I was supposed to go the following day. I found out it was in Bavaria, a –four to six hours' drive, and since I wasn't even picking up a car until seven pm at night and had no idea where I was going, it was time for a bit of re-planning. And besides, Weisbaden looked *so* inviting. So I decided to go to Weisbaden once this little cruise was over. I was very sorry to not be able to get to Rothenburg auf der Tauber, as I had looked forward to it, but it was in Bavaria and was just too far for this old lady to make the trek up and back in two days.

BACK TO MAINZ. Johanna took us to a Cathedral that had been destroyed more than seven times. Each time it was rebuilt, it was done so in a contemporary manner. So there is a Romanesque arch, a Gothic style wall, a Baroque altar, Rococo architecture, and so on.

I learned that the word "sarcophagus" comes from the Greek words that mean "meat-eating"—this is because the first ones were made of limestone, which ate up the bodies. Also, the word "crypt" comes from the words "I hide myself," which of course is what a crypt is. Johanna was just a wealth of esoteric information. This church also had an organ with eight thousand pipes, the sizes of which ranged from five millimetres to nine metres. Wish I could have heard it being played.

WE WENT TO the Gutenburg Museum where we saw a reconstruction of his printing shop. Johanna gave us a demonstration of how to print. People could actually print before Gutenberg, but in a different way. The Koreans used wood blocks, for example. But Gutenberg printed with moveable metal types. He used a matrix. That word, Johanna said, came from the Latin meaning "mother." The real invention of Gutenberg was the alloy using lead, tin, antimony, and bismuth—with this alloy, he could get it very hot and it would cool in seconds, so could be used efficiently for printing.

Johanna demonstrated how a line was made, and placed on a galley to form a page. The whole page was then put on the printing press. The inking brushes they used were made of horse hair covered with leather and had wooden handles. The leather was dog skin, because it had no pores and the ink could not soak in. I got real queasy thinking about dog skin leather.

Before 1851, all paper was made of rags. In 1452, Gutenberg printed a hundred and eighty Bibles; forty-nine exist now, eleven in the US and twelve in Germany. All the pages have forty-two lines and so they are known as B-42s.

The books in the middle ages were always sold unbound. First, when you bought one, you just bought the printed pages. Then you took it to someone who painted in the capital letters and marked new sentences with a red stroke. Then you took the pages to an illustrator who would do the ornamentation and decorations in the columns according to the taste of the owner. Then you would take the pages to a book binder. On the top of the page, Gutenberg wrote the first word of the next page so the binder could match up the pages, as there were no page numbers, and usually, the binders, as well as most others, couldn't read, especially Latin. The first thirty bibles were printed on parchment. In the year 1282, a Bible would sell for thirty guilders or so. In the 1970s An Old and New Testament Bible printed by Gutenberg sold for more than two million dollars.

IN THE TOWN of Mainz was a street system with red signs and blue signs. The red signs were for streets that led to the river; the blue streets ran parallel to the river. It was said that Napoleon did that so that his drunken soldiers could get home, but that probably wasn't true.

If a German was said to be "blue," it doesn't mean he or she was sad, but rather, he or she was drunk. So the blue streets are for drunk people; if you take them you won't ever fall into the river!

In the middle ages, houses had nicknames (street numbers weren't invented yet). Many people would take their surname from the nickname of the house. So it was with Gutenberg—that was not his surname but rather the name of the house in which he was born in Mainz.

In Mainz, there were three hundred Jews. There was no synagogue, but there was a house they used for prayers. There were now 180,000 Jews in Germany; Germany cannot refuse any Jews now. The largest communities are in Berlin, Munich, and Frankfurt. In the past ten years, over 100,000 Jews came to Germany from Russia.

A lot of Mainz, like most of Europe, was destroyed during the war. And every time they built something, or tried to reconstruct a building, they would uncover something interesting, like a Roman road.

AFTER THE TOUR was over, I sat in the square, drinking a latte and waiting for my group to gather. There was so much to look at—beautiful reconstructions of colourful houses with painted facades, a huge square with people coming and going, meeting each other, sight-seeing, a large pillar in the middle of the square with the history artistically depicted in bronze, and a small oom-pah-pah band playing in the square for all to hear.

More and more I felt so lucky and privileged to live in Canada. I would return home with a rekindled love for my country, flawed though it is. Our daily lives are so incredibly different from millions of others—mostly easier, I think, although pain and suffering translates into every language and country in the world, including Canada.

Chapter 25
Lorelei and Goodbye to the Rhine

THE LAST FULL day on the ship was spent sailing the Rhine, a particularly beautiful part of it, full of quaint towns with many castles, vineyards growing along the mountain, and old ruins and ramparts along the water—it was stunning, really. I was so tired, yet I forwent my afternoon nap in my bed to sit up on the sun deck. I did snooze on and off, but kept opening my eyes to see yet another castle. The announcer would tell us, in both German and English, what we were looking at.

The most exciting part for me was seeing the rocks of Lorelei or Loreley in German. The name came from two words—*ley* or *lei*, meaning rock, and *lure* which meant treacherous or lurking. Another explanation was that it came from another German word which meant murmuring. It was thought that the rock made a murmur or humming noise. Whatever the etymology, there was the rock, a very large rock, 433 feet high, which was at the most treacherous part of the Rhine. It was very narrow at that point, and there used to be dangerous reefs just under the surface (they have recently been removed), as well as whirlpools. The fact that there were a lot of shipwrecks there can be explained just by the topography, but there was a legend which I thought was much more interesting.

Lorelei was a beautiful blond maiden, who sat high up in the rocks combing her hair and singing her songs, and so enchanted all the sailors that they couldn't concentrate on navigation, and crashed into the rocks and perished. Lorelei was slighted in love, betrayed by her lover. It was said that sometimes when the rocks in the Rhine valley glowed in the light of the setting sun, or moonlight on the water reflected the craggy rocks in the swirling waters, a slight figure could be seen, high up on a hilltop, and a voice could be heard throughout the valley. This was Lorelei. The hearts of the soldiers trembled with delight; they would sink into the waters and never be seen again. Lorelei's reputation spread, and soon the son and heir of Duke Palantine heard about her. One night he snuck out of his palace with his men in an attempt to try to win the heart of Lorelei. They reached the gorge at sunset and were spellbound by the sight of Lorelei. The Prince commanded his men to land, but they were positively spellbound by the woman. The strength to row left them. The Prince, in his impatience, jumped overboard, the word "Lorelei" on his lips. He disappeared into the swirling waters. His father was more than a little upset. He wanted that betrayer captured, and the next morning, his men surrounded the rock.

The captain took his men to the top and, blocking the path to her grotto, said to Lorelei, "Unholy woman, now you can pay for your sins."

"That does not lie with you," she replied, and took off her necklace of pearls and threw it into the water. The pearls rose out of the water as high as the cliff on which she stood and they carried her away into the evening light. She was never seen again, but if you listen very closely, you can be haunted by an echo which you can hear coming from the rock.

HEINRICH HEINE WAS one of Germany's greatest poets. He wrote a poem about Lorelei. Here is just a small part of it:

> The doomed in his drifting shallop
> Is tranced with a sad sweet tone,
> He sees not the yawning breakers,
> He sees but the maid alone.
> The pitiless billows engulf him,
> So perish sailor and bark.
> And this, with her baleful singing,
> Is the Lorelei's gruesome work.

It was quite an afternoon, listening for the voice of the Lorelei, and watching the rocks and the castles.

WE SAILED PAST Bingen where Hildegarde comes from. Not too many people know of her—does one have to be a feminist first? Hildegarde of Bingen was one of the first women I learned about when I first became part of the feminist movement. She was immortalized as one of the thirty-nine women whose place setting was part of The Dinner Party, the art installation by artist Judy Chicago. Hildegarde of Bingen was a writer, a composer, a mystic, a philosopher, a woman of encyclopedic knowledge. She was thought to be the founder of scientific natural history in Germany, and much more.

The last evening on the ship, we had the captain's dinner, together with the obligatory Baked Alaska, or something akin to that, and then we docked at Konigswinter. We went for a very small peripatetic, into the town and down along the water. Many people stayed in the town, but I elected to return to the ship. My past several months of traveling were catching up with me, and I was beginning to feel *soooooo* tired. I felt as though I could sleep all day, and once I got to Wiesbaden for a few days, I intended to do just that. Or so I thought.

THE FOLLOWING MORNING, we docked at Cologne or Koln in German. We had a two hour walking tour with our guide de jour, Angelica. Cologne was the fourth largest city in Germany, with a population of over one million. It was bigger than Frankfurt, to my surprise. (Although Frankfurt had the largest airport on the continent; Heathrow was the largest in Europe). However, in the city, everything was pretty compact. Part of it used to be an island, so maybe that's why. It was now connected to the mainland (around 1000 AD), but it had a very small town feel to it. Because it used to be on an island and land was at a premium, the houses were very, very narrow.

Agrippina, the Roman Empress, wife of Claudius, had Cologne named after her (somewhat indirectly). The name came from Colonia Agrippina (colonies of Agrippina) and was later shortened to Cologne. Agrippina killed Claudius with poisoned mushrooms. Her son was Nero, who later on set out to kill her. Nice roots. However, they overcame those beginnings.

RIGHT ON THE water was an area called the Fish Market, but there were no fish there now. They used to sell salted herring from the Netherlands there. There used to be, in fact, salmon in the Rhine too. Now, no more salted herring and for sure, no more salmon. There was a joke in Cologne that if you threw your film into the Rhine (in the days before digital cameras and the Green party), you would get it back developed! The river is much better now. In fact, they are trying to restock the Rhine with salmon, but it is not very successful.

Cologne used to be the biggest and richest city in the empire; it was a happening place. It was nicknamed St. Cologne because of all the churches there. They used to joke that there was one church for each day of the year. Angelica says that's not true—maybe one for every other day.

There were a lot of ruins still found in Cologne. The town people joked that if you didn't like your neighbour, throw an old Roman coin in his backyard and all the anthropologists, ethnologists, etc, would come and take over the house and then the neighbour would have to move. Cologne was built on layers and layers of Roman and other ruins.

There was a very strong Turkish minority in Cologne. They didn't identify that much as Germans, but definitely identified as being from Cologne.

Every year the city had a huge carnival. The word "carnival" comes from "*carne*" and "*vaye*"—meat-good-bye, and occurs just before lent and the fasting.

One is supposed to lose all control just before fasting, and everyone was equal, there were no social classes during this time. This carnival drew over one and a half million spectators for the "Parade of Roses." It used to be a religious thing, but now it was a city thing. It had strong political and social overtones. Angelica said the carnival was very important if you wanted to be mayor.

We saw two wonderful sculptures of Tunnes and Schal. I think they are sort the German Frick and Frack, whoever they were. Actually, Frick and Frack were initially two Swiss figure skaters who became famous, came to America, joined the original Ice Follies, and then later appeared in films. Their names have become slang in English used in two ways: the first is two people who are so close that they are virtually indistinguishable and the second way is a term of mild derision, like stooges.

Tunnes and Schal initially came from the puppet theatre of Cologne. Tunnes was good-natured and clever, and Schal, not so nice, actually hypocritical and double-dealing.

Anyway, there were all kinds of Tunnes and Schal jokes going around. An example: The two of them went to Lourdes, and they wanted to smuggle back some Cognac. The customs man asked if they had anything to declare, and they said no, they just had this holy water from Lourdes. When the customs official examined it, he said, "This isn't water, it's cognac!"

"Oh," the pair answered, "that must have been the miracle!"

WE WALKED ONTO a square that used to be the Jewish quarter. We saw a deep, deep hole, with Romanesque arches and Roman-type ruins in it, all covered with protective glass. That used to be the *mikvah* (ritual bath). It was so deep because they needed moving water for it. These ruins dated back from the twelfth century.

There was a strong Jewish population, but in the fifteenth century, the last of the pogroms drove them out, and they didn't return until around 1800. Then they built up a big Jewish quarter which thrived until the Nazis arrived. Karl Marx used to live there. Before the war there were four synagogues and a large Jewish population; now there is one synagogue. The ruins where the old *mikvah* was had previously been destroyed and a new house was built over it, but during the war, the house was bombed and the *mikvah* was rediscovered and preserved.

DURING THE WAR, 90 percent of Cologne was destroyed. That's pretty incredible to think about. The Dom Cathedral was hit fourteen times in WWII, and while everything around it was flattened, it remained standing. That was supposed to be a miracle.

We saw some more Roman ruins with *opus cementitsio*, a concrete type substance the Romans invented to put between bricks. Those Romans were pretty incredible.

Beside the Cathedral, there was, of course, a large square, but there was also a museum that the people of Cologne called the "Shoebox" because it looked like one. So imagine this incredible cathedral with ubiquitous flying buttresses, spires rising heavenward, and this shoe box building in gray concrete beside it. Why? Well, there was a good reason, actually. A huge Roman mosaic was found when they were constructing an air raid shelter. It was so amazing, that they built a museum around it. It was the mosaic of Dionysius. I know, Dionysius is a Greek name, but the Greeks used to be the artists for the Romans, so poor Bacchus could not thusly be named. The mosaic was dated at 213, and was thought to be part of a very rich Roman villa, part of the dining room.

In 1998, there was a political summit in Cologne and the politicians decided to hold a dinner over the mosaic. So Clinton, Blair, and all the other high-ups dined over the mosaic which had been covered by plexiglass. The mosaic was really beautiful. It was more than a dining fixture though—the Romans thought that eternity was dining forever, so the mosaic represents eternity and funereal concepts as well. The mosaic consists of one million pieces. It was fascinating to see.

IN 1164, AN archbishop of Cologne, who was also a politician, went to Milan and stole the bones of the magi from a church there and brought them to Cologne. They displayed the three holy kings, and the Emperor became as strong as the Pope because of these bones. Tourists starting coming to see the bones. In fact, the bones are still in the church, and the vault where they are kept is opened once a year. They did carbon date the cloth that contained the bones, and it was from around the year 300. It was thought that the bones were found by Helena, brought to Constantinople, then to Milan where they were stolen and brought to Cologne.

However, in Milan, the church from which they were stolen said that the original archbishop took the wrong bones, and they in fact had the original bones of the three magi. Did we really care?

AS WE WERE strolling back to the boat, we walked by a very beautiful, very large, very empty square. Angelica explained that the architect made an error. The concert hall and the rehearsal hall were under the square, and every time there was a rehearsal, watchmen surrounded the square and prevented anyone from walking onto it, as the footsteps disturbed the rehearsals! So that's more employment for many people.

THEN WE LEFT Cologne and sailed down the Rhine toward Dusseldorf. We passed by extensive production facilities of the Ford Motor Company and were they ever extensive! And shortly thereafter, there was the Bayer plant, huge stacks, and vats, and pipes. In fact, they were in this town called Leverkusen, which was called the "test tube town" because of all the chemical plants around. And on the other side of the Rhine was the most pastoral scene with many trees and sandy beaches. Then, back across the water, cranes, container ships, factories, vats, catwalks, rails, like an iron forest.

I SOON SAID goodbye to everyone on the ship, Zoltan, Lucia, Stanisalva from Slovakia. In fact, most of the crew on the ship were from Slovakia.

I arrived at the airport and stopped at an information desk.

"Excuse me, if I'm going to Düsseldorf, where do I check in?"

"You *are* in Düsseldorf, ma'am."

"Oh, I guess it's time to go home now."

"Yes, I think so." And so I will. Soon.

Chapter 26
Wiesbaden: From Health Spa to Home

I FOUND MYSELF in Wiesbaden, Germany, my last stop before going home. It was only about thirty minutes away from the Frankfurt airport, and the shuttle to the airport was already arranged. My bags were packed and I was ready to go, across the "Atlantical Ocean" as one of my guides called it.

I was staying in the oldest hotel in Germany, founded in 1486, situated beside the thermal springs that made Wiesbaden so famous for health concerns.

WHEN I FIRST arrived, I was greeted at the desk. "Hello, Miss Simkin."

"Dr. Simkin." I smiled at her.

"Yes, of course. Please sign here, Miss Simkin."

"Dr. Simkin," I urged.

"Yes. Your room is on the second floor, Miss Simkin."

"Dr. Simkin."

"Of course. My colleague will take your luggage up to your room, Miss Simkin."

"Dr. Simkin."

"Yes, of course, Miss Simkin."

The next morning, as I came downstairs, the same receptionist said, "Good morning, Miss Simkin."

I didn't even go there.

THE HOTEL WAS lovely and my room was, well, amazing would be an understatement. It was almost as big as my home, including stairs. There were two steps down in the entry hall into a large foyer, and then one step up to one bathroom, and one step up to another bathroom. I was there for hours and was still discovering new rooms off the hall! It was beautifully appointed, and had, beside a large bed, attractive and comfy sofas, chairs, desks, tables, cabinets, and more. I did overhear some people talking in a restaurant saying that this was only the "second best" hotel in Wiesbaden. It worked supremely fine for me.

I HAD SLEPT a lot the first night and continued to sleep during the day. In the late morning, I did go out to walk down Wilhemstrasse, the famous shopping area, and did a bit of sightseeing. I saw the "World's largest cuckoo clock" which excited me no end, until the anticlimactic "Kook." But I went inside the cuckoo clock store and had an amazing time there. There were very many remarkable things and I left there not just a little bit poorer.

THE CUCKOO CLOCK store folks had recommended a place to eat—Dortmunder. Down that street, turn left through the passageway, across the street, a little to your left, then on the right, and then . . . many more turns. Amazingly, I found it. I sat in the little garden off the pedestrian only street and watched the Wiesbaden world go by while eating a most delicious meal.

When I first sat down, the waitress arrived and I ordered, in German what I thought was an appetizer and a main course.

"Iz zis for one or for two pearsonz?" she asked. Oops. Guess I didn't understand it as well as I thought. I cancelled the "appetizer." Zum Dortmunder Das Haus der Biere was really a good restaurant and I thoroughly enjoyed my meal.

Just across the road, two men set up—a saxophone player and an accordion player. I think they were Slavic, although they played German songs. However, most of the time they each seemed to be playing different German songs. No matter, it was still entertaining, and after about three different ditties, one of them walked right into the restaurant garden passing his hat, collected what he could and they moved on.

THERE WERE LARGE sections of the old town of Wiesbaden that were for pedestrians only, and it was sure nice to stroll alongthem.

Wiesbaden had twenty-six thermal springs and the town dated from the Stone Age, so they say! Two thousand years ago, the Romans built a border there, but it didn't hurt that there were thermal springs there as well. Wiesbaden became a capital of the area and famous as a spa. Then in 1866, Kaiser Wilhelm II started a large city which flourished and the population doubled from 1880 to 1905. As spas became fashionable, so too did Wiesbaden. Currently, beside all the spas, the town is also known for all the medical people here, and the place is very health conscious. But portions of it were not exactly my kind of health; some of it was cosmetic, some were new age, and others just about anything else one could think of regarding health and bodies. However, a good deal of the medical offices, in conjunction with the spas, worked with arthritics and other "real" or "legitimate" medical problems (I understand I could be considered to be a medical elitist). There were many buildings with medical offices everywhere I walked.

I got on the elevator to go up to my room, and standing there was a beautiful black man, in swimming trunks, face all lathered up, shaving in the elevator mirror. "I like to shave in the lift," he joked in a lovely British accent. He then went on to explain something about no power, which didn't make sense since he was using a razor but hey, it was his face. The elevator arrived at my floor and I got off, leaving him scraping off the lather.

THE FOLLOWING DAY in Wiesbaden found me walking and shopping again. I still hadn't bought a present for Reenie, my dog, but I finally found the perfect gift for her—a special doggie Frisbee I knew she would love. I returned to Zum Dortmunder again for a repeat of yesterday's lunch. It really was good. This time, instead of the English-speaking waitress, I was waited on by the proprietor who did not speak much English. So when she brought the menu, I just shook my head, and ordered the whole meal in German. And it worked out just fine that day. I got exactly what I asked for and wanted.

I had probably drunk more beer on this trip than in the last ten years—not that I drink that much but I normally do not drink beer. I drink filtered water at home, but drank beer or wine instead when traveling. I would be glad to get back to my water.

I FINALLY GOT to the *badhaus* (bath house). Wiesbaden is very famous for its spas and mineral waters and health programs. And my hotel had a large *badhaus*. Before arriving in Wiesbaden, I was told that the spas were all "textile-free"—about the funniest euphemism for "naked" I've ever heard. However, once there, I was told to wear my bathing suit. I was glad I brought one—it was the second last day of my trip and the first time I've had it on! This hotel was very large—from the elevator to my room was close to a kilometre (well, it felt that long). From the elevator in the other direction to the *badhaus* lift was about the same distance, so from my room, it was quite a hike, especially in one's robe. However, at the appointed time, off I went, robe over bathing suit, to the *badhaus*. First I was told to go into the "swimming pool." This was a good-sized pool of mineral water, very comfortable, and it was about 1.7 meters (just over five feet) deep. There were maybe four people in the pool and another four lying about in lawn chairs. Nobody was textile free.

I grabbed a noodle, sat on it in the pool, and spent about twenty minutes taking the waters, as they say. Then it was time for my "therapy."

I reported to the desk, and a youngish man welcomed me and showed me into room 4. There in the room was a table for lying on, a smaller table for putting things on, and a deep tub, almost five feet deep and quite wide. It appeared that the young man was going to be involved in my "therapy." I asked his name, and was told it was Thomas.

"Hello, Thomas, my name is Ruth."

"Yes, hello, lady."

Thomas then asked me to take everything off and lie on my back on the table.

"Everything?"

"Yes, lady, everything. It is for the therapy."

Well, why not. So I went textile free and laid down. The ceilings were very high and arched, and the walls were tiled about half way up with decorated tiles in blue and white and tan. It really was a beautiful old building.

Thomas then got this stuff, marine sea mud, and proceeded to cover me with it everywhere. And I mean everywhere. It was a bit weird for me, but an experience, nevertheless. Another woman came in at one point, and although I asked her name twice, all I could get was a long name ending in "ina." Ina poked her head in now and then, but Thomas was really the one doing it. After he totally covered me, I was a very dark green, almost black. I looked like a mate for the jolly green giant. And once I was all covered, Ina came in and she and Thomas proceeded to wrap me up in plastic and then blankets. I did have to keep one hand up and almost out though: it was a little too close to some bad memories of years ago, to be all wrapped up like that. Still and all, I was determined to benefit from this "therapy" and so took a deep breath and tried to relax. Thomas and Ina left and shut the door. It was warm and then I started to sweat. And sweat. And sweat. I think I poured off twenty pounds in one hour.

At one point, Thomas came in.

"Okay, lady?"

"*Ya*, Thomas, *aber genug* (yes, but enough)."

"Yes, good, lady." And he walked out.

He finally did show up after I had been wrapped up for over thirty minutes, and ran the water in the tub. I was totally green/black with marine mud and felt rather yucky.

Thomas unwrapped me. He pointed to the tub.

"Sit, lady."

I sat in the tub.

"Is the temperation okay, lady?" (Thomas did not speak much English.)

"*Ya*, Thomas, the temperation is just fine."

AFTER I WAS all washed off and my normal colour again, I still had a reflexology treatment, but had to go to the bathroom. I told Thomas I needed the toilet. I put on my bathing suit while he was standing there, and must have been in a bit of a hurry as I put both feet into the same leg hole and lurched forward almost falling flat on my face.

Back from the toilet, I once again lay down on the table. Since it was a reflexology "treatment" I just kept my bathing suit on. For some reason, Thomas felt he had to cover me with a towel. I guess naked is okay, but bathing suits need to be covered.

I left the *badhaus* after several hours feeling very refreshed and good, but especially about twenty pounds lighter from fluid sweated out. I planned to return the next morning.

AFTER THE *BADHAUS* I went to the opera house. The Opera House was only about a ten minute walk from the hotel. I knew they were performing Mozart, but had no idea which opera. Even after it started, I still had no idea. I've since discovered that I watched *The Abduction from the Seraglio* or *Die Entführung Aus Dem Serail* by Mozart. It really was excellent. It was done in modern dress, sort of. Hard to tell exactly, because the action took place in a Turkish pasha's palace, and all the women had on *chadors* and were covered up, except when they were at the beach party and had on not much at all. I didn't really know the whole story until I came back to the hotel and read the synopsis on line, but I could figure out pretty much what was happening. It was very good—funny and dramatic and the voices were great! The stage was covered with sand, real sand, like in the desert. It was a fairly modern production. I was actually amazed at how much I could figure out from the words and action (sung and spoken in German) because I'd never even heard of that opera before, much less knew about it.

THE OPERA HALL was interesting also. The ceiling was beautiful—full of multi-coloured murals with 3D relief sculptures of women and cherubs and such. There were three balconies, but each balcony only had but three or four rows, so although the theatre was large, it had an intimate feel to it. The chairs were comfortable and had large wooden head rests so that one wasn't even aware of the row behind. It was a very pleasant evening.

After the opera I had to go to bed so I could rest up for another day at the *badhaus*.

I SPENT THE next morning at the spa again. This time, I had the whole pool to myself, so happily paddled away before Ina had her way with me. I had a mud pack and a massage and a head wrap, whatever that was. I didn't think I had any fluid left in me to sweat out, but I guess I've accumulated several months of travel gunge, because I was sure pouring off the sweat.

I SPENT THAT afternoon walking through old town, which was really quite wonderful: winding cobblestoned streets, lovely houses and shops, lots of outdoor cafes and coffee shops, lots of action on the streets. I could have wandered much more, but the hour had approached for me to pack one final time.

I had lunch at a different place that last day as I was far from Dortmunder. I was going to order *stangenspargel* because I had no idea what it was (it's asparagus) and I liked the sound of it, but instead, I ordered something else that I had no idea what it was—actually I thought it was a sandwich, but they don't really make sandwiches the way we know them. Lunch was fine, but I missed Dortmunder.

AND SO I packed. I was very happy to have gone on this trip and was very happy to be going home. I knew that I would appreciate my home, my friends, and my city far more after this trip than I had done so in the past. I learned a lot and experienced a lot, and had much of the arrogance knocked out of me, a very good thing, I believe. This whole trip was like a quest to find out more about myself, to become comfortable and come to terms with my life on my own. Once I left my sister Judi and went on to Europe on my own, I had to start defining my life the way it would be when I came home. I could easily have had someone join me, or could have continued traveling with Judi, but then things would have been different. When I finally arrived at my home, I had come out the other side of the world, of my quest, to find myself waiting for me. I was really all that I would need. I returned home being the woman I have always known I could be—stronger, kinder, much more self-accepting, easier on myself and much more loving and understanding of others, to the world and to myself.

WHEN I ARRIVED back in Canada, I handed my passport over to the immigration official. There were only two blank pages left in the entire booklet, and two more years to go before the expiration date. I beamed with pride at my travel accomplishments. I was in my sixties, not the healthiest person in the world, with all kinds of strikes against me in terms of pain-free traveling. I smiled—not bad for an older arthritic woman who had filled most of her passport pages, traveling on her own. And loving it. The world out there is an amazing place. Thank you for sharing my adventures with me.

Ruth and her sister Judi

Ruth Simkin's published books include *What Makes You Happy*, a book of short stories, *The Jagged Years of Ruthie J*, a memoir which met with critical acclaim, *Like an Orange on a Seder Plate, a Feminist Haggadah*, *Dear Sophie*, and *The Y Syndrome*. She has written countless medical papers and contributed to textbooks, as well as doing many mixed media presentations. She has published many non-medical articles and booklets on a variety of topics.

She currently lives with her Golden Doodle, Kelly, and when she is not writing, is contentedly reflecting on the ocean, the flora and the wildlife around her home.

www.ingramcontent.com/pod-product-compliance
Lightning Source LLC
Chambersburg PA
CBHW031948090426
42739CB00006B/119